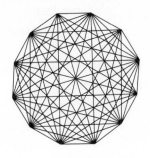

Human Behavior
in the Social Environment

A Social Systems Approach

FOURTH EDITION

MODERN APPLICATIONS OF SOCIAL WORK

An Aldine de Gruyter Series of Texts and Monographs

Series Editor

James K. Whittaker

Ralph E. Anderson and Irl Carter, **Human Behavior in the Social Environment: A Social Systems Approach** (Fourth Edition)

Richard P. Barth and Marianne Berry, **Adoption and Disruption: Rates, Risks, and Responses**

Larry K. Brendtro and Arlin E. Ness, **Re-Educating Troubled Youth: Environments for Teaching and Treatment**

Kathleen Ell and Helen Northen, **Families and Health Care: Psychosocial Practice**

James Garbarino, **Children and Families in the Social Environment**

James Garbarino, Patrick E. Brookhouser, Karen J. Authier, and Associates, **Special Children—Special Risks: The Maltreatment of Children with Disabilities**

James Garbarino, Cynthia J. Schellenbach, Janet Sebes, and Associates, **Troubled Youth, Troubled Families: Understanding Families At-Risk for Adolescent Maltreatment**

Anthony M. Graziano and Kevin C. Mooney, **Children and Behavior Therapy**

Roberta R. Greene, **Social Work with the Aged and Their Families**

Robert M. Moroney, **Shared Responsibility: Families and Social Policy**

Norman A. Polansky, **Integrated Ego Psychology**

Steven P. Schinke (ed.), **Behavioral Methods in Social Welfare**

George Thorman, **Helping Troubled Families: A Social Work Perspective**

Albert E. Trieschman, James K. Whittaker, and Larry K. Brendtro, **The Other 23 Hours: Child-Care Work with Emotionally Disturbed Children in a Therapeutic Milieu**

Harry H. Vorrath and Larry K. Brendtro, **Positive Peer Culture** (Second Edition)

Heather B. Weiss and Francine Jacobs (eds.), **Evaluating Family Programs**

James K. Whittaker and James Garbarino, **Social Support Networks: Informal Helping in the Human Services**

James K. Whittaker, Jill Kinney, Elizabeth M. Tracy, and Charlotte Booth (eds.), **Reaching High-Risk Families: Intensive Family Preservation in Human Services**

James K. Whittaker and Elizabeth M. Tracy, **Social Treatment, Second Edition: An Introduction to Interpersonal Helping in Social Work Practice**

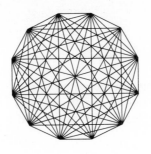

Human Behavior
in the Social Environment

A Social Systems Approach

FOURTH EDITION

Ralph E. Anderson
Irl Carter

ALDINE DE GRUYTER

New York

About the Authors

Ralph E. Anderson is Professor Emeritus of the School of Social Work at the University of Iowa, now living in Oregon. He received his B.A. at the University of Minnesota in 1950 and his M.S.W. at the University of Nebraska in 1953.

Irl Carter is Associate Professor in the School of Social Work at the University of Minnesota, and Acting Director, Center for Youth Development and Research. He received his B.A. at Parsons College in 1955, M. Div. from Drake University in 1960, M.A. (Social Work) at the University of Iowa in 1965, and a Ph.D. in Social Foundations from the University of Iowa in 1975.

Copyright © 1990 by Ralph E. Anderson and Irl Carter

Aldine de Gruyter
A Division of Walter de Gruyter, Inc.
200 Saw Mill River Road
Hawthorne, NY 10532

Library of Congress Cataloging-in-Publication Data

Anderson, Ralph E.
    Human behavior in the social environment: a social systems
approach / Ralph E. Anderson, Irl Carter.—4th ed.
        p. cm.—(Modern applications of social work)
    Includes bibliographical references.
    ISBN 0-202-36065-2—ISBN 0-202-36066-0 (pbk.)
    1. Social systems.   2. Social institutions.   3. Human behavior.
1. Carter, Irl. E.   II. Title.   III. Series.
HM51.A54   1990   70577
306—dc20   89-17999
                                                      CIP

Manufactured in the United States

10 9 8 7 6 5 4 3 2

Table of Contents

v

3   Culture and Society

4   Communities

5   Organizations

6   Groups

7   Families

8   The Person

9   Epilogue

Acknowledgments

The persons most responsible for this book, other than ourselves, are those of our students, past and present, who stimulated us to think more clearly and to attempt to teach more effectively. These students, many of them now our professional colleagues, will recognize ideas and examples that emerged from these interactions.

We are grateful to our colleagues from across the nation, and abroad, who have contributed evaluations and opinions of previous editions. We have taken these seriously and have attempted to respond in kind. Ron Mancoske, Daniel Chan, and Susanna Tsoi colleagues at Chinese University of Hong Kong, provided insights based on their use of this book.

We continue to be especially indebted to the late Gordon Hearn for breaking the ground and sowing the seed.

Introduction to the Fourth Edition

> My book is always one. Except that each new ad-
> dition, so that the buyer may not come off com-
> pletely emptyhanded, I allow myself to add, since
> it is only an ill-fitted mosaic, some extra orna-
> ments. These are only overweights, which do not
> condemn the original form, but gives some special
> value to each of the subsequent ones, by a bit of
> ambitious subtlety.
>
> Montaigne, *Essays*

It has been nearly two decades since this book first appeared. In that
time, social systems approaches have been incorporated as the "conventional wisdom" in a very wide range of disciplines and professions, and
has encouraged an increasingly wide range of cross-fertilization among
the social sciences and related applied fields. Systems ideas are now so
widely accepted that there is a steadily growing body of criticism and
theory refinement, which is important to good scholarship and the
"community of ideas" within colleges and universities, and within the
professions.

We, along with many others, continue to attempt to present more
clearly the fundamental concepts of this approach, and to incorporate
recent contributions to the systems literature. Throughout the past fif-
teen years, we have solicited and received frequent feedback from many
readers: faculty, students, and practitioners. This has greatly influenced
our revisions. One example is the inclusion of film and video suggestions at the end of most chapters, based on our acquaintance with them,
and actual use of many in classes.

Our experience and the experience of others have confirmed our
statement in the first edition that the sequence of use of chapters is best

determined by the user(s). Instructors have used all possible sequences (and so have students, who probably found some new ones, such as sequencing *parts* of chapters).

As usual, we welcome your suggestions and criticisms, sent to us personally or through the publisher.

Finally, we welcome you to the goodly band of systems theorists, a hearty and jovial, if sometimes contentious, group. Just remember, it's only a metaphor!

Ralph E. Anderson
Irl Carter

Introduction

But *you* gotta know the territory!
Meredith Willson,
The Music Man

This book is an attempt to map the territory of human behavior. it is intended to introduce students in the human services to ideas and theories that are fundamental to understanding human behavior. Students in social work, nursing, education, home economics, child development, and other professions providing human services require an acquaintance with a vast body of knowledge about the behavior of humans. Today it is impossible to present enough information in one book to accomplish this.

In our teaching and in our students' learning, we found that we came nearest to accomplishing this task by writing this book and using it as a global map of human behavior. It designates the major levels of knowledge of human behavior and enables students to recognize the human systems that most concern them. It is designed to organize human behavior content into an understandable whole.

Along with most of our students, we have found this book useful as a large-scale map in a "survey" of human behavior. We know from our experience that its utility in a particular sector of human behavior may be limited; therefore, we provide "small-scale maps" in the suggested readings at the end of each chapter. These sources provide more detailed explorations of particular human systems. This book, however, serves to place knowledge of human behavior within a broad context to remind us that one's theory and one's practice are "a piece of the continent, and a part of the main," as the poet John Donne put it.

The manner in which this book and the more specialized resources fit together varies with the terrain. For example, a great many books and articles deal with organizations as systems, and it is fairly clear how the large- and small-scale maps of organizational behavior can be integrated. However, the integration of the two scales is less clear as they converge in the behavior of persons, where the relation of the part and the whole is always at issue. One recurrent question, for example, is whether a person should be regarded as the basic unit (the focal system), a system capable of being subdivided, or only as a subsystem of society. There is disagreement about which scale to use, which perspective to take. Our intent is to demonstrate that these are all legitimate perspectives, to be used selectively in accord with criteria explicated in this book.

Our objectives in this book are to explain how our map is designed and to establish its utility. We have sought an "umbrella" theory under which various theoretical perspectives would fit, or—to shift the metaphor, a "skeleton" framework upon which various theories can be affixed and fleshed out toward a comprehensive theory of human behavior. In our experience, no single theoretical perspective can encompass all aspects of human behavior. Courses in human behavior have had various organizing themes, including:

1. *Normal vs. abnormal behavior.* This perspective provides knowledge of individual and family dynamics, which is invaluable in understanding and dealing with individual behavior but is of doubtful validity when applied to groups, institutions, communities, and societies.

2. *Developmental patterns of the individual.* This perpective includes groups, communities, and society, but only from the standpoint of their effects on the development of the person. Inherent in this approach is a view of the person as an "adjuster" or "adapter." Human behavior is seen as adjustment to social stresses. Intervention possibilities are dichotomized, *either* working toward helping the person to adjust to the social situation *or* attempting to change the social situation so that it would be less stressful to the person.

3. *Social process.* This perspective emphasizes knowledge of the social and cultural patterns that provide the social context of development and behavior. Such understanding is essential to social planning but omits the uniqueness of the individual and patterns of living.

Each of these perspectives and others have served as a structuring theme for ordering knowledge of human behavior. Each enables scrutiny of various theories and hypotheses. Each, however, has limited applicability to the broadening base of human services. There has been an exponential increase of social science knowledge, which varies widely in its quality and reliability. This increase requires a more comprehensive integrative framework than that provided by any of the previously employed organizing schemes. What is now required is an approach that will foster an integration of psychoanalytic, psychological, and developmental perspectives with the burgeoning discoveries from the many disciplines that study human behavior. We have found that social systems is that approach.

The social systems approach is probably best described as a "way of thinking," a theory about theories" (a metatheory), or a "hypothesis about theories," since there is not yet sufficient research to establish it as a theory of human behavior. It is a particular variation of general systems theories, which crosses physical, natural, and social sciences. Emerging findings in many disciplines buttress the validity of general systems theories.

A social systems approach has several advantages:

1. *It is comprehensive.* It offers greater possibilities for description and integration of seemingly disparate theories into a single framework than any other approach we know.

2. Even though it does not map adequately all sectors of human behavior, it does *provide suggestive leads.*

3. It has the potential for *providing a common language* to various disciplines, both within and across disciplines. Students interested in psychotherapy, education, community development, and administration may find social systems a useful common framework. The psychotherapist may not be vitally interested in community development, believing that significant changes occur with individuals; the community developer may believe that significant changes occur only when groups act; while the administrator may believe that change is real only when it is structured and solidified in an institution or program. We believe that each is partially right and partially wrong. Like the proverbial blind men examining the elephant, each has part of the truth. Yet these three specialists can see the relationships between and among their localities if they share a knowledge of social systems. Each might still prefer his or her own domain, but would be aware that it was "part of the main." They would recognize that interactions of persons, groups, and organizations are integrally related in a common system. It is our conviction that human services have lacked such an integrative approach far too long, even though we recognize the historical reasons for the delay.

4. A final advantage is *parsimony.* The social systems approach allows the student to reduce the "blooming, buzzing confusion" of theories of human behavior and methods of practice to a framework that can be mastered. Herein lies the danger, of course. Through reductionism the student may be content with the global map, flying from continent to continent, coast to coast, without encountering the precipices, mudholes, and arid wastes upon which many a theory has foundered. The systems approach cannot replace detailed knowledge of at least some particular sectors of human behavior. After all, people live through the processes of human interaction, not on maps.

This book attempts to describe a systems skeleton and then locate important human behavior concepts upon it. The instructors and students who use this book must flesh out the skeleton so that the approach will be directly applicable to the practice of each respective profession.

HOW TO USE THIS BOOK

This book is, then, a large-scale map, intended to be supplemented in each particular sector of human behavior by more detailed maps. We have used it in this way with both graduate and undergraduate students. We have guided students through the courses in modular fashion, selecting theories that made sense to us and to the students and indicating where each more detailed theory meshed with the large-scale map.

The first two chapters acquaint the student with our social systems approach. The essential systems characteristics are introduced and explained. These concepts, which serve to draw the map, reappear in the subsequent chapters. They are the key ideas that together form the social systems approach of this book.

The subsequent chapters are modules—they can be taught as discrete units, requiring only the first two chapters as precedent. The present arrangement of the chapters is one feasible way of ordering human systems, in descending order of magnitude. If instructors using this book prefer other sequences, the order can be changed or even reversed. By so doing, this course might better integrate with others being taught during the same term, or might better convey a particular theme being emphasized. For instance, instructors in colleges of education may decide to deal with the chapter on the person prior to chapters on group or family.

We have found it advantageous to use other texts with this book to provide additional threads of continuity through the general map, to assure degrees both of latitude and longitude, and to provide a single small-map source for each human system examined. For continuity crossing all human systems we have used *The Autobiography of Malcolm X*, Tillie Olsen's *Tell Me a Riddle;* Ken Kesey's *One Flew over the Cuckoo's Nest*, and Randy Shilts' *And the Band Played On*. For specific systems we have assigned, for example, Erikson's *Identity, Youth and Crisis* for the chapter on the person; Billingsley's *Black Families in White America* for the chapter on family, and Hall's *Beyond Culture* for the culture module. Again, many choices are open to the instructor.

Suggested readings, with brief commentaries on their particular utility, follow each chapter. The readings actually used will depend on the instructor and students involved and on the clock and calendar time available. If the students are unfamiliar with the content germane to particular human systems (such as family or groups), the supplemental materials should be selected with this in mind. For students acquainted with particular content, supplemented readings can give deeper insights into theoretical writings and related research. The listed films and videos may also be helpful to convey particular ideas, or as an opportunity for students to apply the concepts in analyzing the situation portrayed.

The glossary is designed for easy reference to the key concepts used throughout this book. Although most readers will be familiar with most of the terminology, our usage may be unfamiliar. The reader should consult the glossary because these are the definitions used throughout.

The book is intended to be an open system. We assume that each instructor will add and substitute books, articles, films, or other learning aids. This flexibility allows the book to be used in graduate schools, four-year colleges, community and junior colleges, and perhaps in-service training programs.

In other words, this work comes to you incomplete. It not only suggests that students and instructors add their own input to this study of human behavior; the book *requires* it. We hope that this social systems approach to the study of human behavior will be a step toward an integrated body of social science knowledge that will reflect both the complexity of social forces and the uniqueness of the person.

The Social Systems Approach

No man is an island, entire of itself; every man is
a piece of the continent, a part of the main; if a
clod be washed away by the sea, Europe is the
less, as well as if a promontory were, as well as if
a manor of thy friends or of thine own were; any
man's death diminishes me, because I am involved in mankind; and therefore never send to
know for whom the bell tolls; it tolls for thee.

John Donne, Devotions XVII

This well-known passage expresses the sense of this book's systems
theme, a theme that we will refer to as the *systems approach*, or *systems
model*. Since our approach is in fact a loose cluster of theories, axioms,
and hypotheses emerging from various disciplines, the phrase *systems
theory* is inaccurate and should be avoided. *If used*, at most it connotes
only theorizing about theories. Some of this eclectic body of knowledge
has been validated by observation and experiment; some is merely logical and suggestive of hypotheses for investigation. Howard Polsky classified systems theory as metatheory, that is, theorizing about theories;
and as a model applicable to any dynamic, patterned activity (Hearn,
1969:12). Joe Bailey stated, " 'Systems theory' is really a misnomer. It is
really a complicated and elaborate metaphor for describing what seems
to be an inevitable way of thinking" (Bailey, 1980:73). In fact, our social
systems approach is, in its essence, a *way of thinking*.

Much of the utility and explanatory power of a social systems approach derives from the manner in which the metaphor fits with the
thinking about the reciprocal relatedness of persons and their social environment. Gordon Hearn established that a systems approach is partic-

1

ularly well suited to the profession of social work, as exemplified by the following:

> The general systems approach . . . is based upon the assumption that matter, in all its forms, living and nonliving, can be regarded as systems and that systems, as systems, have certain discrete properties that are capable of being studied. Individuals, small groups—including families and organizations—and other complex human organizations such as neighborhoods and communities—in short, the entities with which social work is usually involved—can all be regarded as systems, with certain common properties. If nothing else, this should provide social work education with a means of organizing the human behavior and social environment aspects of the curriculum. But beyond this, if the general systems approach could be used to order knowledge about the entities with which we work, perhaps it could also be used as the means of developing a fundamental conception of the social work process itself (Hearn, 1969:2).

We suggest this conception is useful to other professions as well, for example, psychology, nursing, education, communication, and medicine.

The general systems approach seems to apply to all phenomena, from subatomic particles to the entire universe. We will confine ourselves to one part of the systems approach—social systems—which comprises knowledge about persons, groups of persons, and the human and nonhuman environs that influence social behavior and are influenced by persons.

Auger asserted that a systems approach enables the nurse

> to evaluate the status of the person who is ill and the significance of changes that may or may not have occurred in patterns of behavior. This content will help the student to develop a broader concept of the relationship between health and illness, the wide variations of "normal" behavior, and changes that may occur as a consequence of illness and/or hospitalization (Auger, 1976:x).

Peter R. Monge argued that a systems perspective provides the best theoretical basis for the study of human communication. His reasons

> are based upon my belief that a discipline as young as ours would make a serious mistake to preclude alternative perspectives. That perspective which incorporates the others is, at least until more information is available, the one best suited to guide us in our quest for knowledge about human communication (Monge, 1977:29).

In his essay recommending a new model for biomedicine, George L. Engel stated, "When a general-systems approach becomes part of the basic scientific and philosophic education of future physicians and medical scientists, a greater readiness to encompass a biopsychosocial perspective may be anticipated" (Engel, 1977:135).

The social system model explained in the ensuing pages provides organizing principles for this book. This model enables the reader to recognize similar or identical ideas *(isomorphs)* emerging from different ancestry and provides a scheme for classifying and ordering such related ideas. More importantly, it provides a means to understand human behavior better and points the direction for professional practice.

I. ESSENCE AND ANCESTRY

A classic sociology text stated more than twenty years ago that

> By far the most widely used analytical model in contemporary sociology is that of a social system. System models of various kinds are used in many fields besides sociology, so a social system can be thought of as a special case of a more general system model. A social system is not, however, a particular kind of social organization. It is an analytical model that can be applied to any instance of the process of social organization from families to nations. . . . Nor is the social system model a substantive theory—though it is sometimes spoken of as a theory in sociological literature. This model is a highly general, content-free conceptual framework within which any number of different substantive theories of social organization can be constructed (Olsen, 1968:228).

Munch noted that there has been a "remarkable renewal" of systems theory in sociology since the 1970s, and that the 1980s "brought forth, to some astonishment, several new approaches . . . a new generation of sociologists are once again taking up the Parsonian [systems] theoretical tradition, but in a new way and with a critical and constructive attitude" (Munch, 1987:116). We consider that this book fits within this "renewal" although we do not consider ourselves "Parsonians."

The model itself is probably most easily and efficiently introduced by the basic metaphor common to the sciences: the atomic or molecular model, which is composed of interacting units, each with its own parts, each unit being part of some larger whole.*

Buckley defined a system as "a complex of elements or components directly or indirectly related in a causal network, such that each component is related to at least some others in a more or less stable way within a particular period of time" (Buckley, 1967:41). The model is not descriptive of the real world. It is only a way of looking at and thinking about selected aspects of reality. It is analogous to a map or transparency that can be superimposed on social phenomena to construct a perspective in order to show the relatedness of those elements that constitute the phenomena. It is a means to "make sense" of seeming chaos or puzzlement, a way of thinking, and an approximation. A systems model draws

---

*We call your attention to the logo, which symbolizes the model, on the cover of this book.

attention to dynamic patterns of relatedness of part to whole, foreground to background, and object to environment.

A social system is a special order of system. It is distinct from atomic,
molecular, or galactic systems in that it is composed of persons or
groups of persons who interact and mutually influence each other's behavior. Within this order can be included persons, families, organizations, communities, societies, and cultures. The social systems model,
if valid, should be applicable to all forms of human association.

> Very briefly, a social system is a model of a social organization that possesses a
> distinctive total unity beyond its component parts, that is distinguished from its
> environment by a clearly defined boundary, and whose subunits are at least par-
> tially interrelated within relatively stable patterns of social order. Put even more
> simply, *a social system is a bounded set of interrelated activities that together constitute a
> single entity* (Olsen, 1968:228–229).

Having said that systems exist at all "levels," from individual persons
to cultures and societies, we should specify what we see to be the "basic
unit" of social systems. Within sociology there has historically been polar divergence on the designation of the unit of primary attention. The
macrofunctionalists such as Talcott Parsons tended to view the totalistic
system, the society, as the prime focus and to view the behavior of the
system and its components as being determined by the total system's
needs and goals, i.e., the whole determines the actions of its parts. Simply put, people are determined by the society.

At the opposite pole were the social behaviorists and social interactionists, such as Max Weber, G. H. Mead and Herbert Blumer. They
began with the smallest unit of the system, the behavior of the individual person. In this view, the acts of the individual persons tend to cluster into patterns, or role consensus, and the social system is constructed
out of these patterns, i.e., the whole is the sum of its parts. Again, simply put, persons determine the society.

Thus, of the two polar positions among early system theorists, one
was wholistic, viewing persons as units within the social system and
behaviorally determined by it: the other was atomistic, viewing systems
as the accumulated acts of individuals. The wholistic view implied
"downward" causality, while the atomistic view implied "upward" causality (Hofstadter and Dennett, 1982:197).

The vacillation between these two polar positions has confounded efforts to better the position of the person within society, as Stivers argued:

> If one takes an atomistic view (society as a collection of individuals) evil is always
> and only in the individual. But if one regards society as a totality, for example, the
> nation state as a superorganism above and beyond the individuals who compose
> it, then evil resides in the organism or system as a failure of function. Here the
> individual is reduced to a social cipher (Stivers, 1982:74).

These polarized positions appear in professional education and in professional practice as "social change" versus "individual change." The social change emphasis is grounded in the macrofunctionalist view that behavior is primarily determined by the larger social systems. A clinical or individual change emphasis derives its theoretical legitimacy from the belief that society is constructed from the behavior of its smallest units.

We hold that *both* polar positions must be taken in examining human affairs. There must be simultaneous attention to *both* the whole and the part. Our point of view is that each social entity, whether large or small, complex or simple, is a *holon*.* The term is borrowed from Arthur Koestler, who coined it to express the idea that each entity is simultaneously a part and a whole. The unit is made up of parts to which it is the whole, the suprasystem, and, at the same time, is part of some larger whole of which it is a component, or subsystem. Koestler said that, like the god Janus, a holon faces two directions at once—inward toward its own parts, and outward to the system of which it is a part (Koestler, 1967a:112ff; 1979:23–51). What is central is that any system is by definition both part and whole.

The single individual constitutes the apex of the organismic hierarchy, and at the same time the lowest unit of the social hierarchy. Looking inward the person experiences self as a self-contained, unique whole; looking outward as a dependent part. No man is an island; he is a holon. His self-assertive tendency is the dynamic manifestation of his unique wholeness as an individual; his integrative tendency expresses his dependence on the larger whole to which he belongs, his partness (Koestler and Smythies, 1971: Gray and Rizzo, 1973:302).

We have found the concept of holon to be particularly useful. It epitomizes a consistent theme in this book. *Any system is by definition both part and whole.* No single system is determinant, nor is system behavior determined at only one level, part or whole.

The idea of holon as used in this book extends Koestler's proposition of whole-part relationships to include certain corollaries. First, the systems approach requires the designation of a *focal system*. The focal system sets the perspective; it is the system chosen to receive primary attention. "Holon" then requires the examiner to attend to the component parts (the subsystems) of that focal system and simultaneously to the significant environment (the suprasystems) of which the focal system is a part, or to which it is related. For example, a family may be identified as the focal system. If viewed as a holon, attention must simultaneously be given to both its members and its significant environment such as

*[A note to the reader: We know you will encounter difficulty incorporating "holon" into your speaking vocabulary. Be undaunted; the important thing is that you incorporate its meaning into your thinking so that you always view a social system as both a whole with parts and as part of other wholes; that it always has partness and wholeness.]

schools, community, work organizations, other families, and neighborhood. To deal only with the interactions among family members (family
as whole) ignores the functions of family interactions with larger systems (family as part). A series of simple diagrams illustrates this (see
Figure 1).

The causal network referred to in the preceding quotation from Buckley (see p. 3) does not imply one-way causation. Causation is multiple,
mutual, and multidirectional. A change in any part of the causal network affects other parts but does not determine the total network. In
other words, behavior is not determined by one holon (seen as whole
or part) but rather by the interaction and mutual causation of all the
systems and subsystems, the holons of differing magnitudes.

A nineteenth century German philosopher, Wilhelm Dilthey, concluded, "There is no natural scientific causality in the historical world,
because 'cause' in the natural scientific sense necessarily entails the production of effects according to laws, whereas history knows only the

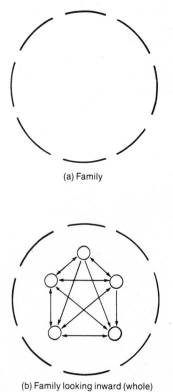

(a) Family

(b) Family looking inward (whole)

Figure 1.   Diagrams of a family system.

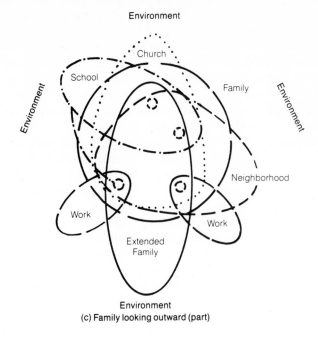

(c) Family looking outward (part)

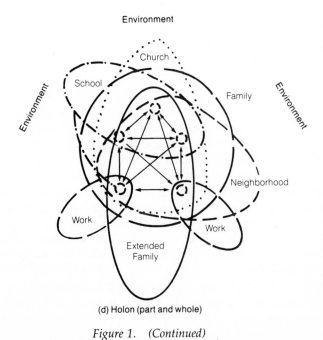

(d) Holon (part and whole)

Figure 1.   (Continued)

relations of effecting and being affected, of action and reaction" (Ermarth, 1978:308).

Consequently, we take the position that it is not useful to think of human behavior as understandable through searching for linear cause— effect relationships. It then serves little purpose to ask why? persons do what they do. A "why" question demands a causal explanation, that is "because. . . ." A more useful form of inquiry is "how?" An example of a systems model that is nonlinear is Forrester's "world dynamics" model, adapted in the controversial study *Limits to Growth* (Meadows et al., 1972). Forrester's model recognized that factors interact in complex *loops* (see glossary), avoiding the use of an oversimplistic causal chain. Alan Watts took a stronger position: "Problems that remain insoluble should always be suspected as questions asked in the wrong way, like the problem of cause and effect. Make a spurious division of one process into two, forget that you have done it, and then puzzle for centuries as to how to get the two together" (Watts, 1966:53).

Happenings or phenomena frequently are labeled "problems" when it is recognized they do not fit theory, belief, or expectation. The "problem" may be a function or consequence of the way of thinking; alter the perception and the "problem" becomes something else. "Solve" a problem and three others replace it. Recognize the thinking that defined it that way and the conditions may exist for real change.

Our stance, then, rather than being either wholistic or atomistic, may be described as contextual, interactional, pluralistic, or perspectivistic (Bertalanffy, 1967:93). The latter term connotes that causation, or the significance of an event, is relative to the focus one has at the moment of assessment; that the interpretation one places on events depends upon where and who one is and the perspective one has upon the focal system. "What we perceive, or overlook, in the field of our potential experience depends on the framework of concepts we have in our minds" (Ichheiser, 1949:2). Werner Heisenberg put it: "What we observe is not nature itself, but nature exposed to our method of questioning" (Lincoln and Guba, 1985:98). Einstein expressed the idea more simply: "It is the theory which decides what we can observe" (Watzlawick, 1976:63).

If one is a social behaviorist, one sees what happens to individual persons as most important. If one is a macrofunctionalist, the essential consideration is what happens to the total system (suprasystem, usually the society). Our viewpoint is that one's perspective at a particular time is what determines one's view of the nature and importance of an event. As events are viewed from other times, or by other observers, meanings are likely to change.

Thus the view we take here, a "holonistic" stance, requires (a) the specification of the focal system, (b) the specification of the units or components that constitute that holon, and (c) specification of the significant environmental systems. This could be called "mapping." The components and environment will have meaning in their effects on the focal system and, of course, the focal system will have meaning in its effect on its component parts and its environment. Further, to achieve an objective description of the focal system, one must state one's own position relative to the focal system, e.g., family therapist, patient's nurse, community's organizer. Such a view is philosophically consistent, we think, with the basic metaphor drawn from Einstein's theory of relativity, that perceptions of events are relative to the position of the observer; and consistent with Heisenberg's principle of uncertainty.

> Things are not as we see them,
> but we are as we see things.
>
> Albert Szent-Gyorgyi (1963:89).

In most dictionaries the first meaning of "system" is "a set of things or parts forming a whole," "a complex unity formed of many often diverse parts subject to a common plan or serving a common purpose," or something similar. Systemic thinking then refers to using the mind to recognize, conceive, and form the coherence of wholeness; to seek to complete the picture. That which is called "system" consists of elements cohering intelligibly, i.e., capable of being understood. Systemic thinking seeks that coherence. Science and the arts, each in their own way, engage in systemic thinking.

Ironically, the requisite beginning process of such modes of thought, as of all thinking, may lead to *in*coherence and *dis*integration rather than coherence and integration. As humankind seeks to find order amid chaos, meaning in the intrinsically meaningless, and to find the quality of whole-some-ness, thought is patterned and imposed on the world as experienced by the thinker. This process can be described in the language of mathematical logic.

> A universe comes into being when a space is severed or taken apart. . . . By tracing the way we represent such a severence, we can begin to reconstruct, with an accuracy and coverage that appear almost uncanny, the basic forms underlying linguistic, mathematical, physical and biological science, and can begin to see how familiar laws of our own experience follow inexorably from the original act of severence (Brown, G., 1979:v).

It can be described in the elegant language of art.

> The universe would appear to be something like a cheese; it can be sliced in an infinite number of ways—and when one has chosen his own pattern of slicing, he finds that other men's cuts fall at the wrong places (Burke, 1935:136).

These quotations refer to a single commonality of thought; to identify a piece, pick it up and look at it. Thinking holonistically would also entail paying attention to what it is, or was, connected to, and when finished looking, to put it back where it came from. Not only to put it back *but* also to be aware that all connections can never be known and the piece can never be fully restored to *exactly* where it came from. This applies to persons as well as other objects of study or intervention. In part, this is the Heisenberg effect, that one cannot observe without affecting the subject being observed.

Holonistic thinking includes those ways of thinking that seek to understand the coherence and connectiveness of all life. A recurrent phrase that conveys this quality of coherence is, "hang together." Here are three uses of that phrase from three quite different kinds of sources (emphases added).

> Consequently: he who wants to have right without wrong,
> Order without disorder,
> Does not understand the principles
> of heaven and earth
> He does not know how
> They *hang together*
>
> Chuang Tzu, poet-philospher of Taoism

> We must *hang together;* or surely we shall hang separately.
> Benjamin Franklin, scientist-philosopher-revolutionary

> The doctrine that everything in the universe *hangs together*, partly by mechanical cause, but mainly by hidden affinities (which also account for apparent coincidences), provided not only the foundation for sympathetic magic, astrology and alchemy; it also runs as a *leitmotif* through the teachings of Taoism and Buddhism, the neo-Platonists, and the philosophers of the early Renaissance.
> Arthur Koestler, philosopher (1979:265)

Comprehension of the part/whole nature of life is the central tenet of holonistic thought. From this core flow most of the propositions of our social systems approach. "Holonology" then is used to mean the study of holon phenomena and holon is a parsimonious description of whole/part matters.

Furthermore, what is here labeled holonistic thinking refers to thinking that includes attending to foreground and background, part and whole, and interdependence and interaction. Although it is not possible to attend to all of these aspects simultaneously, it is possible to take all into account, and the perception of each alters the perception of the others, in the process of perceiving.

II. ENERGY

Consistent with the atomic metaphor, we suggest the basic "stuff" of a system is energy. Just as atoms and molecules are composed of energy, so also are social systems.

The smallest molecular particle gets its dynamic movement from the fact that it consists of a negative and positive charge, with tension—and therefore movement—between them. Using this analogy of the molecular particles of matter and energy, Alfred North Whitehead and Paul Tillich both believe that reality has the ontological character of negative–positive polarity. Whitehead and the many contemporary thinkers for whom his work has become important see reality not as consisting of substances in fixed states but as a process of dynamic movement between polarities (May, 1969:112).

The dynamic movement between polarities accounts for the genesis of energy. What occurs in social systems are "transfers of energy" between persons or groups of persons. The energy in this dynamic process is not directly observable. Its presence is inferred from the effects upon the system and its parts. There is some disagreement among system theorists as to whether energy is a valid concept for social systems. For example, Gregory Bateson did not like analogies of energy since such analogies were derived from nineteenth-century physics; he termed it "misplaced concreteness" (Lipset, 1980:171).

Our use of energy, then, is analog and construct. In this sense, energy may be defined as "capacity for action," "action," or "power to effect change." As previously stated, the presence of energy is inferred from its effect on the system and its parts.

In his systems text, Richard Adams also used the concept of energy:

The central problem is to have a concept that includes everything of interest within a single framework. Energy has been chosen for this (R. Adams, 1988:14).

The term *energy form* will refer to any form of potential or kinetic energy; that is, for those things we ordinarily call matter and those we call energy. The choice of the term *energy form* is, of course,

arbitrary. [James] Miller, in his treatise on general systems, uses the term *matter-energy*. . . . I prefer *energy form* because *form* implies matter and information. In more vernacular terms, an energy form is anything—literally anything—for which we can identify a material form and that has the potential of releasing energy and is, therefore, theoretically capable of doing work (R. Adams, 1988:15)

The question becomes: "Is energy an inclusive enough concept to denote the life of a social system?" We suggest it is, providing the meaning goes beyond the precise idea of active force. To borrow again from physics, the broader meaning includes both information and resources as "potential energy." The nature of both information and resources includes the capacities to activate or mobilize the system and to serve as energy sources.

While most readers would have no problem in conceiving of coal or petroleum as energy forms, the present argument requires that we also regard human beings, human behavior, social groups, and assemblages of social interactions as energy forms. Similarly, mental processes located in the brain, writing on paper, and sound-waves in the air are also energy forms. The inclusion of all these different kinds of things as energy forms is legitimate because all of them meet the definition (Adams, 1988:15–16).

Monane agreed: "The interplay of people on the job, of husband and wife, of nations at war are all social systems that involve the sending and receiving of energy/information. System action will be examined as this movement of energy/information (1) *within* a system and (2) *between* a system and its environment" (Monane, 1967:1–2). To disqualify information as energy is to deny its reality; information is nothing if it provides no potential for action. Hence we proceed on the assumption that social systems do have energy, and that energy transfer is a prime function of all social systems.

Bertalanffy's discussion may assist in resolving the question of the legitimacy of energy as applicable to social systems. He said that living systems must be thermodynamically open, that is, exchange energy across their boundaries and be information carriers (Koestler and Smythies, 1971:71–74). We interpret this to mean that energy and information are not identical, but that they are complementary and inseparable in living systems. Both are necessary although neither is sufficient. Energy must be structured in order to be useful; information, just as its root meaning implies, gives form to the energy. One illustration is that all life carries within itself the code for its own replication; in humans the genetic code, as we are increasingly coming to understand it, is a set of instructions for creation of new systems, embedded in the structure of each system. All systems carry information and instruction, in some form.

One of the first social scientists to apply systems ideas to his discipline was James G. Miller, a psychologist, who wrote that "systems are bounded regions in space–time involving *energy interchange* among their parts. In his last published work, Sigmund Freud said of the concept of energy,

> We assume, as the other natural sciences have taught us to expect, that in mental life some kind of *energy* is at work; but we have no data which enable us to come nearer to a knowledge of it by *an anology with other forms of energy*. We seem to recognize that nervous or physical energy exists in two forms, one freely mobile and the other, by contrast, bound; we speak of cathexes and hypercathexes of the material of the mind and even venture to suppose that a hypercathexis brings about a sort of synthesis of different processes—a synthesis in the course of which free energy is transformed into bound energy. Further than this we have been unable to go (Freud, 1949:44–45 emphasis added).

The exact nature of human energy is undetermined and depends in part upon the particular system being examined. Within a person, we refer to psychic energy; we could analogously refer to the social energy of a family, group, organization, or community. What is meant is the system's capacity to act, its power to maintain itself and to effect change.

The energy derives from a complex of sources including the physical capacities of its members; social resources such as loyalties, shared sentiments, and common values; and resources from its environment.

For example, a military organization's energy would include the persons available for service, the military hardware it possesses (weaponry, transportation facilities, communications equipment), money appropriated for its use, and public sentiment favoring support of the military (such as "support our boys" campaigns). Other energy sources may be ideological support for military activity ("we must make the world safe for democracy") and legal or diplomatic sanction to conduct war (as provided by a declaration of war, a United Nations declaration as in the Korean War, or the Gulf of Tonkin Resolution, which expanded the United States involvement in Vietnam). The trials of Oliver North exemplified, in part, the conflict over whether or not to provide energy (money, weapons, ideological support) in an undeclared war.

Energy sources for a personality system, to give a further example, could include food; the physical state of the body; intellectual and emotional capabilities; emotional support from friends, family, or colleagues ("I Get by With a Little Help from My Friends" and "Bridge Over Troubled Waters" are two songs expressing this); cultural and religious sanctions for one's beliefs and activities; recognition of one's status by society and one's colleagues in an organization; and perhaps most important, one's own sense of worth and integrity.

At this point, essential concepts that bear on the topic of energy in a social system should be introduced. *Entropy* is the tendency of an unattended system to move toward an unorganized state characterized by decreased interactions among its components, followed by decrease in usable energy. Entropy is a measure of the quantity of *energy not available for use*. *Synergy* refers to increasingly available energy within a system derived from heightened interaction among its components. Whether or not the law of entropy is applicable to organic and social systems has been a lively issue among general systems thinkers. Schrodinger, a physicist, postulated the mind-boggling concept of *negentropy* (or negative entropy) to counter the tyranny of the law of entropy. He stated, "What an organism feeds on is negative entropy," and argued that living organisms "build up" instead of run down as they create complex structures from simple elements (Anderson, 1981:90). Biologist Szent-Gyorgyi coined the less complicated term *syntropy* to connote an innate drive in living matter to protect itself, to seek synthesis and wholeness.

Entropy is a concept from physics that does not apply precisely to social systems. This limitation was recognized early by general systems theorists.

Physical proceses follow the second law of thermodynamics, which prescribes that they proceed toward increasing entropy, that is, more probable states which are

states of equilibrium, of uniform distribution and disappearance of existing differ-
entiations and order. But living systems apparently do exactly the opposite. In spite
of irreversible processes continually going on, they tend to maintain an organized
state of fantastic improbability; they are maintained in states of *non*-equilibrium;
they even develop toward increasing differentiation and order, as is manifest in
both the individual development of an organism and in evolution from the famous
amoeba to man (Bertalanffy, 1967:62).

The emerging multidisciplinary science of *Chaos* has cast the debate
over entropy in a new light. Chaos theory holds that randomness (entropy) has its own underlying order, its own patterns of complexity.
Chaos as a science attempts to account for the nonlinear behavior of
systems through identifying and describing the recursiveness of those
phenomena that seem to be random, to find the order in chaos. Commenting on the application of entropy to social systems, James Gleick
stated, "These secondary metaphorical incarnations of the Second Law
[of thermodynamics] now seem especially misguided. In our world,
complexity flourishes and those looking to science for a general understanding of nature's habits will be better served by the laws of chaos
(Gleick, 1987:308). However, one of the laws of chaos is termed *turbulence*. "What is turbulence then? It is a mess of disorder at all scales,
small eddies within larger ones. It is unstable. It is highly dissipative,
meaning that turbulence drains energy and creates drag. It is motion
turned random" (Gleick, 1987:122). This is very similar to what we are
here referring to as entropy. We will continue to recommend the usefulness of the concept of entropy, again cautioning that it and its corollary
concepts be used as analogy and metaphor, *not* as employed in physics
as literal fact.

An example of the usefulness of the notion of entropy can be seen in
the concluding phases of the Vietnam War, and the Contra war against
the Nicaraguan government. As opposition to the war gained momen-
tum, energy for making war became disorganized and depleted. In un-
knowing recognition of this process, the phrase "winding down" was
used regarding the Vietnam War. That phrase is a fair description of
entropy, worded as if it had been planned and controlled.

Synergy is appropriate to open, living systems (and thus to social systems). One advertisement proclaimed, "We're synergistic. We do a lot
of things at Sperry Rand. And we do each one better because we do all
the rest." An open system does not deplete its energy, but it actually
compounds energy from the interaction of its parts. Abraham Maslow
credited Ruth Benedict, an anthropologist, with the first application of
the idea of synergy to social interaction. She used it to denote the ampli-
fication of goal-directed activity where there was a fit between the individual goals of persons sharing a culture and the goals of the culture
(Maslow, 1964:153–164). Again, we emphasize that the concepts of en-

tropy and synergy should not be used literally with regard to social systems, but rather as analogies.

For example, it may be apparent that an organization is becoming increasingly static and predictable and could be described as entropic. Another organization may be increasingly unpredictable and fluid, with internal shifts of concentration of energy and power that result in "dynamic growth"; this could be described as synergistic. The same analogy could be applied to a person as well. Rigidity and maintenance of psychological defenses could be evidence of entropy, while absorption of new stimuli and constant adaptation to the environment, with resultant stimulation of new attachments and ideas, could be evidence of synergy or syntropy. Both energy and entropy are imported across system boundaries. One system's (person's, town's, organization's, nation's) energy may be another system's entropy. A prime example is the escalating controversy over waste disposal, whether it be household, industrial, medical, or nuclear waste. High concentrations of energy collection and use are inevitably connected to high concentrations of entropy, nuclear waste being the foremost problematic example.

Systems require energy in order to exist and carry out system purposes. This can be diagrammed simplistically as occurring through four energy functions (see Figure 2). This diagram is intended to illustrate the interrelatedness of energy functions and is applicable to all human systems.

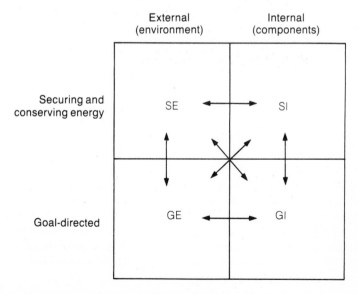

Figure 2. Four energy functions (S: securing; G: goal; E: external; I: internal). See glossary for definitions of terms.

A. Functions SE and SI

The first pair of functions (cells SE and SI) pertain to the securing of energy (as opposed to the *use* of energy, cells GE and GI, discussed below). SE represents the function of securing energy from outside the system, that is, importing energy from the environment. This importing function roughly corresponds to Parsons' idea of "adaptation" (Parsons, Bales, and Shils, 1953:182). The SE function involves GE as well, since the importation of energy occurs through a transactional process between the human system and the environment. SI denotes securing energy from inside the system and requires access to energy sources from one or more component parts of the focal system. A variety of possible outcomes are probable with SE and SI functions. The SE function is well-illustrated by the fossil fuel situation facing industrialized nations in the recent past and the forseeable future. If less fuel is available externally (imported oil), more must be conserved and secured internally (SI function) through domestic oil, wood, coal, or solar energy to achieve national goals. An example in a family is that if family members become unemployed, all must "pitch in" to pool resources. Fathers may babysit while mothers work, children's earnings become family income, and everyone may have to "make do" with what they have. The utilitarianistic family in Hong Kong (see Chapter 7, Families) is an excellent example; resources are pooled by members who are related by sharing rather than by blood alone.

If internal system energies are in short supply and energy from the subsystems is critically needed, energy-consuming frictions and conflicts among subsystems must be prevented or reduced. If the focal system has a surplus of energy available from its components, then the system can tolerate diversion of energy into subsystem conflicts. Such conflicts between components may be, to focal system goals, the lesser of two evils. Diversion of energy to suppress one subsystem may be preferable to allowing the subsystem to go unchecked. The operation of defense mechanisms of the personality is an example. Suppression of impulses or wishes may be preferable to allowing them free expression, which in turn could endanger the "survival" of the personality. Racial supremacy in a nation is another example. Although the amount of available energy required to maintain conditions of segregation and second-class citizenship for a racial minority (United States) or a racial majority (South Africa) is great and thus dysfunctional for the attainment of some goals, continuation of the system as it is (morphostasis) may take priority for the privileged because of fear of the anticipated consequences of changing it (morphogensis).

Parsons referred to the function of securing energy internally as "integration" (Parsons et al., 1953:182), which means reduction of internal conflict to maximize available energies to direct toward the goals of the focal system. This phenomenon can be seen in those circumstances where a system is in danger of being destroyed or radically changed. Pulling together, tightening the ranks, and forgetting past differences are found in the family, city, and the nation when circumstances or events threaten continued existence. Such was the rationale given for both President Ford's pardon of former President Nixon and President Carter's granting of amnesty to Vietnam era draft evaders. Reduction of conflict within a personality in order to achieve better ego orientation to reality, thus heightening the likelihood of achieving goals, is yet another example. According to some observers, President Reagan's greatest achievement may have been a symbolic reintegration of United States society, a reduction in internal divisiveness. Reagan's words frequently conveyed a patriotic call to unity, often in seeming disregard of actual (and perhaps useful) internal conflicts (Goodman, 1989a). Whether Reagan's creation of the massive federal debt reduces integration by depriving the Unites States of internal resources is yet to be seen.

B. Functions GE and GI

The second pair of basic functions (cells GE and GI of Figure 2) pertain to the *use* of energy, that is, the uses to which energy is put. One of the characteristics of living systems is the purposefulness of activities. They operate in a goal-directed manner. This pair of functions may be called goal achievement or "goal attainment" (Parsons et al., 1953:182). As in the first pair of functions, these two are performed both internally and externally; GE refers to goal-directed activity outside the system and is interrelated with SE, SI and GI. The holon must carry on transactions with the environment to achieve its own goals as whole and as part. It must achieve as much reliability and control over the linkages between system and environment as possible. The American Medical Association, for example, collects money and efforts from its constituent parts (its membership) in order to engage in lobbying activities to influence and control its environment to achieve system goals. The Iran–Contra scandal was, in part, an attempt to use internal resources (private funds as well as governmental) to control anti-United States governments in Nicaragua and Iran, to "neutralize" antagonistic foreign governments; this was GE activity (to achieve external goals) through the use of SI (securing energy internally), at the cost of considerable disagreement about internal goal achievement (GI), that is, the subversion of democratic processes through concealment from the Congress.

In another example, a child mobilizes internal resources to please parents and to achieve the goal of attaining security, love, status, and a position of influence in the family system, which is the child's primary environment.

GI refers to goal-directed activity inside the system. Here energy is employed to subordinate the subsystems to the goals of the focal system in order to be consistent with the nature of the system and the environment. This is similar to Parsons' labeled function of "pattern maintenance" (Parsons et al., 1953:182).

The declaration of a state of martial law in a nation is an example of goal-directed activity within the system. Because system survival is supposedly at stake, energies are directed inward to reduce or eliminate disequilibrium, which is perceived to threaten the existence of system patterns. Military takeovers in Chile, Argentina, Poland, Haiti, and Burma are examples. A professional organization requires its members to align their goals and behaviors with the goals and patterns of the system. If members fail to do so, they are subject to expulsion or disciplinary measures. Social workers are regulated by a code of ethics and subject to sanctions by the National Association of Social Workers; psychologists are regulated by the American Psychological Association. A family system that holds a goal of educational achievement will direct energies to control a member who rejects education as a goal, for example, denying use of the family car unless grades are satisfactory.

C. Interrelatedness of Energy Functions

It should be emphasized that these four functions are not discrete; that is, a system performs all of these functions at the same time. In any exchanges between whole and parts, all elements receive some energy and have some goals met. The reciprocal nature of the transactions and exchanges should be kept in mind. If one function is dominant, the other functions are neglected to the detriment of the total system. For example, the family system that concentrates energy only on the SE function through securing and importing energy from the external environment may experience internal disintegration. This make take the form of both parents devoting excessive time and energy to jobs at the expense of internal family functions. One estimate, for example, is that about 20% of children in the United States "return from school to an empty home (without adults present) and had no other form of afternoon care" (Popenoe, 1988:200). The parents may not have a choice: their survival and that of the children may depend upon the efforts they exert at work; but all parties pay a price. It has been suggested that good day-care for their children at affordable prices at convenient locations (SE) would reduce workers' stress and concern about their children (GI) and allow them to be more stable and productive (GE).

An excellent example of a person-system concentrating all energies on internal functions is Paul Simon's lyrics, "I Am A Rock":

I've built walls:
A fortress deep and mighty
That none may penetrate.
I have no need for friendship—friendship causes pain.
Its laughter and its loving I disdain.
I am a rock . . . I am an island.

Don't talk of love.
I've heard the word before.
It's sleeping in my memory.
I won't disturb the slumber of feelings that have died;
If I'd never loved I never would have cried.
I am a rock . . . I am an island.

I have my books.
And my poetry to protect me.
I am shielded in my armor.
Hiding in my room, safe within my womb
I touch no one and no one touches me.
I am a rock.

I am an island.
And a rock feels no pain.
And an island never cries . . . (Simon, 1966).*

The energy functions portrayed in this song can be diagrammed in the style introduced under "Energy" earlier, or by Figure 3, to illustrate relative imbalance of functions being performed in the person-system.

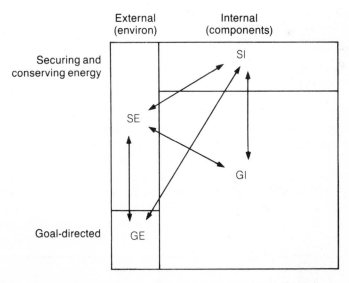

Figure 3. "I Am A Rock" Energy Functions (S: securing; G: goal; E: external; I: internal).

III. ORGANIZATION

Just as energy is the basic "stuff" and the necessary element of a system, organization is the sufficient element. A total absence of organization would mean a total absence of system. Randomly distributed energy cannot be mobilized to further the purposes of the system. A more or less closed system, a rock (to continue the metaphor) for instance, can be only immobile because its energy is unorganized. In order to move the rock, energy must be exerted from outside. To be a social system means to have a degree of organization. The word *organization* refers to the grouping and arranging of parts to form a whole, to put a system into working order. System organization secures, expends, and conserves energy to maintain the system and further its purposes.

Monane, in discussing the cybernetic concept of organization, asserted that it pertains to the degree of the system's intrarelatedness, that is, the degree of impact a component's actions have upon the other components of the system. He distinguished between high and low organization (Monane, 1967:21). In a highly organized system—a particular family, for example—the components are strongly interdependent; what one does is crucial for others. In systems of relatively low organization—some neighborhoods, for example—components are independent and autonomous. Monane's notion of high organization and low organization are similar to E. T. Hall's conception of "high" and "low" context.

> A high-context (HC) communication is one in which most of the information is either in the physical context or internalized in the person, while very little is in the coded, explicit, transmitted part of the message. A low context (LC) communication is just the opposite; i.e. the mass of the information is vested in the explicit code (Hall, 1977:91).

The comparative sets of "high and low" of Monane and Hall are akin to Tönnies' (1957) characterizations of community (*gemeinschaft* and *gesellschaft*) as explained in Chapter 4, and the distinction between traditional and modern families drawn in Chapter 7.

Thus there are two polar aspects of system organization that have been applied to communities, organizations, and families. One side of the duality is less formal, based on relationships over time with a high degree of interdependence among components, and where meaning is largely derived from the particular context. The other side of the duality has system organization based in formalized structures, with explicitly stated expectations of required behaviors, and relatively autonomous components. In reality, all systems will organize with some mixture of these two polar aspects.

The founding of a social system, that is, the delineation of a new entity from its environment, can generally be expressed in the familiar phrases, "Let's get organized," "Let's get it together." The first action of the components of a burgeoning system must be to order randomly distributed energies. The Constitution of the United States organizes the component systems into a suprasystem. The Preamble sets forth the general purpose for forming a new system and then specifies system goals:

> We the People of the United States, in Order to form a more perfect Union, establish Justice, insure domestic Tranquility, provide for the common defence, promote the general Welfare, and secure the Blessings of Liberty to ourselves and our Posterity, do ordain and establish this Constitution for the United States of America.

The various articles and amendments of the Constitution specify the conditions of intrarelatedness of the components (states and individuals) to system. The goals of the national system as specified in the Preamble are, and must be, congruent with the goals of its components. It was precisely this organization and interrelatedness that were at issue in the Civil War (or War Between the States), Nixon's "New Federalism," the effort of the Reagan administration to refer "general welfare" programs back to the states, and the Supreme Court's 1989 reconsideration of the *Roe v. Wade* decision regarding abortion, to allow states wider discretion. Revenue sharing was designed to decentralize federal control, and that has been followed by a weakening of the federal regulatory agencies; both are attempts to redefine relationships and linkages between the federal government and the various component states. The Equal Rights Amendment was an attempt to redefine organizing principles prescribing the relationships between system and components and among components. Ultimately, the Watergate issues and the Iran–Contra trial of Oliver North dealt with the balance among the three branches of federal government. In the latter instance, the executive branch engaged in unilateral foreign policy operations without the "advise and consent" of Congress. This has been termed a "constitutional crisis" by those who saw such activity as violations of the constitutional provisions organizing the interrelationships among the branches of government. The metaphor of "branches" suggests the organic nature of the nation conceived by the writers of the constitution.

Organization is a concept that does not implicitly carry the message of ever-increasing complexity, although complex systems with a higher order of differentiation usually require complex organization. "A complex society is not necessarily more advanced than a simple one; it has just adapted to conditions in a more complex way" (Farb, 1968:13). A personality with complex defenses is not necessarily better or worse than an "uncomplicated" personality, but certainly the two function differently. There is a rapidly expanding literature advocating reduction of scale and specialization in society (Illich, 1973; McRobie, 1981; Schumacher, 1973; Slater, 1974; Sale, 1980). Such authors propose reorganizing society in various ways in order to promote less complex patterns of living. "Voluntary simplicity" is a Thoreau-like secular version of the religious injunction to "take no thought for the morrow," that is, cultivate less complex lifestyles.

The measure of the effectiveness of organization is its capacity to enable the fulfillment of the system's goals as well as the goals of the component elements of the system. (See discussions of "effectiveness" and "efficiency" in Chapter 5, II, A, " Goal Direction"). Effective organization enables the energies of the system not only to be generated and purposefully used but also to secure energy from the environment (i.e., SE and GE functions).

Disorganization of a system—whether person, family, or neighborhood—does not mean totally unorganized. It means not *sufficiently* organized. The system's energies are not in working order; the components of the system do not stand in sufficient relatedness to one another; energies are randomly distributed and expended; the system is tending toward a state of entropy. Vernacular terms for this in a person are *spaced out*, or *losing it*.

In the Freudian personality system, id, ego, and superego are the triad of organizers that must work in harmony, with the ego dominant. If the id were dominant, energies would be directed toward goals not in keeping with the goals of the total system. If the superego were dominant, energies could not be sufficiently mobilized to fulfill total system goals.

Erikson's (1963) formulation of identity can be viewed as the expression of an organizing principle that enables the components of the personality to "get together" to fulfill the goals of the person. The "identity crisis" is defined by the bipolar dimension of "identity vs. diffusion" (see Chapter 8, I,A,1,c "Erikson", regarding polarities). In systems terms this could be expressed as organization versus disorganization. The word *identity* is defined as personality components drawn together to form a working whole; *identity diffusion* refers to disharmony among personality components, that is, randomization. The person diagnosed as schizophrenic is seen as a disorganized system—not all together, "not all there."

The family with problems is generally a disorganized family. The members (internal energy sources: SI,GI) are operating in a system–defeating manner. Among the possible reasons for family disorganization are the following:

1. The goals of one or more members are in opposition to system goals.
2. The elements of organization (communication, feedback, role expectations) are disrupted or unclear.

3. Available energies from within the system are not sufficient for the demands on the system.
4. The family is not adequately organized to obtain additional energy from outside its own system.
5. Pressures from the environment (the suprasystem) exercise a disorganizing influence on the family system (e.g., oppression).
6. Energy is denied or not available from the suprasystem, e.g. poverty.

The dimension of organization—the fact of organization—is characteristic of all social phenomena that can be designated as social systems. If there is no organization present, there is no system. If organization is insufficient or dysfunctional for the goals of the system, the term *disorganization* is used. Organization refers to the ordering of the energies of the component parts in some fashion that results in a whole.

SUGGESTED READINGS

Adams, Richard N.
  1988 *The Eighth Day: Social Evolution as the Self-Organization of Energy*. Austin: University of Texas Press.
    "A study of human society," "an exercise in applying to human social evolution concepts that have originated elsewhere." Compatible with our systems approach.
Bertalanffy, Ludwig Von.
  1967 *Robots, Men and Minds*. New York: Braziller.
    The "father of general systems" deals with the central ideas.
Buckley, Walter, ed.
  1968 *Modern Systems Research for the Behavioral Scientist*. Chicago: Aldine
    A comprehensive collection of the major writings of early general systems theorists. The reader must understand basic terminology before tackling this work.
Capra, Fritjof.
  1977 *The Tao of Physics*. New York: Bantam Books.
    A creative attempt to reconcile Eastern philosophy and Western science. A search for unity which extracts the commonalities of world view in these seemingly disparate cosmologies.
Hearn, Gordon, ed.
  1969 *The General Systems Approach: Contributions Toward an Holistic Conception of Social Work*. New York: Council on Social Work Education.
    The seminal monograph that established the relevance of the general systems approach to social work. The articles by Hearn, Gordon, and Lathrope provide essential background to a social systems approach to the nature and knowledge of social work.
Koestler, Arthur.
  1979 *Janus: A Summing Up*. New York: Random House.

In this book Koestler developed his final conception of holon and expanded the applications.

Koestler, Arthur, and J. R. Smythies.

1971 *Beyond Reductionism: New Perspectives in the Life Sciences.* Boston: Beacon. This is for the student who wants to delve into the complex issues inherent in general systems. It is a report of an international symposium held in the Austrian Tyrol in 1968. The invitations were confined to "personalities in academic life with undisputed authority in their respective fields." They included Jerome Bruner, Bertalanffy, and Piaget.

Saxton, Dolores F., et al., eds.

1977 *Mosby's Comprehensive Review of Nursing,* ninth edition. St. Louis: The C. V. Mosby Company. Review of concepts and sources fundamental to the practice of nursing. Chapter 5, "The Behavior Sciences" includes systems ideas and is an excellent listing of concepts applicable to all levels of social systems.

LITERARY SOURCES

Forster, E. M.

1954 *Howards End.* New York: Random House. This symbol-laden novel with its oft-quoted theme, "Only connect," beautifully describes systemic properties. It is one of many literary sources that are available for testing out the ideas presented in this chapter. From this book: "Only connect the prose and the passion, and both will be exalted, and human love will be seen at its height. Live in fragments no longer. Only connect, and the beast and the monk, robbed of the isolation that is life to either, will die."

Mailer, Norman.

1979 *The Executioner's Song.* New York: Warner Books. Mailer's biography of Gary Gilmore written in novel form is an excellent portrayal of the complexity of a person's part/whole aspects interacting across the range of systems: family, group, organizations, communities and society.

Romains, Jules.

1961 *Death of a Nobody.* New York: New American Library. Another of many literary works that portray the interlacing of human systems as they converge through a particular system, in this instance a person whose life seemed of little consequence.

Aspects of Social Systems

> Man is related to everything that he knows. And everything is both cause and effect, working and worked upon, mediate and immediate, all things mutually dependent. A bond that is both natural and imperceptible binds together things the most distant and things the most different.
>
> Blaise Pascal, 1658
>
> Everything flows; nothing remains. . . . One cannot step twice into the same river.
>
> Heraclitus

Energy and the organization of energy are the prime characteristics of social systems. We now discuss in more detail aspects of social systems that follow from these prime characteristics. All systems are composed of energy interchange. Structural and functional aspects of social systems are merely descriptions of this basic interchange. Those processes of energy interchange that are slower and of longer duration and thus appear to the observer to be relatively static can be called *structural;* those processes that are of relatively fast tempo and short duration can be called *behavioral.* This is a distinction employed by John Dewey, whose discussion is worth reading (Dewey, 1966). We call these processes behavioral rather than functional to avoid confusion with the energy functions described earlier. Those processes that change slowly over time but are not apparently static (that is, they move faster than structural but slower than behavioral changes), we label *evolutionary* aspects. For example, a structural change in the family may be from extended family to nuclear family over centuries; evolutionary change may be from traditional nuclear family to single-parent families over decades in the twentieth century; and behavioral change includes any particular family's functioning during its life cycle.

I. EVOLUTION OF SOCIAL SYSTEMS

As with other dimensions of social systems, change and maintenance are not diametrically opposed in reality. Systems never exist in a condition of complete change or complete maintenance of the status quo. Systems are always both changing and maintaining themselves at any given time. The balance between change and maintenance may shift drastically toward one pole or the other, but if either extreme were reached, the system would cease to exist. As philosopher Alfred North Whitehead said, "The art of progress is to preserve order amid change and to preserve change amid order." This is similar to Erikson's (1963) "bipolarities" of personality growth and Piaget's "assimilation" and "accommodation" discussed in Chapter 8.

A. Steady State

Steady state, a systems concept borrowed from physics, is the most adequate term available to describe what Laszlo referred to as "the particular configuration of parts and relationships which is maintained in a self-maintaining and repairing system. . . . It is a state in which energies are continually used to maintain the relationship of the parts and keep them from collapsing in decay" (Laszlo, 1972:37).

Steady state occurs when the whole system is in balance. In such a state, the system is maintaining a viable relationship with its environment and its components, and its functions are being performed in such fashion as to ensure its continued existence. The word *steady* is somewhat confusing because it implies some kind of fixed, static balance. The balance is, however, dynamic and always changing to some degree, as just noted concerning change-maintenance. The use of the word *state* in its singular form also is mildly confusing. Actually the concept involves a series of states in which the system, as a complex of components, adapts by changing its structure. It is not exactly the same, but somewhat the same, from one time to another. The steady state is modified along with the system's goals and the system's purposive, self-directive efforts (syntropy) to maintain integrity. Steady state is characterized by a sufficient degree of organization, complexity and openness to the environment.

The concept of steady state applies to all social systems. One example of it is Erikson's (1963) concept of *identity,* which is a steady state of the personality system. Karl Menninger's view is consistent with this. He devoted an entire chapter to demonstrating how systems concepts are compatible with psychiatry and the succeeding chapter to a discussion of ego's function in maintaining steady state (Menninger, 1963: Chapters 5 and 6).

The terms *equilibrium* and *homeostasis* have meanings similar to steady state but with important differences. They denote a fixed balance in which some particular adjustment is maintained, and the structure of the system is not altered significantly. Steady state does not include a fixed balance; the system can find a new balance and new structure radically different from the previous one.

The three terms may be illustrated by analogy to transportation, using the human body and the means of transportation to represent a system. Equilibrium is like a teeterboard; balance can be achieved, but the limits of being in balance are narrow. No movement is possible on a balanced teeterboard. To maintain balance, it is necessary to protect it from environmental factors such as wind or swaying. A possible exception may be acrobats on a tightwire, but even in this case, it is hazardous to attempt to move a fixed balance. This was illustrated by the tragedy of the Wallenda family when their pyramid of balancing acrobats fell from the high wire and some of them were killed.

Homeostasis denotes a more variable balance; that is, the system's balance may change within narrow limits. Balance is maintained by movement and by encounter with the environment. Homeostasis may be illustrated by a motorcycle. The rider has some latitude and remains upright by leaning against centrifugal force (leaning into a curve) or by altering the machine's center of gravity on a banked curve by tilting the machine. Within some limits, which are determined by the weight of the machine, wind velocity, speed, and road angles, the bike is maintained in balance. *Zen and the Art of Motorcycle Maintenance* (Pirsig, 1975) contained a description of the delicate art of balance, both of a motorcycle and of a personality.

Steady state is movement and balance like a space shuttle, transported slowly, by feet per hour, to its launch pad; then hurled into space by huge rockets at increasing speeds; held in space by centrifugal force, but traveling roughly 17,000 miles per hour relative to the earth; and finally descending to earth in a long, controlled fall. It changes its configuration during each of these periods: first, an appendage of the huge fuel tanks, then a space ship and cargo carrier, and finally a glider. It is a vehicle for moving people and machines throughout, but changes its mode of movement and its function to a significant degree.

The concept of *ecological balance* also is appropriate here. Forms or structures may change in and of themselves and in relation to one another in order to survive, but there are strong tendencies for the ecological system to continue in some form.

Buckley (1967) called the two tendencies involved in balance "morphostasis" (structure-maintaining) and "morphogenesis" (structure-changing). Again, no system reaches either extreme, although it may tend toward one pole or the other. All systems must maintain a shifting balance between status quo (morphostasis) and change (morphogenesis) and likewise a balance between order and disorder.

In his book, *Finite and Infinite Games*, James Carse puts it this way: "change is itself the very basis of our continuity as persons. Only that which can change can continue." (Carse, 1986:37). When order destroys or prohibits disorder, other forms of disorder will probably emerge.

Another important distinction among steady state, equilibrium and homeostasis is that equilibrium demands a minimum of stress and disturbance and seeks minimal interchange with the environment. The verses previously quoted from "I Am A Rock" are the expression of a person seeking a state of equilibrium. Homeostasis also requires minimal stress and disturbance but does require moderate interchange with the environment. Steady state does not require minimal stress; social systems may prosper from stress and disturbance. In fact, human systems tend to seek situations that are stressful as a means toward "building up" (negentropy) or to "seek synthesis and wholeness" (syntropy). You well may be experiencing stress as you are studying these systems concepts. More than likely you have encountered this book as a consequence of actively seeking to acquire information/energy as you seek steady state. Interchange is essential to the existence of steady state. Equilibrium implies closed and static systems, homeostasis implies open and static systems, and steady state denotes open and changing systems (see Table 1). What we mean by steady state is the "identity" of the system, its continuity with the previous states through which it has passed, its newly emerged elements, and the states through which it will pass in the future.*

Table 1.   Comparison of Equilibrium, Homeostasis, and Steady State

	Equilibrium	Homeostasis	Steady state
Stress	Least possible	Minimal	Optimal and necessary
Structure	No change	No change	Wide possibility of change
Interchange with environment	Least possible	Minimal	Optimal and necessary
Openness	Closed	Minimal	Open

*There is a familiar French saying, translated as "the more things change, the more they remain the same." If one explains that from a social systems perspective, the idea of steady state will be clearer.

II. STRUCTURAL CHARACTERISTICS

This discussion of structural characteristics is related to the preceding sections, especially the discussion of holon, and Chapter 1, III, "Organization."

A. Boundary, Linkage, and "Open" and "Closed" Systems

In order to be identified as distinct from its environment, a system must have some limits, that is, locatable boundaries. Consistent with our view that energy or activity is essential to social systems, we define a *boundary* as being located where the intensity of energy interchange is greater on one side of a certain point than it is on the other, or greater among certain units than among others. The intensity of energy transfer between units within the boundary is greater than the intensity of exchange across the boundary. For example, members of a family are distinguished not only by blood relationships, but also by frequency and intensity of personal contact. A neighbor would usually be considered outside the boundary, but may become "a member of the family" by participating in family activities and sharing emotional ties of the family. A household pet may be "like one of the family." An adopted child is another example of a person not related by blood who crosses the boundary and is incorporated within it.

Boundaries can be defined only by observation of the interaction of the parts of the system and the environment. Some boundaries are visible because of their impenetrability, for example, the rigid personality that permits little modification by the environment. Some religious orders have boundaries defined clearly by behaviors such as dress, marital status, and allegiance to group beliefs. The Old Order Amish are set apart by dress, modes of transportation, and style of beard. The fact that boundaries may change is evidenced in the Roman Catholic Church by changes in dress (abandonment of some traditional nuns' habits) and by some indications of change in group beliefs such as attitudes toward birth control as evidenced in opinion polls, ecumenical relationships to other denominations, and roles of women, although women still cannot be priests.

It is important to distinguish between the location of a boundary and its nature. Boundary does not necessarily mean barrier. A social system may have a readily discernible boundary and yet be very open to transfers of energy across its boundary (e.g., the boundary of male–female). Some social agencies survive by drawing clear boundaries (e.g., they serve teenage pregnant women, but not delinquent girls, and hence can qualify for certain federal funds). Another example is the boundary between generations that has become an important tenet in systems approaches to family therapy (Bowen, 1978; Minuchin, 1974).

Other boundaries are difficult to identify because interchange is frequent and intense across the boundary. For example, "Who is a Jew?" is a question both unsettled and important religiously and politically to the state of Israel.

The boundaries of being "American" were at issue during the Vietnam War. For some persons, support of, or opposition to, the war constituted a boundary. Usually no single interaction defines a boundary. Obviously, more than one criterion is involved in being "American": Such behaviors as paying taxes, voting, and acknowledging "American" values and responsibilities are some criteria to be considered. The issue of amnesty for draft evaders raised the question of such boundaries in a tangible and dramatic form. President Carter attempted to resolve the residual issues of the war by granting amnesty under a broad construction of the boundaries of "American," similar to President Lincoln's attitude toward Southerners after the Civil War.

When two systems exchange energy across their boundaries they are *linked* or have *linkage* with each other. Their linkage may be for a very limited and peripheral purpose or may constitute a vital linkage, e.g., a family's association with a work organization. A family's memberships in social clubs and civic groups may be important links to community activity and resources. Their religious affiliation may be a vital social, emotional, and ideological link as well.

Energy transfers by way of linkages are rarely, if ever, one way. Reciprocity of energy, or true exchange, is present in virtually all linkages. The church, club, or industry draws energy from its linkage to the family, hence industry's willingness to contribute to families' welfare through Social Security, United Fund drives, mental health campaigns, or ecological improvements. Increasingly, industries provide services directly in support of family welfare (e.g., day-care, social services, and retirement preparation). (See discussion of organizations' relationships to other systems in Chapter 5.) Similarly, religious organizations maintain their role as prime defenders of family and marital stability; the linkages are vital and central.

Open and *closed* are largely self-explanatory terms. A system or its significant environmental systems can be receptive or nonreceptive to the movement of energy across their boundaries. In actuality, of course, no system is completely open since it would then be indistinguishable from its environment (as families previous to the Industrial Revolution in Europe; see Chapter 7). Nor is a system ever completely closed—it would cease to exist. We use open and closed with these reservations in mind; what we really mean is "relatively more open" or "relatively more closed" than some other system or than some standard by which we are judging the system. A person is an open system but, from a teacher or counselor's point of view, may be less open (or more so) than is desirable for his or her own growth. For example, a child may be less open to interaction with peers than he or she "should" be and more open to interaction with parents than is expected at a certain age. Community organizers might wish for a social agency to be more open to ghetto residents and less open to interchange solely with white, middle-class clientele. This latter example illustrates that it is often not sufficient to generalize that a system is open or closed; it is frequently crucial to specify one's point of view and to specify "open to what" or "closed to what."

B. Hierarchy and Autonomy*

Parts of systems are related to each other in various ways. One of these kinds of relationships is vertical or hierarchical, meaning that parts are arranged in the order in which energy is distributed. For example, parents in a family ordinarily have greater access to the family's income than do the children. Because they receive larger shares of public goodwill and public resources, state universities have an advantage over welfare and penal institutions in receiving public funds. This might be qualified by public reactions to campus protests because university teachers and students became identified with controversial social issues such as the "nuclear freeze," abortion, or women's rights, or because of perceived extravagant expenditures by university officials. At the moment, community colleges may be rising in public favor while universities may have declined somewhat, over issues of access by potential students.

Another hierarchy is that of power and control. Some parts control others by regulating access to resources or by regulating communication. For example, the executive officer of an organization has rank not only by title but by virtue of controlling the allocation of responsibilities and resources. Power wielded by members of the White House staff who control presidential appointment schedules and screen incoming information is yet another example. The "gatekeeper" function is of central importance to a system; it is the locus of control of the flow of information and the crossing of system boundaries from both inside and outside. In contrast to Presidents Nixon and Johnson, it appeared that Jimmy Carter sought to establish a greater degree of openness of information flow through personal contact. President Bush is more accessible to news reporters than was President Reagan, who restricted access by frequently meeting members of the press in situations where he would be unable to hear their questions through the din of helicopter rotors.

A third form of hierarchy is that of authority. Some parts serve as sources of sanction and approval through acting as "defenders of the faith" (a phrase applied to the monarchs of England, whose status far

*Hierarchy and autonomy are emotionally laden words; refer to the definitions in the glossary.

exceeds their actual power). Religious institutions and schools serve this function. Within a family, part of the mother's role has traditionally been that of imparting and representing certain values of the society—hence Mother's Day has been observed with a certain prescribed reverence and respect. Traditionally fathers also have imparted certain societal values; there has been some change from "macho" values to father's role as counselor, friend and "pal" or confidante.

A forth form of hierarchy is a fixed sequence in which development must occur. Some events or functions must occur before others can be attended to. One example of this is Maslow's hierarchy of needs within the person:

> Needs or values are related to each other in a hierarchical and developmental way, in order of strength and of priority. Safety is a more prepotent, or stronger, more pressing, more vital need than love, for instance, and the need for food is usually stronger than either. . . . [a person] does not know in advance that he will strive on after this gratification has come, and that gratification of one basic need opens consciousness to domination by another, "higher" need (Maslow, 1968:153).

The physiological development of the human organism follows a hierarchical sequence of emergence and integration. Similar forms of hierarchy are found in Erikson's developmental tasks (1963) and Piaget's cognitive stages (1932), both of which are discussed in Chapter 8.

There are, then, several varieties of hierarchies. Most frequently we will discuss hierarchy in one of the forms just described. We will discuss instances in which the hierarchy is one of control and power and in which the parts are dependent upon other parts for some vital resources. The relationship in these instances will be that of subordination–superordination, or submission–dominance. That is, the hierarchies most often examined will be those in which control is exerted in a "chain of a command" (e.g., bureaucracies or communities with elected leadership), or personality, in which ego functioning provides control and direction.

Not all parts, however, exist in such chains of command. Some parts are relatively autonomous from a centralized control agent. Children are relatively autonomous after reaching legal status as adults, yet they remain part of their parents' family. In classic cases of "split personality" or dissociative reaction, some significant portions of the personality function autonomously without control by the ego. The military organizations of some countries function largely independently of the elected political hierarchy and are autonomous. Such autonomy in a social system may mean great power, as in the case of a military or intelligence organization (some people have described the CIA as an example) that is increasingly less responsible to the society, or it may mean irrelevance and powerlessness. This is seen, according to some observers, in the case of a caste or racial minority such as African Americans or American Indians.

It should be noted that, as Miller says, "It is the nature of organizations that each subsystem and component has some autonomy and some subordination or constraint from lower level systems, other systems at the same level, and higher level systems" (Miller, 1965:222). In one way, this repeats what was said earlier about holonistic relationships and the fact that causation is mutual; each system is both a superordinate whole and a subordinate part.

C. *Differentiation and Specialization*

The terms *differentiation* and *specialization* are similar but not identical. Differentiation means "dividing the functions," that is, assigning functions to certain parts and not to others. Specialization adds the further stipulation that a part performs only, or predominantly, a particular function.

Differentiation is not the same as, but is always related to, allocation or distribution of energy. For example, assigning particular societal goals (GI function) to the Department of Health and Human Services is not the same as providing the necessary appropriations. Income maintenance of the elderly, as provided for in the Social Security Act, cannot be realized without the allocation of necessary revenues; the perennial debate over Social Security illustrates this very well.

Differentiation may apply to any of a large number of aspects of system functioning. There may be differentiation by age in regard to earning income for the family. Typically, adults are expected to earn, teenagers are expected to provide their own spending money, and the elderly and children are not expected to be self-supporting.

As society becomes more complex, it becomes necessary to differentiate functions. Modern professions such as nursing, home economics, social work, and law enforcement have come into being as part of the evolution of particular societies. In these societies, problems of social welfare and problems in social relationships are the concern of these newly minted professions.

There are several other important facts about differentiation that merit discussion. As a social system becomes differentiated, at some point the need arises to reintegrate and to establish communication between the differentiated parts. The more differentiation occurs, probably the more internal exchange of energy/information is necessary. This is one of the seemingly insoluble problems in governmental provision of human services. There has been a high degree of differentiation of function, without accompanying specialization, which has resulted in the necessity of increasing amounts of energy being devoted to communication. A whole communications "industry" has been spawned to coordinate functions. Despite that, not because of it, services remain largely uncoordinated, duplicative, and random as experienced by the consumer/citizen.

Differentiation may be reversible; a system may reorder its structures to perform functions more satisfactorily, e.g., the belated efforts of the U. S. automobile industry to modify the assembly line. The highly specialized assembly line had provided the means to mass produce automobiles and greatly increase the volume of sales. Now, in order to redress the resultant problems of quality control and alienation, the industry is merging and combining previously differentiated and specialized functions, e.g. through autonomous work groups and "quality circles". In a sense, the field of medicine is acting similarly in broadening specialties, e.g., family practice or the nurse practitioner as is social work, in licensing clinical social work in many states.

There are levels of differentiation according to the stages of development of the social system; the more complex, the more fully the functions are differentiated among the parts, and this leads to discussion of specialization. As noted earlier, specialization means exclusivity of function—as a popular song puts it, "I can handle this job all by myself." Professions stake out their boundaries, who shall administer medication, who shall give legal advice, who shall approve adoptions, who is an expert witness in court. In that sense, professions are specialties, but they are not completely specialized in that all of them are performing integrative SI and GI functions in the society.

An example of societal specialization from ancient history is found in a manual for farmers written in the second century B.C.: "tunics, togas, blankets, smocks, and shoes should be bought at Rome . . . tiles at Venafrum, oil mills at Pompeii and at Rufrius's yard at Nola" (Lenski, 1970:255). This might have been the first paid commercial or the first consumer protection announcement in history. Occupational specialization is most pronounced in modern industrial society, but in Paris in 1313, there were already 157 different trades listed on the tax rolls (Lenski, 1970:256).

The extent of occupational specialization in modern society has become problematic. As Darwin and later scientists proved, the utility of specialization is always dependent upon particular environmental conditions. When these conditions shift, the highly specialized adaptation is no longer functional. Similarly, if technology replaces or supersedes a specialized occupation, the previous workers are no longer valued or needed (e.g., local telephone operators and service station attendants). It is possible for the technological environment shift to restore an occupational specialty; during oil shortages, there was a shift back to the use of wood as heating fuel and the occupation of chimney sweep was again in demand.

As with differentiation, specialization is necessary to perform functions, but certain dangers also arise. One such danger has been referred to as "tyranny by specialists," when people are divided into expert and ignorant, able and unable. As the physician may tyrannize the patient, the auto mechanic or the electrician may tyrannize the physician. An indication of such tyranny is found where the expert assumes the matter is too complex for the nonexpert to make decisions.

Archie Bahm has emphasized another danger of overreliance on specialization.

> As more specialists appear, more areas in which other specialists are ignorant exist. This implies a relative growth in ignorance. The more new fields which emerge about which one has no knowledge, the more ignorant one is, no matter how successful one is in improving one's knowledge within one's own field (Bahm, 1977:72).

Others have stressed that greater specialization leads to greater dependence on the products of other groups and the greater importance of systemic linkage: "The more highly specialized a group's activities the more its need for the products of other groups and more important systemic linkage becomes. The ultimate of the kind of systemic linkage occasioned by cooperative specialization is reached in centralization" (Loomis and Loomis, 1961:228).

It is risky to specialize completely. Systems may have to rely on other systems that do not perform adequately: the family upon the school, or the school upon the family; some persons choose not to risk family life, for example; some families choose to emigrate to safer countries. In order to reduce risk, systems integrate vertically, both upward and downward. Thus we come full circle to hierarchy as an aspect of structure.

III. BEHAVIORAL ASPECTS OF SOCIAL SYSTEMS

Behavioral aspects are those interchanges that are of shorter duration and faster tempo. Three of these seem to us most significant: They are related, but not identical, to the basic energy functions, and they are the subfunctions that seem to be most important for this book.

A. Social Control and Socialization

Social control and *socialization* occur in all systems and can have the purpose either of securing energy for the system from its components (SI) or of achieving goals (GI, GE). This process of securing energy or expending it to achieve goals can be done in either a coercive or cooperative fashion. The system can secure energy or achieve goals coercively either by threatening the component's survival and functioning or its goal achievement, or cooperatively by supporting the component's goal and encouraging its harmony with the system's goal. An example of this is the "gentle persuasion" that a religious organization can apply to its members to summon their efforts in supporting the system's goals, such as a building fund, yearly budget, or attendance at a revival. Or the religious organization may employ coercive means—excommunication or expulsion from membership—if the member interferes with its goals by refusing to rear children in the faith, failing to contribute financially, or violating its ethical standards as in the cases of "televangelists" Jimmy Swaggart or Jim Bakker. In 1989, Iran's Ayatollah Khomeini called for the killing of Salman Rushdie, an author whose book *Satanic Verses* "blasphemed" the beliefs of Islam (and coincidentally also satirized Khomeini in the book), and thousands of Muslims offered to enforce this extreme example of social control.

Coercive control is usually labeled "power" (see the discussion of power in Chapter 5, II, C, "Power and Control.") Traditionally, the helping professions have espoused cooperative approaches, holding up the value of "self-determination," but in practice, decisions are sometimes made for clients. When these decisions are forced upon the client and fulfillment of the client's own goals or the client's access to needed resources is threatened, the professional person is using power and is an agent of coercive social control.

One form of social control is socialization. This is the induction of persons into the social system's way of life, whether the system is a family, community, organization, or society. A bargain is struck: The system "promises" support or noninterference with the person's goals as long as they are consistent with the system's goals. The purpose of socialization is to get the work of the system done; the more successful the socialization, the less control is necessary because the person's goals will be harmonious with or identical to the system's goals. A certain degree of aggressiveness is tolerated and sometimes valued in our society if it is expressed in approved ways (football, military action, or self defense, e.g.). If we interfere with society's functioning by threatening people's lives, disrupting transportation, or preventing law enforcement personnel or firefighters from performing their tasks, we are liable to be controlled in some manner consistent with our "offense."

B. Communication

Communication is discussed in Chapter 3, II, C, "Language," in regard to symbols and language and in the appropriate chapters for functions of communication in communities, organizations, and families. Here we only wish to point out the necessity of communication and energy transfer in systems. Organization depends upon effectiveness of communication. We often think of communication as conveying emotional warmth and bringing components together. It certainly may, but it may also alienate and separate people by its content. The point is that *communication* is the transfer of energy to accomplish system goals. The effect of communication depends upon the context in which it occurs. For example, "You're under arrest!" hardly seems likely to encourage affection—it expresses control. The professionals who say they "communicated" with clients usually mean that positive affect was conveyed. But the professional and the client also communicate when the communication exerts control as in, "Stop it, Jimmy, I won't *let* you run away!"

Systems develop means to send and receive information. *Feedback* is the primary means by which systems accomplish self-direction and seek goals. Feedback is a term that has been bankrupted in popular usage. "Give me your feedback" or "I really want your feedback" are corruptions that, at best, deal with only one aspect of feedback (see glossary). Feedback is not, as the popular definition suggests, merely the echo received in response to one's actions, like a radar blip. In cybernetics and systems thought, feedback includes not only the echo but the adjustment made to the echo. It is "feed" and "back"; a newer way to put it is "feed forward."

In social systems thinking, feedback is the means by which systems accomplish adaptation and self-direction. Feedback has been referred to as the secret of natural activity, that is, adaptation and self-direction in natural systems. It refers to the process of interaction whereby information is received and processed; behavior is validated (morphostasis: assimilation—see the discussion of Piaget in Chapter 8) or changed (morphogenesis: accommodation). Feedback enables a system constantly to monitor and adapt its own functioning, which is the means to steady state. As noted in Chapter 1, feedback and the monitoring of feedback are the basis for *Chaos* theory, in which the behavior of a system is not predictable because it constantly responds to incoming stimuli, within some general range of behavior.

The use of the quality terms *positive* and *negative* in describing the nature of feedback varies among systems authors. Some view positive feedback as that which impels behavior in desirable directions and negative feedback as discouragement. Others describe negative feedback as characteristic "of homeostasis (steady state) and therefore [it] plays an important role in achieving and maintaining the quality of relationships. Positive feedback, on the other hand, leads to change, i.e., the loss of stability or equilibrium" (Watzlawick, Beavin, and Jackson, 1967:31). Still others, including the authors of this book, label feedback as positive if it confirms or encourages existing behavioral patterns. Negative feedback, then, discourages or invalidates current behavior; it encourages change, and the adaptive response is one of change (accommodation).

One example of the use of feedback processes is the planned "news leak" or material attributed to "a White House source." Information is released in order to assess what the reaction would be to official statements, actions, or shifts in policies. If there is minimal public reaction or favorable reaction, the adaptation is to proceed in the suggested direction. If reactions are negative, that is, unfavorable, the adaptation is to modify or cancel the proposed course of action or to postpone to a more auspicious time. Effective use of such "trial balloons" and the inherent aspects of feedback cycles enable a system to steer a course toward its goals with minimal need to rescind actions in the face of opposition. This whole process is feedback, not just the public response.

Feedback operations and mechanisms are familiar to people in the human services. Some commonly encountered concepts are reaction formation and overcompensation; looking-glass self and generalized other; positive reinforcement; unconditional positive regard; cycle of poverty; dynamic modeling; deviation-amplifying, deviation-counteracting, and deviation-reducing mechanisms.

An example of deviation-amplifying feedback is the following: A boy from a poor family wears clothing that makes a negative impression, and his teachers conclude that he is probably not very intelligent. He is treated as though he is not, and he responds to this, confirming their view, in order to "get along." His behavior confirms their opinion, and so they provide him with less attention and simpler, less demanding material. He performs at this level and, when he is tested, his scores confirm that he does not perform as well as other children. Teachers continue to regard him as less capable than other children, and he continues to fall behind. Eventually, he withdraws or is expelled from school. (See the comments on Truffaut's film, *The 400 Blows*, at the end of Chapter 8.)

This example serves to illustrate the differing uses of "positive" and "negative" labeling of feedback. As this boy is confirmed in and accepts the position of "poor student," this status becomes a central element of his conception of himself. Each time he receives further recognition of being an inadequate or unwanted student, that is "positive" feedback. It is "positive" since it validates his self-conception. In this instance "negative" feedback would be information the impels him to reappraise himself and change sufficiently to cause others to revise their expectations of him. Since such change is more difficult than remaining the same, the first adaptation to this sort of negative feedback is to accentuate the familiar patterns of adaptation. Thus with the boy in the example, a teacher or counselor may ambitiously attempt to use strategies to manipulate the feedback cycle through informing the youth that he really is capable of better performance, and then becomes discouraged when the boy's response "proves" he is indeed a poor student. One example of this feedback cycle is Malcolm X's encounter with Mr. Ostrowski, who discouraged Malcolm's interest in becoming a lawyer (Malcolm X, 1966). Again, the point being emphasized is that feedback processes are not simple causal chains; they are complex cycles of mutual interactions.

Feedback is an integral part of all teacher–student relationships or all counselor–client relationships, as it is of all human relationships. Therapy consists, in part, of interpreting signals from the client and "feeding back" carefully selected responses that are neutral, positive, or negative to stimulate the occurrence of behavior that is consistent with the goals of the two-person (or agency) therapeutic system. The therapist assumes the client will be similarly interpreting and feeding back.

C. Adaptation

Feedback could be considered identical to adaptation, but adaptation is discussed separately to emphasize two points. First, adaptation is viewed by some theorists (including Parsons) as being of paramount importance because systems must adjust to their environment. While it is true that there must be adjustment between systems and environment, we reject the view that the adjustment must be made only by the system and not by the suprasystem or environment. (Our position was stated earlier in the discussion of holon.) Therefore, we do recognize the importance of feedback as a mechanism of adjustment but do not make adaptation *the* primary function.

Second, adaptation takes two forms: *assimilation* and *accommodation*. These are discussed in Chapter 8 in the section on Piaget. These two terms indicate whether the system accepts or rejects the incoming information without any change on the part of the system, or whether it modifies its structure in response to the incoming information. In reality, systems do both of these at the same time in some mixture; as with other polarities, no system does one or the other exclusively. In the nineteenth century, Samuel Butler wrote,

> All our lives long, every day and every hour, we are engaged in the process of accommodating our changed and unchanged selves to changed and unchanged surroundings; living, in fact, in nothing else than this process of accommodation; when we fail in it a little we are stupid, when we fail flagrantly we are mad, when we suspend it temporarily we sleep, when we give up the attempt altogether we die. . . . A life will be successful or not according as the power of accommodation is equal or unequal to the strain of fusing and adjusting internal and external changes (Butler 1942:288—289).

CONCLUSION

This chapter has introduced those concepts we judge to be essential to a social systems approach to understanding human behavior. These are fundamental ideas that will be developed further in subsequent chapters. A few other key concepts will be introduced in later discussions of particular systems.

It is important to note in conclusion that *evolutionary, structural,* and *behavioral* aspects are three ways to slice the same apple; they are not separate but complementary dimensions of a system. A board that is long, wide, and thick is not three separate boards; nor can one dimension exist without the others.

SUGGESTED READINGS

Carse, James P.
  1986 *Finite and Infinite Games.* New York: The Free Press.
    An interesting and entertaining inquiry into the nature of closed and open interactional patterning.
Gleick, James.
  1987 *Chaos: Making a New Science.* New York: Viking Penguin.
    Based on findings from many scientific fields, this book summarizes newer views of natural and social events. "Chaos" describes the variation of events, demonstrating that particular events can be predicted only within some general parameters, because systems are extremely sensitive to initial conditions, and respond to minute changes in the feedback cycle. Chaos theory brings the natural and social sciences much closer in their views of causation, randomness, and predictability of systems.
Malcolm X (with Alex Haley).
  1966 *The Autobiography of Malcolm X.* New York: Grove Press.
    This moving autobiography exemplifies all levels of human systems and a person's interactions with them. It highlights how systems affect the person and how a person can influence wider systems.
Zukav, Gary.
  1979 *The Dancing Wu Li Masters.* New York: William Morrow.
    Another stimulating attempt to reconcile differing ways of knowing. A book written for lay persons, explaining the evolution of the quantum relativistic physics of today. It stresses that experience is never limited to two options; there is always an alternative between every "this" and every "that."

LITERARY SOURCES

Warren, Robert Penn.
  1946, 1982 *All the King's Men.* New York: Harcourt, Brace, Jovanovich.
    Written by the late poet Laureate of the United States, and loosely based on the later years of political boss and governor Huey Long of Louisiana, this novel has as one of its fundamental themes the "web" of consequences

that follow from human actions. "What goes around comes around" is another way to state it, or one can view it systemically: All actions reverberate, and affect the rest of the system.

FILMS AND VIDEOS

Dangerous Liaisons (1988)
Magnificently acted and photographed, this is a film about the "closed system" of the French court, and its intrigues, sexual, social, and political (and the overlap of all three): an entropic system in which everyone loses. Again, all actions have consequences, often unanticipated.

3

Culture and Society

Men commonly feel according to their inclina-
tions, speak and think according to their learning
and imbibed opinions, but generally act according
to custom.

Sir Francis Bacon

You observe a lot watching.

Yogi Berra*

INTRODUCTION

This chapter explores human behavior at the broadest, most general
level—that is, as a species. We will examine ideas from a number of
disciplines, ideas that seem particularly pertinent to human services and
a systems approach. These disciplines include biology, sociology, lin-
guistics, psychology, ethology, communications, and especially anthro-
pology.

A. Definitions

First, we should explain how we use the terms *culture* and *society*. To
be consistent with the systems approach, we use the term culture in two
ways. First and generally, culture refers to those qualities and attributes
that seem to be characteristic of all humankind. Culture denotes those
things unique to the species *homo sapiens* as differentiated from all other
forms of life. Humans, by contrast to all other species, evolve and adapt

*Quoted in Van Maanen (1988).

through culture rather than changes in anatomy or genetics, primarily. We employ this general usage of culture to underscore the notion that the human evolutionary timetable is unique in that it is through culture that the human is immediately affected by and subject to the evolutionary principle of natural selection. As Konrad Lorenz, the widely known ethologist, put it, "historians will have to face the fact that natural selection determined the evolution of cultures in the same manner as it did that of the species" (Lorenz, 1963:260). Sociobiologists have derived formulas of cultural diffusion and demise based upon maximization of selected cultural traits through breeding and mate selection (Boyd and Richerson, 1985). This approach is hotly disputed as lending itself to a theory of cultural (or racial) superiority. In general, we can say that a culture survives if it can accommodate to changing conditions. If its ways are rigidly matched to a particular set of environmental conditions, the survival of the culture is dependent upon the continuation of those conditions. One reason for the decline and near disappearance of some Plains groups of American Indians is that the buffalo were exterminated by white hunters and there was no adequate substitute. Another example might be the demise of western, industrial cultures as we know them, should supplies of cheap oil disappear within the next fifty years—would our culture survive the demise of the private automobile and cheap electricity?

The human, then, is a social being, uniquely possessing culture. Cultural forms—not the species—are changed, synthesized, radiated, and extinguished. This does not preclude the possibility of the human species being subject to the laws of species survival as well, but the time scale is much different for biological evolution. According to this broad definition, then, culture is viewed as a macrosystem here for purposes of discussion and speculation.

A *society* refers to a group of people who have learned to live and work together. Society is a holon, and within the society, culture refers to the way of life followed by the group (society). This, then, is the second usage of culture—that which binds a *particular* society together, and includes its manners and morals, tools, and techniques. To repeat, culture may refer to either of two levels: that which is characteristic of the species, and that which is characteristic of some specific group within the human species.

B. The Nature of Culture

According to sociologist Peter Berger, culture is a group phenomenon. While individual persons may originate ideas or behavior, they do not create cultures alone. Cultures evolve from the interactions of persons and others, and a person's belief or behavior becomes part of a culture when it is "externalized" and "objectified" (Wuthnow, Hurter, Bergesen, and Kwrzweil, 1984:24ff.) Externalization is the process by which human ideas are presented to others and become accepted as part of the culture. Once the ideas are built into a culture, and act upon the people within the culture, they have been "objectified," as part of the external world: "This world as an objective reality manifests itself most unmistakably in its coercive power, in its capacity to direct behavior, impose sanctions, punish deviance and at the extreme, destroy human life (Wuthnow et al., 1984:39).

A culture evolves as each person encounters four "poles":

1. One's own body, or somatic process, which includes the biological constitution and genetic endowment.

2. Other persons, or society; this encounter can be described in such terms as the feedback cycle, "looking glass self," and "generalized other," discussed later in this chapter. This includes the behavior of others as mediated by symbols and interpretations.

3. The material world of non-human objects, experienced as Piaget described them (see Chapter 8); this world exists independent of each person (although some philosophers might disagree), but, must be interpreted by each. It includes tools and other objects created by humans, as well as the natural environment.

4. The universe of socially constructed meanings, which must be interpreted by each person. This includes language, customs, and institutions. Berger's is a generally accepted view:

> It is important to note what Berger regards as essential in culture. The very heart of the world that humans create is socially constructed *meaning*. Humans necessarily infuse their own meanings into reality. . . . In concert with others, these meanings become objectified in the artifacts of culture—ideologies, belief systems, moral codes, institutions, and so on. In turn, these meanings become reabsorbed into consciousness as subjectively plausible definitions of reality. . . . Culture, then, is at base an all-embracing socially constructed world of subjectively and *inter*-subjectively experienced meanings. Without the intended and subjectively meaningful actions of individuals, there would be no such thing as culture (Wuthnow et al., 1984:25).

These "poles" are similar to Erikson's description of the three processes of organization: ego processes, somatic processes, and social processes (see Chapter 8,I,A,1). This can be diagrammed as a spiral, in which the self evolves within a field that has the four poles just described (see Figure 4). This conception can, by analogy, be pictured as an atom evolving in a dynamic field. As one atom evolves in interaction with its environment, it changes, as does the environment; simultaneously, other atoms interact with the first, and with their environments, of which this atom is a part. Thus, cultures evolve simultaneously with their components, the persons who inhabit them. In this process, objects, artifacts,

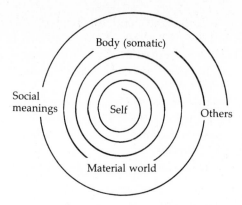

Figure 4.   Evolution of Self in culture.

conventions, and language (layers of meaning) accumulate, but some are dropped or modified; these elements are part of the culture only as long as they are employed by someone who inhabits the culture.

The spiral in figure 4 might be seen like the path of a pinball as it caroms across the playing surface of the pinball machine, bouncing from one pylon to another, sometimes "hung up" at one spot and sometimes suddenly hurled toward another. Is a person similarly determined by the forces of society? Berger denied this:

> Though Berger would acknowledge society is the stronger partner . . . he also contends that the individual is not passively shaped by his [sic] world. He is a participant in the process, co-producing with others not only the social world but himself as well. More important is Berger's repeated insistence that individuals can say "No" to the institutional imperatives. The consequences in the end may be grim, but . . . the individual, while a product of society through socialization, is, according to Berger, capable of genuine acts of freedom (Wuthnow et al., 1984:46–47).

How free? Can a person transcend the playing field, escape culture and its poles? Can a person be "beyond systems?" Apparently not. Contrary to Abraham Maslow's conception of the person who transcends culture as "self-actualizing," and Lawrence Kohlberg's similar view of the most advanced stage of moral development, Erikson's analysis of persons such as Gandhi, Luther, and Jefferson indicated that these creative people externalized and objectified (and internalized) the most universal values of their respective cultures, but did not escape them. At most, they experienced other cultures sufficiently to internalize significant values of those cultures also.

As in the examples Erikson analyzed, cultures change through the actions of persons whose ideas and behavior "fit" the culture, and were adopted by the culture because (as Erikson said) these new ideas and behaviors solved a problem for the culture (see Chapter 8,I,A,1) and hence were adopted. Change can also occur as a result of cataclysm, either physical as in famine, war, epidemic, or natural disaster (the "four horsemen of the apocalypse"). It can also change as a result of a "paradigm shift" (Kuhn, 1970) in fundamental understandings by those in the culture; one example is secularization as occurred in Western societies; another is scientism as believed in the "modern world," and discussed later in this chapter. The acceptance of Freud's views constituted such a "paradigm shift," grounded in the two examples just given.

The two major sections following deal with, first, those aspects of culture which are uniquely human; and second, dimensions by which culture can be analyzed.

I. SPECIES AND CULTURE: UNIQUE ASPECTS OF THE HUMAN SPECIES

Human beings have certain attributes in common regardless of time or place. These common attributes can be parsed and explicated in a number of ways. For our present purpose, we will generalize these attributes under four headings: (A) the capacity to think, (B) the family as a human universal, (C) language/communication, and (D) territoriality.

A. The Capacity to Think

The capacity to think is perceived as the most distinctive attribute as witnessed by our identification of the species as *homo sapiens*, thinking man. In 1948, Julian Huxley commented that "the first and most obviously unique characteristic of man [sic] is his capacity for conceptual thought, if you prefer objective terms, you will say his employment of the true speech but that is only another way of saying the same thing" (Huxley, 1964:8). The capacity to think and communicate thoughts sets humans apart from most other forms of life. In recent research, it appears that humans are not unique in this ability. Dolphins' language, e.g., is being decoded by means of computer; it appears whales have an elaborate set of sounds, consisting of songs and "whistles" by which they communicate over long distances.

Gross impairment of the capacity for thought in humans is a grave matter. Much of child rearing is devoted to the refinement and development of this capacity (as is apparent in the discussion of cognitive theory in Chapter 8). Perpetuation of tradition and use of tools is dependent upon members of the culture having the capacity to think.

Humans are unique in that not only can they think, but that they can externalize the thought process itself, possibly in three ways. One implication of the viewpoint expressed earlier about culture is that each thing created by humans is an externalization of human thought and, in some particular way, reveals some aspect of the human thought process. As discussed later, tools are amplifications of human capacities, and the tool that comes closest to fully externalizing human thought is the computer. We can discuss the human brain as a computer, but this is backward; the computer is an externalization of the brain and nervous system, and a relatively poor copy, at that. Scientists have constructed computers from mechanical switches, vacuum tubes, transistors, silicon chips, and magnetized film, and are experimenting with living cells as the material from which computers can be constructed (Angier, 1982). Should this prove successful, human beings will have externalized human thought through the creation of human biocomputers in the second way available to them. The first way is through human reproduction; every baby is, in a very limited sense, a human biocomputer. The third way for humans to externalize their thought processes would be through cloning. The implications and possible dangers to human culture in such undertakings have been expressed by science fiction writers, notably Mary Shelley, in the novel *Frankenstein*. The fundamental question raised by Shelley persists: What is distinctively human about human thought?

B. The Family as a Human Universal

The family is biologically based and is the primary social (and socializing) unit. The *fact* of the family is a constant; the *form* of the family is a variable. Anthropological studies have demonstrated convincingly that although the family as a primary socializing unit is a universal phenomenon, there is no "normal" form. As ethologists have learned about the mating, reproducing, and rearing patterns of a range of species, they have uncovered a number of factors that seem to influence the pairings and groupings of various species. These factors include:

1. The number of offspring per mating—the reproductive rate.
2. The length of the gestation period, which influences the number of matings.
3. The length of the period of the immaturity of the young, expressed in ratio to total life span.

As the first factor reduces (smaller number of offspring per mating) and the other two factors lengthen (gestation and length of time of immaturity), pair bonds and family rearing of the young increase. Among humans, the existence of the family is, of course, a necessary element for the development of culture because culture is transmitted from one generation to the next through teaching, not through the genes (La-Barre, 1954: Chapters 2 and 7).

As LaBarre emphasizes, the *cultural form* of family must never be confused with the *biological norm* of the family; the cultural forms vary tremendously (La Barre, 1954:113). The nuclear family, consisting of the biological parents and their offspring, is only one of these forms and not the most prevalent at that. The city of San Francisco, in the spring of 1989, became the first governmental unit in the United States to recognize the union of two homosexuals as legal. San Francisco leads the nation in recognizing rights of gays and lesbians, and it is likely that other communities will follow its example. If gay or lesbian marriages were to be legally sanctioned, recognition of new family forms presumably must follow, with new definitions of filial responsibility, inheritance rules, and custody provisions for any minor children (it is becoming more common for lesbians to choose artificial insemination in order to bear children). The form of the family is influenced by the culture in which it exists; in turn, the family form influences the culture. The human family, then, is a system, a holon, and it has a simultaneous existence as part and whole. Its form organizes the energies of the family members, and it must engage in transactions with its suprasystems.

The following is an example of how cultural aspects influence the family system. Our economic system, with its accent on production and distribution of goods achieved through the standardization of organization of energies, requires a mobile work force. Adaptation to this single cultural artifact has been extremely stressful to the form of the family during the past generation and has been amply discussed in both popular and technical literature. (See our discussion of this subject in Chapter 7.) The cultural bind experienced by emigrants from Appalachia is a prime example. To seek and find gainful employment required a move to an industrial city, but the cultural expectations and norms for expected behaviors remained the same at home. The nature of the mutual obligations between the emigrants and those who remain behind, especially those obligations to family, require the emigrants' presence at certain times of need. As these occur, the emigrant may decide to leave work to "go down home." This is a phenomenon also noted among American Indians.

The main point here is that family is a universal characteristic of the human species and is necessary to the maintenance of human culture, but the form of the family varies from one culture to another, and among subcultures within a single culture.

C. *Language/Communication*

Etymologists broadly define language as any transfer of meaning, but general usage refers to spoken and written messages. Appreciation of

the universality in the broader sense—that is, any transfer of meaning—
is particularly important to those who deal with persons rather than
objects. Since persons with troubles often have their troubles because
they rely on other means of communication without conscious intent,
attunement to unspoken and unwritten language forms is essential. A
person may express feelings and ideas with signals rather than with
consensual symbols of communication. Consequently, such ideas as
"body language" and "listening with the third ear" (Reik, 1948) become
important.

There are explicitly arranged language forms other than spoken and
written verbal messages. A driver's exam for illiterates uses colors and
sign shapes rather than the printed word. On the road, the conventions
for indications of one's intent to overtake and pass another vehicle are
communicated through codes of blinking lights. The automobile driver
can overtake a truck and signal to the truck driver a wish to pass. The
truck driver, based on a better view of the road ahead, can signal the
driver behind either to remain behind or that it is safe to pass. And the
variation from dim to bright lights indicates that it is a "done deed."
The key to nonverbal language is the consensus of meaning attached to
symbols and their manipulations. An important aspect of socialization
into a new system is to become acquainted with such symbolization and
learn the attached meanings. Excellent examples are the sometimes subtle and complex, silent or audible signals exchanged at auctions, and the
coded signals employed by baseball coaches.

There are also implicitly understood conventions and symbols that
require even more consensual agreement than the explicit symbols. The
initiation of a social transaction between equals can be signaled by the
shaking of hands, an embrace, or mutual acknowledgment of deference,
such as bowing or the removal of hats. The culturally conditioned "em-
bracer" learns very quickly in a "handshaking" culture that the meanings of gestures are culturally defined and are not universal.

Communication seems to be present in other life forms, as noted earlier. The dancing flight of the bee and the singing of birds to announce
territorial prerogatives to other members of their species are well
known. Such phenomena seem distinguishable from human language
in respect to the thought and meaning signified. The evidence thus far
is that bees and bird signals, operating from instinct, evolved for purposes of species survival.

Etymologists have an interesting time with cross-cultural comparisons
of word meanings and in the process provide interesting insights. For
example, in his fascinating book *The Story of Language* (1984) Mario Pei
dealt with the symbolism of color and how symbols vary from one language to another and one culture to another. Why are we "blue" when
depressed, "yellow" when cowardly, "red" when radically inclined? In
Russia, red is beautiful, and both "red" and "beautiful" come from the

same word root. White is the color of purity and innocence (and surrender) to most European cultures, but to most Asians, it is the color of mourning and death. In the Russian civil war, the Reds had a gigantic psychological advantage over the Whites because of the symbolic overtones. This kind of information carries implications for attempts to understand racial conflicts. Those who launched the "Black is Beautiful" campaign in the 1960s were attuned to the cultural importance of color symbolism. How much racial prejudice is attributable to the cultural artifact of color symbolism is unknown, but it appears to be an important factor.

In considering language and thought as species characteristics in humans, the thesis propounded by Whorf and Sapir is worthy of note. Their hypothesis was that language structures reality; the form and variability of the language determines how members of the culture will view reality and structure their thoughts (Whorf, 1956). This hypothesis is generally accepted. E. T. Hall, in developing his thesis about territoriality and its importance to people, did an analysis of the words listed in the *Oxford Pocket Dictionary*. He found that 20% of them could be classified as referring to space and spatial relations (Hall, 1969:93).

Bruner said that the Whorf and Sapir formulation sets up the pins in the wrong alley (a cultural metaphor). He held that attention should really be focused on *how* language determines thought, regardless of which language is being considered (Bruner, 1968). There is a close, demonstrable relationship between culture and language. This relationship is not necessarily causal in either direction. As often cited, modern English and American language structures attend closely to the passage of time. In the study of grammar, tenses are of utmost importance, since time is so essential to aspects of the culture. Some cultures make no provisions for tenses—the precise measurement of time is of little importance to them.

La Barre presented intriguing facts and speculations about language as symbolic communication (LaBarre, 1954: Chapter 10). He accepted the Whorfian hypothesis and stated that the structure of reality is, much of the time, merely imputed to reality by the structure of our language. As soon as the human infant learns to speak any language at all, it already has a "hardening of the categories," or "they are different, this we know, for our language tells us so" (LaBarre, 1954).

La Barre developed the idea that language is so flexible that a word can put into semantic equation any two disparate objects in the universe. If the society accepts the equation by consensus, semantically it becomes the essence of reality; if the individual does this without societal consensus, the person may be labeled schizophrenic and thus not attuned to reality (the person may, alternatively, be a creative genius, of course). "A psychotic's truth is one 'I' make it, and cultural truth is what by unwitting vote 'we' make it; but ultimate truth still remains in the outside world of that which is" (LaBarre, 1954:266). Robert Merton expressed the same idea in his Thomas theorem, "If men [sic] define situations as real, they are real in their consequences" (Merton, 1957:421). Koestler commented:

> The prejudice and impurities which have been incorporated into the verbal concepts of a given universe of discourse cannot be undone by any amount of discourse within the frame of reference of that universe. The rules of the game, however absurd, cannot be altered by playing that game. Language can become a screen which stands between the thinker and reality. This is the reason why true creativity often starts where language ends (Koestler, 1967a:177).

D. Territoriality

Territoriality refers to the tendency of people, in their social systems, to seek and maintain a territory. Some authors deal with territory as primarily spatial (Ardrey, 1966; Hall, 1969), while others stress the interactional aspects (Lyman and Scott, 1967). The definition of spatial and interactional territories is a paramount feature of any culture.

One simple example is the definition of territorial elements as squared or rounded. It seems that this choice is simultaneously determined *by* other features of the culture and is a determinant *of* culture, as well. The "home territories" within a given culture give clues to other aspects of the culture. The sedentary and specialized culture with much differentiation of function tends to organize living and work spaces in squares with specialized uses. The square house has its bedrooms, bathrooms, kitchen, living room, den, and so forth. The nomadic, unspecialized culture lives in round houses (igloo, wigwam, cave, or round hut) without specialized compartments. Arranging territories in squares tends to close boundaries. In the 1960s and 1970s, two examples of apparent shifts in culture were the building of geodesic domes as homes, and the design of public schools in "pods," "clusters," or "modules."

The spirit of equality, fidelity, and camaraderie embodied in the King Arthur legend is symbolized by the table round. Formal dining tables are usually rectangular, while tables in small, intimate bars are round. Youth's expressions of dissatisfaction with the impersonal, highly structured role relations and specialized functions of the bureaucratic system or organization were expressed in the 1960s epithet "square." Dictionaries show that the meanings attached to this epithet by immediately preceding generations were "justly," "fairly," and "honestly," as in a "square shooter." These meanings reflected the primary purpose of the impersonality of the bureaucratic system—to protect the person from unjust and arbitrary decisions. The Paris negotiations concerning the resolution of the Vietnam War were delayed for many months while it was decided whether the talks would be conducted over a rectangular

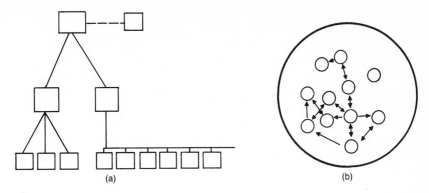

Figure 5. A typical representation of a bureaucratic structure is depicted in (a). A typical sociogram is represented in (b).

table or a circular one. In part, this dispute symbolized crucial differences in cultural traditions and beliefs between the contending systems.

Relationships are symbolized by diagrammatic representations intended to concretize interactional territories (Figure 5). The components in Figure 5a are arranged in a vertical hierarchy and each component (person or department) is designated by title or role rather than by name. Specialization and differentiation are designated by these labels. In Figure 5b, the components would be labeled by name (or number, to protect the innocent). The hierarchy here is represented in the circular plane and conveys positive, negative, and absent patterns of relatedness. Each of these diagrams is illustrative of interactional territorial arrangements and relationships.

It is hypothesized, then, that all systems have a territorial dimension. This territory may be spatial or interactional, not static, objective, or observable. It probably is a "sense of territory," and as such is congruent with the particular culture. Territoriality refers to the cultural ways people locate themselves in their universe and establish the boundaries of their various human systems.

II. ANALYTIC DIMENSIONS OF CULTURE: QUALITIES OF A SOCIETY

Definitions of culture abound and frequently conflict. Kroeber and Kluckhohn (1952) devoted an entire book to a listing of definitions of culture. They concluded that the definition given by Edward Tylor in 1871 was as good as any. Tylor's definition was that culture is that complex whole that includes knowledge, belief, art, law, morals, custom, and any other capabilities and habits *acquired by a human being as a member of society.* The italicized words represent an important qualification occasionally overlooked by enthusiastic culture determinists. Konrad Lorenz considered this qualification to be of the utmost importance, and stated that "human behavior, and particularly human social behavior, far from being determined by reason and cultural tradition alone, is still subject to all the laws prevailing in all phylogenetically adapted instinctive behavior" (Lorenz, 1963:237). Rather than choosing a definition of culture from the myriad that have been offered, or trying to formulate another, we will discuss five dimensions of culture. These dimensions are expansions on what Jerome Bruner termed "the five great humanizing forces" (Bruner, 1968:75ff.): toolmaking, social organization, language, management of the prolonged human childhood, and the human urge to explain the world.

These dimensions are important facets of any culture. One can approach the analysis of culture through examining these dimensions regardless of the time and place, or kind of culture being studied. In regard to a subculture within a culture, such as a peer group or professional culture, certain of these dimensions may seem less applicable; but each of the five seems applicable to some extent. We are then viewing culture as the ways of doing, being, and explaining, in a particular system.

A. Tools

Tools are amplifiers of human capacities, whether the tools are invented or synthesized. They fall into three classes:

1. Amplifiers of *sensory* capacities; for example, microscopes, telescopes, telephones, television, clocks, spectacles, radar, conch shells, and "mind-expanding" drugs (such as peyote in some cultures).
2. Amplifiers of *motor* capacities; for example, hammers, wheels, the lever, rockets, and automobiles.
3. Amplifiers of *reasoning* and *thinking* capacities, for example, mathematical systems, logic, the abacus, the computer, and the chalkboard (a major educational invention).

Tools, then, are devices, objects, and procedures that are extensions of human natural capacities. The crucial, most important aspect is not the tool itself but rather its function, that is, the use to which the tool is put. A hammer is generally assumed to be of use to pound nails and, if it is a claw hammer, to remove nails as well, but it can also be used as a lethal weapon or to prop open a door or window. Books generally are assumed to be for the purpose of reading, but they can also be used to press flowers, impress people, or level the short leg of a table. Understanding the tools of a culture includes, therefore, not only understanding their seeming intrinsic or built-in purpose but, more importantly, how the tools are used (i.e., their purpose to the user). Some years ago one of the authors worked in a small Indian reservation where the occupants had been given a refrigerator for each household and electricity was available. The purpose of food storage by refrigeration was not then part of the way of life of that culture. The refrigerators were used for other purposes—for decoration in a few instances—but mostly for storage. They were perceived as attractive boxes with a door, but the "built-in purpose" was not the purpose of the users. A current example is the function of exercise bicycles, often unused, as clothing racks or end tables in living rooms; they maintain an air of potential if not actual fitness.

Peter Farb, a cultural anthropologist, analyzed the evolution of cultures in a remarkably readable book. One of his theses was that a new tool or technique must have a counterpart in social organization or knowledge to become functional. He used the example of the introduction of the horse into two quite different cultures. The first of these cultures, a hunting tribe, mounted the horses and used them to pursue the bison. This amplified human motor capacities, making them much more efficient hunters, and rapidly the culture evolved toward one in which the horse became central. The second culture merely slaughtered the horse and ate; it had no function in this culture (Farb, 1968:29). A more homely example might be the dust-covered computer in thousands of homes, unused because the owners were reared in a pre-computer-literate society, and have found no function for it in their lives. Their children, however, may find uses for it, for games or for word-processing, having been born into a computerized society.

Tools, then, are a key dimension by which a culture may be analyzed. They extend the uses of energies within the cultural system toward fulfillment of the system's goals. It may be equally significant and analytical of a culture that certain tools do *not* exist. For example, the absence of written languages, or of the wheel, were significant in some North and Central American Indian cultures.

B. Social Organization

All cultures, being social systems, have organization. They may be organized, be in the process of organizing, or be in the process of disorganizing. But in any event, the dimension of organization is present. As previously stated, the structure is not fixed, and any analysis of structure is like a still photo. At the moment of analysis, the social organization of a culture is not what it has been nor what it will become. It is structured in the sense of a system of interacting elements, and any change in one element or single pattern of relationships affects all other elements directly or indirectly.

The theory of evolution, in its essence, describes the increase of complexity, whether from simple to complex biological organisms or from simple to complex cultures. The social organization of an evolving culture becomes more complex because of an increased volume of relationships among the various elements of the culture. A "stagnant culture" is one in which the relationships are static and interaction of the cultural elements is unchanging. Some have postulated that bureaucracy appears as an organizational structure when society reaches a given state of complexity, regardless of the form of government. The bureaucracies of ancient China, Rome, the Roman Catholic Church, the Russian monarchy, and most recently western democracies and communist states can all be cited as illustrations. Bureaucracy seems to have as a major function the reduction and containment of forces that may lead to change. As such, bureaucracy is probably used as a "buffering" device by all complex societies. The systems term *equifinality* (see glossary) applies to this phenomenon; Beer defined it as "the proven ability of certain *open* systems to reach the same characteristic result, despite differences in initial conditions, and despite different rules of conduct along the way" (1981:191). Chaos theory also suggests that despite variances in initial conditions, systems behave in similar, highly ordered, ways within certain characteristic parameters (Gleick, 1987).

Certain important concepts related to social organization are commonly employed. These are the interrelated ideas of *class, status,* and *role.* All societies have schemes of ordering human interaction and ways of defining and communicating expected behaviors. As with definitions of culture. many theorists have proposed hypothetical *social class* structures. Perceptive observers have identified life styles (Loeb, 1961; Mitchell, 1983), socioeconomic indices (Hollingshead, 1969); and values among social classes (Kvaraceus, 1959).

T. H. Marshall, an English sociologist, worked out a scheme based on Max Weber's writings (Marshall, 1964). Marshall believed that there are three aspects operating: economic status, social status, and political power. When the groupings of these three coincide (multibonded), then social class is a visible thing. If the boundaries between the social classes are clear and closed, the result is caste. The idea of social class suggests a group consciousness on the part of members, both of their own social groups and other groups, and of their general position in the social hierarchy. Many writers have noted the emergence of a "permanent underclass" in American society, made up of those who persist in poverty for several generations. It is true, for example, that while African American incomes rose from 52% of white family incomes in 1959 to 64% in 1970, they fell back to 55% in 1982 (Farley, 1984:199), thus tending to fix many such families in a low socioeconomic status.

John Rowan followed the classical distinctions of Pitrim Sorokin in characterizing a social class as a multibonded group:

> One bond is occupation, incuding such things as career chances; one bond is income and wealth, particularly important at the extremes; and the third bond is a matter of the collection of rights and duties, of privileges and disenfranchisements. These things tend to run together and give a certain social status (Rowan, 1978:85).

Social status does not necessarily imply the existence of groups at all; it refers to a consensus of social ranking. Status, of course, can be achieved or ascribed, but the organizing mechanisms for acquiring or granting status, as well as the recognition thereof, seem to be present in all cultures. To understand the culture, it is important to know the key determinants of status.

Role relates to and derives from status. Ralph Linton described role as "the sum total of the cultural patterns associated with a particular status. It thus includes the attitudes, values and behavior ascribed by the society to any and all persons occupying that status" (Linton, 1945:76 77). The complexity of a status is manifested partly by the complexity and differentiation of role expectations. Bureaucracy is one of the organizational forms devised to reduce this complexity. In the bureaucratic structure, the role often becomes more important than the person occupying the status, but it is only through occupying the status that the person can assume the role. Beyond the family, continuity depends less on the characteristics of the person and more on the role being occupied.

Role expectations, then, are culturally defined by the system and its components and incorporated by the persons filling the role. A culture may allow greater or lesser latitude in deviations from the expected behaviors. Certain cultures rigidly define role behavior, but more often the rigidity or flexibility of role definition is dependent on what else is transpiring within the system. For example, there was a time in the United States when expected role behavior of children in relation to adults in their lives was expressed by the phrase, "children should be seen and not heard." More recently, children are expected to be heard, and if this role behavior is not forthcoming, they are considered withdrawn or at least shy.

In a dynamic, open cultural system, role occupants constantly seek flexibility of role definition with or without the encouragement of the culture. As the cultural system is threatened from either internal or external quarters, strings are drawn more tightly on the expected role behaviors. One dramatic example is the behaviors of students in Beijing's Tienamen Square in May and June, 1989; their behavior was proscribed so severely that many were killed, and others hunted by means of nationwide searches. As Woodruff analyzed it, this was part of a series of student demonstrations beginning in 1985, and is part of a pattern of cultural change involving a contest for power between the Communist party, the People's Liberation Army, and newly arisen managerial middle class (Woodruff, 1989: especially Chapter 7). Students, some of whom have traveled or studied abroad, represent this new class which threatens Chinese Marxist ideology and control by demanding social and economic freedom.

Another example of a perceived need for social control of youth is the "wilding" by a group of youth in New York's Central Park in Spring, 1989, in which they attacked several people, injuring some, and raping and nearly killing one woman. Public reaction predominantly demanded severe punishment to stop such incidents; the role of "youth" does not include uncontrolled violence in the wider society, although in the more limited context of some youth gangs, "wilding" is a frequent pastime.

All persons occupy a complex of roles, the total number of these being influenced by the quantity of networks of relationships they are involved in. At any given moment, a person is likely to be more actively fulfilling one or another of the roles but carries them all at one time nevertheless. When a person experiences excessive conflict in fulfilling varying role expectations, or if society judges the person to be failing in this respect, the person and the society both have troubles.

A contemporary example is the strong cultural emphasis on the work role expectation. Work is quite narrowly defined as contractual employment, profession, or own business, and it is expected that each adult, unless manifestly disabled or past an arbitrary age, will fulfill such a role. The work role is fused with the economic role. There are an insufficient supply of such work roles (i. e., jobs). Even though members of the society accept the prescribed role expectations, a significant number are not able to fulfill the agreed-upon role. The culturally prescribed remedy is to attempt to generate more jobs (i.e., work roles). Another culture may seek to broaden the definition of work ("mother's work," e.g.) or to separate work from economic participation (social security or the guaranteed income, e.g.).

If any significant minority of the members of a society (some have suggested 10% is sufficient) do not do what the consensus requires for a length of time, the system is in difficulty and the survival of the culture is in question; or it may change steady states. In such instances, energies of the system must be devoted to maintaining the organization and redefining the expectations of those in the particular status. In the latter years of the Vietnam War a significant minority refused to fulfill the expectation for military service. Subsequently, the draft was terminated and expectations modified. It may not be clear for a generation what effect the revolt of Beijing's young educated elite against the regimentation and militarism of China's culture will have; almost certainly it will have a profound effect. In Hong Kong, which is to return to China's control in 1997, about 20% of the population took to the streets in reaction to events in Beijing; more than the 10% suggested by some as sufficient to modify the larger society.

C. Language

Here again we refer to language in its broader sense, that is, as transfer of meaning. The structures of language strongly influence the content conveyed—language is composed of symbols and the meanings are learned and transferred through social interaction. *Symbolic interaction* refers to this process. The communication of symbols and their attendant meanings represents the major form of transaction between human systems.

Most of the work of the symbolic interactionists is built on the insights of George Herbert Mead and Charles Horton Cooley (Meltzer, 1967; Cooley, 1967). Mead stated that we do not simply respond to the acts (including speech, of course) of others; rather, we act on our *interpretations* of their intentions and judgments. Gestures are an important kind of symbolic communication, and we respond to the meanings not necessarily as they are intended but as we interpret them. When a gesture has a common meaning (some measure of consensus), Mead termed it a *linguistic element*—a significant symbol. Common examples include the kiss as an expression of affection; the drawn-back, clenched fist as threat of aggression; the smile as an expression of pleasure; and the frown as an expression of displeasure. Because of the consensus of meaning, we attribute the quality of pleasure to the smile of a baby even though it may be an expression of gas in the stomach.

The term *generalized other* is central to Mead's formulation. This refers to a generalized stance or viewpoint imputed to others that one uses to evaluate one's own behavior. A person responds not only to others who may be present, but to the general expectations of one's reference group (that is, a group to which one belongs or wishes to belong).

Another key concept is *self*. An individual may act socially toward self as toward others. The self is composed of the *I* and the *me*. The *I* is the impulsive, spontaneous, and unorganized part of the self. *Me* is the incorporated other. The *I* energizes and provides propulsion, whereas the *me* provides direction, in other words, controls function. These are similar to, but in important ways different from, id and superego. The emphasis is on social rather than intrapsychic functioning.

The *looking-glass self* is Cooley's construct and refers to the idea that we interpret what others think of us. It involves the following sequence: (1) the imagination of our appearance to others; (2) the imagination of their judgment; and (3) a self-feeling in response to this imagined judgment (e.g., pride or mortification).

The symbolic interactionists, as represented by Mead and Cooley, go far toward explaining the process of transfer of meaning. Their formulations clearly demonstrate that meaning derives from interaction between the sender and receiver at both verbal and nonverbal levels. These are, in essence, elements of the descriptions of feedback cycle as transacted between systems. If there is little or no feedback from outside the focal system, then the assessment of appearance and judgment must be projected from inside. For example, the paranoid person is not able, or is not allowing self, to participate in this feedback cycle with outside systems and must rely on his or her own imagined judgments. As Philip Slater put it, "Without air we die, without love we turn nasty, without feedback we go crazy" (Slater, 1974:49). The same can occur in nations that are cut off, with feedback projected from within, and therefore become isolated and chauvinistic. This may have been part of the dynamic of China in Summer, 1989, as its army killed its own citizens, to the dismay of other nations; it may have been reacting to its own internal feedback, due to millenia of cultural norms of order and centralized control. In the United States, the Watergate investigations indicated that isolation and closed, internal feedback cycles characterized the Nixon administration. This is a frequent criticism of the societal context of Washington, D.C.; that is, the feedback cycle is overly restricted and tends to be "out of touch." This is often referred to as "within the beltway," the ring of freeways that surrounds the federal district.

Language, then, is the vehicle for transfer of meaning between the components of a cultural system and between one culture system and other cultures. That which is considered important enough to symbolize and communicate is as important to understanding a culture as is the understanding of the methods of communication. Furthermore, language is a means of setting and maintaining cultural boundaries as well as a major means of organizing the energies of the system. Subcultures universally employ their own jargon and argot, and one of the major tasks of socialization into a subculture is to become acquainted with the special language. Certainly the subculture of social work is an example with such jargon as "personal–social needs," "relationship," and "intervention." The special language of a subculture may serve to exclude others from participation in the culture. Because it prevents interaction, this "linguistic collusion" is an effective way to close a boundary. (Incidentally, we hope that this systems approach helps prevent such boundary closures between helping professions, although we recognize the initial difficulty in learning the jargon of systems thinking.)

The importance of "screening" and interpreting symbols in working with people is abundantly clear. Much of the literature of the helping professions, for example, is devoted to making the reader sensitive to the possible meanings of symbols received from the person being helped. Theodore Reik's idea of "the third ear," in which the therapist's own emotional reactions give clues to unspoken messages being sent by the patient, is a time-tested example (Reik, 1948), Another example is psychological testing, especially "projective" tests such as the Rorschach, Thematic Apperception, or House–Tree–Person tests. In these tests, the responses of the subject being tested are interpreted in order to provide clues about the subject's personality structure and what treatment methods may be most useful in dealing with this person. In these instances, between the professional person's reception (input) of the symbols and response (output) to them, the interpretation (processing) that occurs is formalized and takes on the character of scientific problem-solving—or at least, this is what professional schools hope their graduates are capable of doing.

In such professional techniques, obviously some standardization of language and symbols is necessary, and thus each theoretical approach, such as psychoanalysis, transactional analysis, or behavior modification, must devote much energy to training professionals in some standard terminology (and so must the systems approach). This is necessary so that the results of professional efforts and the theoretical elaboration of them can be conveyed in some common language. Certainly the history of psychiatry is replete with examples of attempts by Kraepelin, Freud, and others to standardize terminology. Menninger listed such attempts in the history of medicine (Menninger, 1963: Chaps. 1 and 2, and Appendix). A major problem for each of the developing helping professions has been the training of professionals to apply the same labels to similar phenomena so that terms have some consensual meaning—that is, so that one psychiatrist's "schizoid" is not another psychiatrist's "passive–aggressive." Despite such efforts as the American Psychiatric Association's standard nomenclature, however, serious disagreements on interpretations of symbolic behavior do occur within that profession. Consensus of meaning with a high degree of precision is difficult to achieve; if it were not so, probably books like this would not need a glossary.

D. Child Rearing: Management of the Prolonged Human Childhood

Anthropologists, sociologists, and psychologists have exhaustively researched forms of child rearing in various cultures. Although most of these studies focus on the family system, many deal with other educative and socializing social systems as well. Writers in ethology compare the human family structures with those of other animals, seeking generalities and unique attributes (Ardrey, 1966; Lorenz, 1963). The human family is always found to be highly organized, in the sense that Monane uses this phrase to connote intense intrasystem relatedness (Monane, 1967; and our discussion in Chapter 1, III, "Organization"). There is a predominance of sentiment in this interaction and not merely biological need gratification and response, although these are always related.

The management of the human's prolonged childhood is a major characteristic of any culture and, as such, must fit with other aspects of the
culture and interact with these. As a culture becomes more complex and
differentiated, so too does child rearing, and other social provisions appear. There are numerous examples in the recent evolution of United
States society. As the economic system required greater mobility, the extended family began to dissipate (see the discussion of this sequence in
Chapter 7). This was accompanied by the advent of the babysitter. Currently, the demands of the economic system and shifts in role definition
of the female are leading to rapid growth of day-care centers, the emergence of the "househusband" (in two comic strips, e.g.), and demands
for federal legislation to support wider availability of day care centers.

New social institutions such as day-care facilities are accompanied by
changes in family functions, but this is not necessarily tantamount to family breakdown. These new systems arise to realize more effectively the
complex of values of a culture. Usually, certain values are in conflict with
certain other values, leading to tension and strain in the various systems.
The historical development of the public school is an excellent illustration. The belief that a certain amount of formal education should be the
right of every person developed over centuries in a number of places, particularly Western Europe. This was related to values such as "equality"
and "the importance of knowledge." An informed citizenry became a national system goal in the first half of the nineteenth century. As the belief
became a cherished system value held by a significant portion of the components of the system, provisions were implemented to fulfill the value.
This was followed by the adoption of the "common school" in a majority
of the states during the decade of the 1850s. Since then, the public school
as a child-rearing social subsystem (if not a subculture, almost) has continued to evolve, becoming more complex and differentiated. The current
controversy over the transmission ‑f culture, manners, and morals related
to education about AIDS and sexual behavior generally, and whether this
should be a family or school responsibility, exemplifies the process of culture change and the inherent value conflicts. One community in Minnesota recently defied state law by refusing to have AIDS education provided in its school. There is also increasing concern about the role and
effect of television and movies upon children as well as a growing controversy over the issue of prayer in the public schools.

E. The Human Urge to Explain the World

Berger said that there is "a human craving for meaning that appears
to have the force of instinct. Men [sic] are congenitally compelled to
impose a meaningful order upon reality" (Wuthnow et al., 1984:26).
This major dimension of culture is often overlooked or minimized in

explication of the concept of culture. Much of the energy of a culture system is expended in this effort. Religion, philosophy, science, and superstition are some of these pursuits. This quest to explain the unexplained can be viewed as an integral aspect of the adaptation of a system to its environment.

In our present-day culture, science continues to be the dominant means of exploring, explaining, and changing our world. (The scientific method, empirical observation, and inductive reasoning are, of course, highly valued only in certain cultures.) It is believed dogmatically that the scientific method or technology can solve all important problems. Major religious organizations in this culture have been responsive to the currently accepted way of explaining the world and have engaged in social problem-solving in the "scientific" way. One denomination, of course, refers to "Christian Science."

In recent years, however, there has been a renewal of interest in other ways of knowing and explaining the cosmos. Popular manifestations include astrology, numerology, and meditation; many of these interests have been labeled "New Age" thinking. Adherents of creationism are pressing to juxtapose their explanation with scientism in the curriculum of the public schools.

CONCLUSION

Today, there is recognition by all professions and disciplines concerned with human behavior that culture must be attended to and understood. The concept of culture has become politicized in the past two decades by racial minorities and ethnic groups that have called attention to the vitality and integrity of their own cultures and have reasserted their impact on "mainstream" culture (although the mainstream becomes more difficult to identify as the contributions of subcultures to the society are increasingly recognized). At the same time, the "melting pot" description of United States society—an unfortunate metaphor to the extent that it denied subsystems their own distinctiveness and integrity—has been replaced. Some theorists construed our multicultural relationships to be "beyond the melting pot" (Glazer and Moynihan, 1970).

Obviously, these changes in our thinking about culture have implications for the human services. Without an awareness of the power of culture, it is very difficult to care for, teach, learn from, or assist anyone whose cultural experience has been significantly different from one's own. At the same time, it is difficult to avoid the human proclivity to overgeneralize from the culture to the person (e.g., Latinos are emotional; he is Latino; therefore, expect him to be emotionally unstable). One example is a comment by an American Indian girl, that "you are welcome in the homes of your white friends, as long as you don't get into the refrigerator." Sharing a common culture does not make people identical. We honor that principle in interacting with other members of our own culture, but with members of a foreign culture, we tend not to expect differences among persons.

The pioneering anthropologists tended to study cultures markedly different from their own; these were so-called "primitive" cultures. The unfamiliarity allowed them a measure of objectivity in reasoning from symbolic behavior to related meanings. Even so, they were frequently confounded by what they observed or inferred meanings grounded in their own cultural experiences. Margaret Mead, in her intimate biography (Mead, 1972), makes the statement that her field studies were conducted so that Americans might better understand themselves. This is consistent with E. T. Hall's contention that to be able to see one's own culture, it is first necessary to experience a foreign one (Hall, 1977). This is true for the simple reason that one's native culture becomes "normal," "sensible," "natural," and "right." Moreover, it feels natural. It feels natural to shake hands, to smile when pleased, to bathe frequently; but, of course, all these conventions are peculiar to particular cultures.

Almost everyone has experienced the sensation of being "out of culture," as a fish out of water. This may be expressed as not knowing what to expect from others, vague physical discomforts, longing for the familiar, and disorientation. The traveler in Europe looking for a proper hamburger (and finding sausage with swiss cheese on it) is a popular example. Coca Cola has gone wherever United States citizens have gone, and Kentucky Fried Chicken is adjacent to Tienamen Square in Beijing. In the same vein, in the wake of an earthquake shock in Guatemala City, many people from the United States, without prior plan or communication, congregated in the Dairy Queen parking lot.

How one applies the concept of culture depends on one's vantage point, what one is prepared to see, and perhaps most important, the knowledge used to interpret one's observations. Visualize the three-dimensional atomic model as a system and then consider the study of culture. If you are somewhere within the cultural system you can see some components well, others less well, and others not at all. If you are outside the system your perspective may help you better see the "big picture," but the further out you are, the more danger there is of reductionism and oversimplification. Popular adages express this dilemma (e.g., "they can't see the forest for the trees").

There is no solution to this dilemma. To understand best a culture in any of its forms (e.g., a primitive society, an ethnic group, a peer group, or a profession), observers must strive for objectivity if they are themselves components of the system, or strive for involvement if they are outside the system. It is through this process of reasoning that social work, education, and other human services recently have concerned themselves again with greater involvement in the "client system" and its particular culture, be it family, neighborhood, or community.

SUGGESTED READINGS

Cohen, Bernice.
  1988 *Global Perspectives: The Total Culture System in the Modern World.* London: Codek Publications.
      She says "culture is a system," and we are now in a worldwide culture, a "total culture system," which we must understand.
Farb, Peter.
  1968 *Man's Rise to Civilization as Shown by the Indians of North America from Primeval Times to the Coming of the Industrial State.* New York: Dutton.
      In this very readable book, with its foreboding title, Farb illustrated how cultures evolve.
Hall, Edward T.
  1969 *The Hidden Dimension.* Garden City, NY: Doubleday.
      Extremely interesting and stimulating work that deals with the structure of experience as it is determined by culture. The particular theme examined is the human use of space. We have used this book as the "small map" for this chapter. Students have found the content directly applicable to their professional practice.
Hall, Edward T.
  1977 *Beyond Culture.* Garden City, NY: Doubleday Anchor.
      Hall's synthesis of his own research and the research of others, and his theorizing about culture.
Hewitt, John P.
  1979 *Self and Society.* second edition. Boston: Allyn and Bacon.
      A useful source for a symbolic interactionist approach to social psychology.
LaBarre, Weston.
  1954 *The Human Animal.* Chicago: University of Chicago. (The 1968 edition has minor differences.)
      The author, an anthropologist, examined human culture from an evolutionary viewpoint. He combined findings from anthropology, psychiatry, linguistics, and human biology into a controversial thesis. His arguments are particularly thorough as he deals with family, symbolic communication, and deviant behavior.
Lyman, Stanford M., and Marvin B. Scott.
  1967 "Territoriality: A Neglected Social Dimension." *Social Problems* 15:236–245.
      A definitive statement of a typology of human spatial arrangments. In addition to describing classifications of territory, this article well illustrated varieties of boundary definition and boundary maintenance.

Van Maanen, John.

> 1988 *Tales of the Field*. Chicago: University of Chicago Press.
>
> A practitioner's guide to methodological and conceptual issues in ethnography, the study of culture in the field. Witty, wise, and useful to the student of cultures. It surveys most of the major works of cultural field studies.

Wuthnow, Robert, James Davison Hunter, Albert Bergesen, and Edith Kurzweil.

> 1984 *Cultural Analysis: The Work of Peter L. Berger, Mary Douglas, Michel Foucault, and Jurgen Habermas*. Boston, London: Routledge & Kegan Paul.
>
> Clear, concise analysis and comparison of these pre-eminent theorists. Presumes familiarity with basic concepts of sociology. The chapter on Berger is virtually a summary of mainstream thought on the nature of culture, and highly compatible with our systems approach.

LITERARY SOURCES

Dorris, Michael.

> 1987 *A Yellow Raft in Blue Water*. New York: Warner Books.
>
> A novel of American Indian culture related through the experiences of grandmother, mother, and daughter who move through life together. Vine Deloria, Jr., said it "shows us the humorous, ironic side of reservation life as it has rarely been portrayed."

Erdrich, Louise.

> 1985 *Love Medicine*. Toronto, New York: Bantam Books.
>
> This is a powerful novel of a complex American Indian family and rich culture, in which meanings become evident only after the fact, in the understandings of others.

FILMS AND VIDEOS

The Cutting Edge: Portraits of Southeast Asian Adolescencts in Transition (1983)

> Portraits of three Asian refugees: Hmong, Vietnamese, and Lao. Each describes the survival of his culture in the new United States setting. Music, instruments, costumes, and rituals are part of the background.

Dreams on Hold (1986)

> This documentary examines the growing gap between rich and poor in the United States, and the shrinking middle class. Underemployment, and the need for two paychecks in a family, are examined. The implications of employment of mothers of young children are discussed. The dream of security, growth, and upward mobility seems to be fading.

Farewell to Manzanar (1976; made for television)

> Superb portrayal of the internment of Japanese-Americans during World War II. Pictures well their plight as acculturated *Issei, Nissei,* or *Sansei* (first, second, or third generation) Americans, and their humiliation by their chosen country.

Gandhi (1982)

British and Indian cultures, and the transformation of both by a powerful set of ideas embodied in one person, vividly portrayed. The dramatic events convey well a sense of how change occurred.

Maids and Madams (1986)

Apartheid in South Africa is viewed in the relationship of the Black household worker and the white employer. More than a million Black women are economically bound to such jobs. The psychological battle for dominance is waged in intimate settings in white homes.

Powwow Highway (1989)

A small, unpretentious film that is a gem. Believable characters, plausible plot. A unique film in that contemporary American Indian cultures are presented accurately, sympathetically, and with humor.

Quest for Fire (1982)

This is an imaginative and plausible recreation of human life in the Ice Age. Anthony Burgess created a language, and Desmond Morris *(The Naked Ape)* devised a body language.

Communities

Making your way in the world today
Takes everything you've got.
Taking a break from all your worries
Sure would help a lot.
Wouldn't you like to get away?
Sometimes you wanna go
Where everybody knows your name,
And they're always glad you came.
You wanna be where you can see
our troubles are all the same.
You wanna go
where everybody knows your name.*

INTRODUCTION

Both communities and organizations are macrosystems as contrasted with the microsystems of persons, families, and small groups. Both are intermediate (or "mediating") systems between society and the small groupings in which intimate affective transactions occur. Historically, sociology has had difficulty defining and distinguishing among community, organization, and society (Hillery, 1968). The major distinction between community and organization that we have in mind is one made by Ferdinand Tönnies: "A community is held together by feeling and sentiment, primarily, while an organization is sustained by 'rational' considerations, usually explicit in formal contracts, usually written" (Tönnies, 1957).

I. COMMUNITY AS SYSTEM

Probably the most difficult systems to define with precision are *community* and *small group* (which will be discussed in Chapter 6). The term community has become overly used, with broad and vague applications. It is frequently employed to impute commonality of interest to what in fact are disparate groups of people, e.g., the "intelligence community," the "community of elders," the "farm community." Possession of one common defining quality does not in and of itself form a community.

Because the community is at the interface between society and microsystems, it is of concern to all social disciplines and professions. The family is a person's primary field of interaction during childhood; in adulthood, the other major field of interaction is community, or at least significant sectors of community. Such sectors include the financial, commercial, religious, educational, social, and legal institutions (among others) in which the person participates. French said of community that "at one and the same time it is an important building block of society, and it is society itself. It represents culture to the individual and as such shapes him [sic], and it is subject to the will of the individual who as a citizen can enact changes in his community" (French, 1969:5). Notice the emphasis upon mutual causation here; the citizen and the community influence each other through mediation of family, small group, and organizations.

A. Kinds of Communities

Communities differ in several respects. First, Tönnies described them as being held together by two sorts of bonds—*gemeinschaft* and *gesellschaft*. A gemeinschaft community is characterized by implicit bonds that relate all community members to the others. These bonds include common values and beliefs, mutual interdependence, respect, and a shared sense of status hierarchy. Rules regarding relationships are not formalized but rest in cultural traditions and complementary social expectations rather than written codes or contracts. An American Indian tribal community may be an example in that behavior often is greatly influenced by tradition and culture; however as tribes have "modernized," they too have become somewhat more formalized with Reservation Business Committees (as required in the 1934 Indian Reorganization Act) and parliamentary structures. Yet, there remains for many a gemeinschaft feeling of place, as for Roland Lussier, who wrote this as a sixth grader in Northern Minnesota.

> There is no place better than the Indian reservation. It's so beautiful, the land is covered with dark green pine trees and other kinds of trees. At dawn we can watch the sun, and we will see beautiful colors around the sun. We are proud of our reservation and we thank God for giving it to us (Brill, 1974:56).

A gesellschaft community is characterized by bonds that are both formal and specific. Community members relate to each other through formally structured relations within community institutions such as work organizations, professions, and civic organizations (Nisbet, 1966).

A second way that communities differ from one another is in the degree of attachment to a specific location. This variable can also be used to determine specific types of communities, but the reader should keep in mind that these categories, like all typologies, are ideal and not real. In reality, attachment to place or location is more or less present in all communities. Tönnies described the following communities:

1. *Place Communities.* Tönnies also called this community a "locality." One form of community organization has been called "locality development" (Cox et al., 1987). This type of community has also been called a *geographic* or *spatial* community. It is based upon a common habitat and occupation of adjacent (or nearby) properties. Examples of "place" community are neighborhoods, villages, towns, and cities.

2. *Nonplace Communities.* Tönnies also called this community a "mind" community. This "implies only cooperation and coordinated action for a common goal," without reference to "place" (Hillery, 1968:77–78). Examples of nonplace communities include religious orders and professions. A spirited debate continues among sociologists as to whether "social networks" are nonplace communities.

Beginning with J. A. Barnes' study of the social structure of the fishing community of Bremnes, Norway, researchers have found social networks a fruitful topic of study (Barnes, 1954). His definition of social network is still the most useful:

> Each person is, as it were, in touch with a number of other people, some of whom are in touch with each other and some of whom are not. Similarly each person has a number of friends, and these friends have their own friends; some of any one person's friends know each other, others do not. I find it convenient to talk of a social field of this kind as a *network*. The image I have is of a set of points some of which are joined by lines. The points of the image are people, or sometimes groups, and the lines indicate which people interact with each other (Barnes, 1954:127).

Figure 6. Diagrams of unbounded networks.

The diagrams in Figure 6 represent Barnes' ideas. The fact that it was a fishing village may have influenced Barnes' choice of the term *net*work rather than other possible terms, such as *web*. In Barnes' view, a network consists of the relationships between pairs of people. This is, of course, an atomistic view; some later network theorists have attempted to apply network concepts to larger social groupings with some sucess (e.g., Granovetter, 1977; Miller, 1978). Barnes' definition is perspectivistic; each person has a unique social network defined by the dyadic relationships the person has. In much of the current usage of the term social network, the term is clearly synonymous with nonplace community; it "implies only cooperation and coordinated action for a common goal, without reference to place." This is the sense in which it is used in discussing "networking" as a technique for changing the personal and work conditions of women (Kleiman, 1980; Welch, 1981).

In a social work context, Eilene McIntyre described a social network as consisting of, "a set of people all of whom are linked together, but not all of whom know one another. This inclusion of indirect links differentiates a network from a group" (McIntyre, 1986:422).

All such networks are not necessarily social desirable. For example, illegal drug distribution is carried out through just such a social network.

Network was also a phenomenon observed by the late Virginia Hine of the University of Minnesota, who studied social change. She noted the emergence of "segmented, polycephalous, ideological networks" (abbreviated to "SPIN") which were loosely organized alliances with bonds based on strongly held ideology. This is sometimes referred to as "loose coupling"; at the same time, observers discuss the "strength of weak ties" in such loose couplings. Our discussions of boundaries in Chapters 1 and 2 are relevant here, in that linkages can be intense for short periods of time, for specific purposes. Hines speculated that

this was a new form of non-hierarchical organization, perhaps an unsuspected political model of a world desperately seeking less vertically-structured methods of governance. A SPIN, she noted, functions effectively, does not disintegrate in the face of opposition (indeed the bond gets stronger), and provides meaningful action that is also rich in shared relationships and devoid of subservience on anyone's part (*Tarrytown Newsletter*, 1982:4–5).

This may be an idealized version, but to the extent that they are stable and function as significant environments for their members, such networks clearly qualify as nonplace communities.

3. *Kinship.*   As Tönnies described it, this third kind of community is one in which members have blood relationships. An example might be an American Indian reservation, a barrio or community as portrayed in the movie, "The Milagro Beanfield War," or an Amish community. It might also include immigrant groups that, though geographically dispersed in the new country, still support each other; examples include Chinese communities which comprise members in Hong Kong, Vancouver (Canada), and San Francisco, and Vietnamese (or Lao or Hmong) communities that include Los Angeles, Minneapolis-St. Paul, the Phillipines, and Vietnam. Barnes' definition of social network includes both the "networking," goal-oriented social system (which might also be viewed as a loose-knit organization) and kinship networks.

As mentioned, these categories are not exclusive. Nonplace communities and social networks have geographic ties, even though members may never convene in one location at one time (indeed, cannot, in the case of refugees and those left behind) and do not consider this aspect of their relationship to be primary or constant. For instance, the "academic community" does not reside in a single location, but it does have ties to college campuses. Similarly, the "scientific community" and the "medical community" have ties to laboratories and other research facilities.

Other examples of nonplace communities, such as the barbering profession, are protected from intrusion by custom or by law, as symbolized by the striped pole and the barber's license (although hair stylists, among others, have gained legal status performing many of the same tasks). Another example is the academic community's jealous protection of academic freedom, as when one professor went to jail rather than reveal his vote on giving another professor tenure. This case illustrated that academic freedom is a highly abstract and symbolic territory that some persons will defend with their liberty, if not their lives. The Polish labor union, Solidarity, is another example of nonplace community for which people are prepared to risk imprisonment or die; in this case, of course, there is a geographic tie, the nation of Poland. The students of Beijing who risked imprisonment or death in spring, 1989, are another example, defending an abstract community called "democracy," symbolized by the Statue of Liberty; another example is American Indians who, at the risk of their lives, exercised their treaty rights to spear fish despite the anger of white fishermen in Wisconsin, in Spring, 1989.

A third way in which communities differ is in the breadth of activities, interests, and needs that they encompass. The place community encompasses virtually all human interests and needs; the nonplace community is usually concerned with one, or few, of these. Almost every kind of human activity, in one form or another, is to be found in Chicago, for example, while the nonplace "business community" or "academic community" concerns itself with a narrower range of interests and needs.

II. DEFINITION OF COMMUNITY

We suggest the following composite definition: *Community* is a population whose members consciously identify with each other. They may occupy common territory; they engage in common activities. They have some form of organization that provides for differentiation of functions, which allows the community to adapt to its environment, thereby meeting the needs of its components. Its components include the persons, groups, families, and organizations within its population and the institutions it forms to meet its needs. Its environment is the society in which its exists and to which it adapts (and which it also modifies) by energy exchange, and other communities and organizations outside itself that impinge upon its functioning.

A recent book on community and social work, with which we generally agree and find compatible with the systems approach in this book, stated that "From a systems perspective, a community constantly seeks a level of stability or equilibrium" (Fellin, 1987:30). We agree that social systems seek stability (or steady state), but not equilibrium in the narrower sense of being static at rest. We discuss the energy functions in the following section.

A. Energy Functions

1. For Components/Subsystems. The functions the community performs include the maintenance of a way of life or culture (in the second usage of "culture" in Chapter 3). Another important function is the satisfaction of common needs, interests, and ambitions. A striking example of the recognition of common interests and needs was Malcolm X's redefinition of the community to which he belonged. He found common interests and needs unexpectedly in a new community:

> That morning was when I first began to reappraise the "white man." It was when I first began to perceive that "white man," as commonly used, means complexion only secondarily; primarily it described attitudes and actions toward the black man, and toward all other nonwhite men. But in the Muslim world, I had seen that men with white complexions were more genuinely brotherly than anyone else had ever been.

That morning was the start of a radical alteration in my whole outlook about "white" men (Malcolm X, 1966:333-334).

Further, the members of a community must be aware of its "we-ness" (French, 1969); in other words, there must be a social consciousness or "sense of community." This assists the community to meet the social identity needs of the persons who are its components. The community must provide for them "full opportunities for personal development through social experimentation. . . . This conception falls close to Erikson's views on ego identity and ego integrity as well as to Sullivan's emphasis on a full repertory of interpersonal relations" (Stein, 1960:335-336).

Erik Erikson, Harry Stack Sullivan, the social psychiatrist, and Karen Horney, psychoanalyst, recognized the importance of the social environment, including the community, in providing a medium for the evolution of the person. They were a distinct minority among early psychoanalytic theorists in the importance they placed upon the social environment. Stein elaborated, "A community must . . . provide its members with, at the least, meaningful sexual and work identities if it is to ensure its own continuity as well as the psychic integrity of its members" (Stein, 1960:266). Many communities are incapable of providing opportunities to develop work identities because of lack of jobs, e.g., inner city ghettos, many American Indian reservations, the "rust belt" of industries related to steel production from Gary, Indiana, to Pittsburgh, Pennsylvania, or the Appalachian region. If Erikson, Sullivan, and Stein were correct, some persons in these communities will fail to develop ego integrity since they are prevented from viewing themselves not only as productive members of the community but also as worthwhile persons individually. While some social theorists and policy-makers accept this as an inherent risk in a capitalist industrial society, others regard this as unjustified damage to the community as a system and to its members.

We do not yet know the effects of such failure by the societal system and the community system to provide adequately for its members' identity needs, although the effects of previous economic depressions are known to some degree. Some suggest that we now see the effects of economic marginality in a sharp rise in violent criminal behavior, and in the institutionalization of an illicit drug trade whose participants number in the hundreds of thousands. Some writers have suggested that the effect of such societal neglect may be to produce severely alienated persons and groups who turn to authoritarian ideologies for security and as a means of participation in some form of community. Erich Fromm, Hannah Arendt, and other writers on "alienation" have stated strongly that such alienated groups are breeding grounds for fascism (Arendt, 1962; Fromm, 1942, 1955; Giner, 1976:138–144). The recent burgeoning of "Skinheads" in the United States may well reflect such a

turning toward fascist ideology. Those identifying themselves as skinheads are alienated white young adults who subscribe to, and act upon,
a racist and antisemitic ideology:

> American skinheads are as likely to be middle-class as working poor. But in other
> respects they are typical gang members. They tend to come from broken homes,
> and a high proportion were abused as children. They are creatures of dysfunction,
> casualties of a Burger King economy with no room at the top (Coplon, 1988:56).

Other components such as families, organizations, and groups must
also be able to identify with, and find common cause with the community's way of life in order that their energies may be used to meet the
community's needs. The term *common cause* was adopted as the name
of a national citizen's action organization that explicitly recognizes the
necessity to involve citizens and to draw upon their energies. This organization mobilizes energy in the form of funds and lobbying activity
from its citizen-members to attain agreed-upon goals. It meets the definition of a system, specifically a social network, or nonplace community, in this respect.

Presthus emphasized these functions that the community performs
for its components. He noted that there is

> in every community a certain ongoing network of fairly stable subsystems, activated
> by social, economic, ethnic, religious, and friendship ties and claims. Such systems
> of interest, values, and power have desirable consequences for their members to
> the extent that they satisfy various human needs. In a sense, however, such subsys-
> tems are suprahuman, in that they tend to persist indefinitely and, more important,
> that their members may change but the underlying network of interrelated interests
> and power relations continues (Presthus, 1964:5).

2. For Environment/Suprasystems. A community must also meet the
needs of its environment in order to survive. It is clear from "central
place" theory in geography and economics that place communities function as parts of hierarchical, relatively stable economic and political systems, and that alterations in one community affect other parts of the
region as well (Christaller, 1966; Dunn, 1980). The rise of Chicago ("that
toddlin' town, the town that Billy Sunday could not shut down") as a
major industrial and railroad center affected the commercial and social
development of communities within its region. It became, as Carl Sandburg put it,

> Hog butcher for the World,
> Tool maker, Stacker of Wheat,
> Player with Railroads and the Nation's Freight Handler . . .
> Carl Sandburg (1955:442-443).

Smaller communities nearby adapted, sometimes unwillingly, to Chicago's emergence as a trade center, both supplying and being supplied

by Chicago's services and industries (see Sennett, 1974). Communities unsuited to adapt to new economic and transportation networks, or unable to compete with new centers of power, declined or ceased to exist. In the American West in recent years, "boom towns" have arisen as the demand for minerals or new sources for oil have increased; some have failed to prosper. Others have survived, some with serious social problems (Davenport and Davenport, 1982).

Religious communities, as examples of nonplace community, have also been confronted with the need to adapt to their environment. Within the Roman Catholic Church, some orders that formerly were relatively removed from society have become socially active, performing less specifically religious tasks such as teaching and social service in prisons and hospitals. A few orders have disbanded as their members have returned to lay status, some members in order to marry and others to carry on secular work as part of their religious commitment. The Roman Catholic "community," however, maintains some clear boundaries. Priests and nuns are still forbidden to marry (except when released from their vows), and procreation is still the purpose of marriage. The following news item illustrates the latter boundary:

PHOENIX, ARIZ. (AP)—The Roman Catholic Diocese of Phoenix has refused to marry a couple because the man is a quadriplegic unable to consummate the union, the church says. Jose Sosa, 28, and his fianceé, Barbara Albillar, 23, both of Mesa, are Catholics who want a church wedding. Sosa said the diocese's decisions was a shock to both of them. Sosa said he didn't understand the church's decision and "I never thought there would be this sort of trouble". . . . Larry Bonvallet of Kankakee, Ill., after initial rebuffs in a publicized case, won approval for a Catholic wedding and was married in May. Church officials said they believed he might eventually be able to consummate the marriage. . . . Sosa and Albillar plan to be married in October in a civil ceremony if they are denied a church wedding (*Iowa City Press Citizen*, July 2, 1982).

In another example of boundary-setting and adaptation for this community, the Pope banned priests from holding elective office, which has occasioned strong reactions from some Latin American priests, in particular, who subscribe to Liberation Theology; in their view, priests must participate in the civil community to fulfill their responsibilities in the religious community.

Boundary maintenance and adaptation are crucial functions for the survival of communities. Between 1968 and 1973, approximately half a million people were involved in some kind of communal living. Approximately 30% of the communes survived that five-year period, leaving about a thousand communes by 1975 (Gardner, 1978:240ff.). In 1989, there are still estimated to be about the same number. Virtually none of the urban communes survived; the survivors were almost entirely rural, and were secular rather than religious.

In the United States, currently, religiously based rural communes appear to be increasing in number. The Rajneeshee in Oregon were a striking example of an intentional community offering an opportunity to relinquish one's previous identity and reconstruct a new self. The Rajnesshee commune organized around the person and teachings of Bhagwan Shree Rajneesh and at its peak claimed to have a population of seven thousand members at its site in Oregon. It was utopian and attracted a well educated core of members: "some 75 percent of the Rajneeshee had attended college, two thirds had bachelor's degrees and 12 percent had doctorates" (Fitzgerald, 1986:264). Those who voluntarily joined the commune contributed their liquid assets, were awarded new names, and donned the red garb that attested to their status as members. The Rajneeshee were in constant dispute with local and state governments over jurisdictional governance of their territorial expansion.

With the increasingly affluent, expanding population of retired elders, a new kind of intentional community has emerged, particularly in Florida, Arizona, and California. These are settlements of older citizens who strive for a community restricted to people of a certain age bracket and degree of affluence. Often, as in the case of Sun City, they are physically removed from the general community and have their own governance. They provide facilities and activities for their residents, in a secure and quiet environment.

> ZEPHYRSHILL, FLA. (AP)—Fourteen year-old Staci Elmer left for school Wednesday "tired, angry and sad" because she was kicked out of her parents' home in a court battle over a rule barring children from her small subdivision. On Tuesday, Pascoe Circuit Court Judge Wayne Cobb rejected Beverly and Thomas Elmer's request to delay a Jan. 6 order. He said if Staci wasn't out of the house by 5 p.m., the couple would go to jail for 10 days.
>
> "We have nothing against the girl; it's the principle," said Aline Murray. She is one of the neighbors who sued to preserve the adults-only status of the tiny mobile home settlement on the back streets in this quiet retirement community. "We bought here with the idea of peace and quiet in our old age" (Eugene, Oregon, *The Register-Guard*, February 2, 1989).

The history of utopian communities is replete with examples of those who attempted to isolate themselves from the social environment and thrive as closed systems, unsuccessfully. Without energy exchange with the environment, a system is certain to become entropic and die. Amish communities in Pennsylvania, Indiana, Iowa, and other states have survived by maintaining energy exchange with the environment in certain carefully limited ways; this is an excellent illustration of boundaries that are relatively more closed than other communities but still open to exchanges of energy.

In the past twenty years, some successful communes in the United States adapted to their environment, performing economic functions in the wider society and obtaining needed energy from other systems.

Some cooperatives and communes begun during the 1960s and 1970s attempted "freak capitalism," producing and selling leather goods, ceramics, clothing, art, furniture, or vegetables to support the community. In some communes, such as Twin Oaks in Virginia, members alternated in taking employment in nearby cities for financial support of the community (Kinkade, 1973). Twenty years after its founding, Twin Oaks continues to be a thriving community with its main industry being the manufacture of hammocks.

The "Moonies" (members of Reverend Moon's Unification Church) made conspicuous efforts to adapt to their environment through participating in commerce and industry, owning office buildings and a major newspaper and establishing a fishing industry on the east coast of the United States. The Rajneeshee did not successfully engage in similar exchanges with their environment.

American Indian reservations are examples of communities that were excluded from the general society and suffered entropy. In recent years, economic and social development by the tribes have opened the boundaries. Both American Indians and the general society have found it to their advantage to cross the boundaries. While white society may wish to remove the boundaries entirely (the "assimilation" or relocation policies), American Indians have consciously encouraged maintenance of open, but clearly recognizable cultural boundaries, especially during the past two decades. From a systems perspective, the assimilation policy was unworkable because it would have required only the Indian societies to accommodate (to change their schemas), after which white society would assimilate them. A systems perspective would indicate that mutual accommodation would be necessary, and each culture would both have to accommodate and assimilate. The Indian Child Welfare Act of 1978 is an example of accommodation by the general society, by recognizing the rights of tribes to control the disposition of Indian children's adoptions and foster care placements.

In general, the functions that a community performs for its environment are the energy functions described in Chapter 1, giving, getting, and conserving energy. The community supplies energy to its environment and its components in the form of persons and products to be used by those systems. A community may supply students for higher education who become leaders while also supplying political support for organizations outside the community and taxes for state and national governments.

A large part of the debate about President Reagan's "new federalism" concerned whether communities and states supply too much of their resources to their suprasystem, the federal government, leaving too little to meet the needs of the communities' own components. President Reagan's answer (and thus far, President Bush's, also) is that, yes, too much has been taken by an overgrown federal bureaucracy. The position of many liberals is that only the federal government can be trusted to redistribute these resources equitably because communities and states are more vulnerable to pressure groups and more likely to deny resources to the powerless and disadvantaged components within communities and states. This liberal–conservative debate will continue for the foreseeable future; it illustrates well the need for an energy exchange which meets the needs of each, among suprasystem, system and components, if all system levels are to function satisfactorily. A large part of the debate, also, of course, is over the definition of "satisfactory" functioning, and which functions should be performed at what system levels. It seems likely that the community system will be the arena in which a great deal of this controversy will occur during the 1990s and past the year 2000.

B. Aspects of Community Systems

1. Evolutionary Aspects. The first cities were burial places to which wandering tribes returned at certain times to perform ceremonies that ensured the stability of the universe. From that symbolic beginning, place communities evolved to encompass all human needs and functions. Following Max Weber, Hans Paul Bahrdt and Fernand Braudel contend that the city had its genesis in the market. Thus, a city is a settlement with a resident population that regularly satisfies economic and social needs for energy exchange through the device of a local market (Warren, 1977:25ff.). We could combine these speculations by saying that cities began as locations that were sites of seasonal rituals, which became permanent market sites as agriculture evolved (see Rutherfurd's [1987] large, historically-based novel, *Sarum,* for an enjoyable description of the evolution of settlements on the Salisbury Plain in southern England).

The character of a particular community is determined by its relationships to other communities and the society within which it exists, by the characteristics of its components, and by its own preceding steady state. That is, it is a holon. B. F. Skinner's *Walden Two* (1948) described a fictional utopia (copied by several real communities) that evolved into a complex, planned community. The Lynds' *Middletown* (Muncie, Indiana) evolved toward being a satellite in the regional system of New York City, because decisions about industries were increasingly made outside Middletown (Lynd and Lynd, 1929, 1937). When Theodore Caplow and associates re-examined Middletown fifty years after the Lynds' studies, they found the major change to be the degree to which the federal government determined economic and social conditions. By 1979, "about one-third of all the income received by Middletown families came out of the federal treasury" (Caplow, Bahr, Chadwick, Hill and Williamson 1982:26).

Doxiadis described the evolution of large cities through five stages, differentiated by "kinetic fields," that is, the distance a person can travel within a certain span of time (Miller, 1972:117–118):

A-level organization: The city encompasses 2 by 2 kilometers and has a population of no more than 50,000. No more than ten minutes are required to walk from the center to its periphery.

B-level organization: The city emcompasses 6 by 6 kilometers and has a population of more than 50,000. Examples are capital cities of empires such as Rome, Constantinople, and Beijing. Walking time in these cities at this stage of development was no more than half an hour; paved roads and horse-drawn carts moved people (and in Beijing still do). Such cities were difficult to govern, slums grew, and mobs frequently controlled the city.

C-level organization: These cities depend upon subways or elevated trains to extend the "kinetic field." This is satisfactory only briefly, as cities evolve and freeways are built to accommodate automobile traffic. It is entirely possible, of course, that cities may return to this mode of transportation, but if so, the largest cities would probably use high-speed subways to compensate for distances; San Francisco, Washington, D.C., and Hong Kong are among the cities that have done this. Paris, Tokyo, and London are among older cities that have provided rapid, efficient transportation for several decades.

D-level organization: This is the "modern" metropolitan city, beset by the myriad urban problems with which we are all too familiar. The growing urban population exceeds the capacity of the freeways, resulting in the now ubiquitous gridlocks and air contamination. Modes of public transportation must be augmented or new ones developed, such as the Light Rail system in Portland, Oregon. Examples include Mexico City (soon the world's largest city), Beijing, Bombay, and Shanghai.

E-level organization: This is the megalopolis, the modern urban complex that comprises several cities with a total population of several million. In the United States, the so-called "BosWash" (Boston to Washington) megalopolis is almost a single, continuous urban area. This urban level is marked by the pathology that remains from having failed to solve problems at the D-level.

Presumably, the "universal city" or "ecumenopolis" would be the ultimate city and would require highly centralized planning. In such a system, technology would solve the problems of transportation, distribution of energy supplies, and waste collection. How a sense of community would be maintained is not clear. Others have noted that our microchip technology, most importantly the computer, will enable us to continue to participate in advanced technology working at home, even in relatively isolated communities. Like many people today, the authors of this book, for example, compose on computers at home, utilize a university library via a telephone line, and correspond with colleagues in other parts of the country and overseas via computer and satellite. McLuhan's "global village" is a reality (McLuhan, 1965); another way to describe it would be a nonplace or "mind community."

The shape taken by cities of the future is being determined by experiences and crises in cities today. Many wonder whether the seeming exodus from cities to the suburbs is a permanent trend, especially given a long-term shortage in petroleum fuels. Others suggest radical solutions: The science fiction writer, Isaac Asimov, suggested underground cities may be the future. Another science fiction writer fancifully suggested whole cities may emigrate into space, like spaceships. Architect Paolo Soleri, creator of the futuristic community of Arcosanti in Arizona, suggests massive structures (resembling bee hives in some respects, and similar to a "Buck Rogers" future) are the answer. Like other systems, cities are subject to multiple factors that influence growth and decline.

Community decline.   In our nation's history, some communities have declined and others have died because of their inability to adapt to rapid change. Oliver Goldsmith's eighteenth century poem, "The Deserted Village," illustrated that this began with the Industrial Revolution. Today, ghost towns that were formerly mining camps, small farming villages, or fishing villages attest to the alternative of disintegration for the community that does not have, or does not use, resources to adapt.

Harry Caudill's *Night Comes to the Cumberlands* painfully illustrated the process by which rural Appalachian communities became the lowest level in a hierarchy of industrial power, subject to decisions made in Pittsburgh, Detroit, Washington, and New York (Caudill, 1963). One thorough study analyzed the history of Coos Bay, Oregon:

> Resource capital in the United States has been extremely mobile; it has contributed to the development of towns and then devastated them. The mounting social and economic problems of those troubled communities are witness to that truth.
>
> Immediately after the Second World War, the timber resource was extensive and there was still time to develop a long-range resource-management strategy. However, as this study has made clear, the market prevailed and the social and economic stability of the region was never a major consideration in private and public decision making. Now that the resource base has been severely depleted and nineteenth-century social theories are fashionable in state and federal capitals, there is even less likelihood that those communities will escape from the strategies and investment decisions of the private corporations who control much of the land (Robbins, 1988:167–168).

Some communities like those just described have turned to tourism as a major source of revenue (e.g., Central City, Colorado; Bayfield, Wisconsin; Gatlinburg, Tennessee; Victoria, British Columbia; Kyoto, Japan; Chartres, France; and the Portugese colony of Macao). Other examples of cities that have adapted to survive (in the sense of "steady state") include Iowa City, Iowa, first the state capital and then the site of the state university; and Duluth, Minnesota, a "boom town" dependent first upon lumber, then iron ore, grain, and coal, and now upon tourism. Still other localities are seeking survival through developing a "retirement industry," specializing in housing, goods and services for the expanding population of active elders.

The same principle of adaptation applies to nonplace communities. Certainly the history of Christian and Moslem sects or denominations illustrates the evolutionary process of such nonplace communities. The current unrest in Iran is an example of evolution because of competition between contending factions within Islam.

2. *Structural Aspects.* Included here are some systemic aspects of community that have a slower rate of change (see the discussion of structure, behavior, and evolution at the beginning of Chapter 2).

a. Boundaries. The boundaries that separate communities from larger and smaller social units—the so-called vertical hierarchy—are often difficult to establish precisely. Minnesota's Red Lake Reservation is, by treaty law, a separate, sovereign nation within the United States, and by tribal law one must have a Red Lake passport to enter legally. As one enters the reservation, one encounters signs like this:

> Warning. This is Indian land. No trespassing. No fishing, hunting, camping, berry picking, peddling or soliciting without authorized permit from Red Lake Tribal Council Office. Violators and trespassers will be prosecuted under Federal Law 86-634 (Brill, 1974:22).

The sign indicates that the interactional boundary between the reservation and the federal government is open. The sign further indicates that the geographic boundary is relatively closed, but in reality is closed only in certain ways:

> Red Lakers are not isolated from the outside world. I am always amazed when someone asks me, "Can the Indians leave the reservation?" There are no fences around the reservation; the roads to Bemidji and other cities in the area are well traveled. . . . It is common for Red Lakers to drive to larger cities to shop in the supermarkets and discount stores; to bowl with the league on Tuesday and Thursday evenings. . . . Some commute to classes at Bemidji State College. In addition to the *Redlake Neighborhood Centers Newsletter* . . . many people subscribe to the *Bemidji Pioneer* and the *Minneapolis Tribune.* Television is popular and reception is generally good (Brill, 1974:22).

Their ancestors were wise to refuse to break up the reservation into smaller parcels that could be individually sold to outsiders (as proposed in the 1887 Dawes Act); other reservations did, and many of the parcels were bought by whites. Red Lake continues as a "closed" (tribally owned) reservation. Not all communities have retained their independence from the "outside world." Increasingly, as noted earlier in this chapter, communities are subordinate to larger, regional networks and to industrial and communications centers in their economic and social affairs. Within large communities, the internal structure may comprise relatively autonomous bodies such as corporations that function as private, independent governments (Bird, 1966, Chapter 10; Galbraith, 1968; Wright, 1979).

Boundaries within the community include those between institutions that differentiate tasks. These horizontal boundaries include, for example, the uniform worn and the choice of specific colors and tasks. Firefighters' gear is adapted to their task, but it also distinguishes them from police. What function does the bright, fire red of the fire department's pump truck serve, especially since red is a low visibility color? (Many departments have chosen to use yellow, which is more visible.) Presumbably the color says, "We fight fires. We don't baptize children with our hoses, pick up garbage with our trucks, or fight off mobs with our axes and poles!" Sometimes the boundaries between differentiated institutions are not so clear: Are parochial schools entitled to public funds? Should schools provide sex education? Should police conduct drug education programs? Should health clinics do AIDS testing and should they be required to report the results? These continue to be controversial questions in many communities.

   b. Institutions.   Differentiation of functions by assigning them to specialized subsystems leads to the emergence of institutions within communities. Such institutions usually originate in several communities in slightly different forms. Since the community is a holon between society and "microsystems" such as families and ethnic groups, it contains fundamental system processes such as Miller described (Miller, 1978). In particular, the community performs basic systems functions such as socialization and social control through the church, school, and police; these institutions are prescribed in our culture. The form the institution takes in a particular community depends upon the community's components, previous steady state, and environment (an institution is a holon also). Our society prescribes that education shall be performed by formal schools, but the form of the school varies from community to community. It may be a one-room country school or an urban elementary school; it may be single-sex or coed. The mode of instruction may be the Montessori method or the traditional "3 Rs"; the instructional equipment may be slate blackboards or satellite television and lasers.

Certain communities may evolve distinctive institutions. Pine Mountain Settlement School in Kentucky began the "Little School," a forerunner of the national Head Start program. Significant portions of the War on Poverty of the 1960s were modeled on the Mobilization for Youth program in New York City; hot lines and youth crisis centers originated in a number of cities at about the same time; Berkeley, California's Shanti Project was a model for services to AIDS patients (Shilts, 1988:123). Free experimental schools of various kinds continue to spring up in communities across the country. Internationally, several Austrian communities are known for their Children's Villages, a unique response to the need to care for orphans. The process originates as a recognized need that is unmet by existing institutions; the community (or some influential component) differentiates a new institution to incorporate the new service. In some communities, hot lines are part of mental health clinics, and "crash pads" for runaways are maintained by churches, while housing for the homeless may be more of a cooperative endeavor.

Some institutions almost escape our notice because they exist in most communities, but their functions are overlooked. Examples are taverns or bars (pubs are more visible in England's society), e.g., Small's Bar, which Malcolm X protected by turning himself in, an important institution in Harlem's social structure as were the nightclubs Malcolm mentioned. Think of the bar as a setting for radio and television shows: "Archie Bunker's Place," "Cheers" (based on an actual bar in Boston's Beacon Hill), "Duffy's Tavern," long a staple on radio, and Miss Kitty's bar in the long-running television series "Gunsmoke." The laundromat serves a socializing function in many neighborhoods. Restaurants serve a similar function, as portrayed on the television series "Frank's Place," "Tattinger's," and Mel's diner in "Alice."

Community institutions pose special difficulties to social workers and other professionals acting as change agents. Institutions are systems and seek to maintain themselves. This may be done by modifying structure and function to better fulfill community needs (morphogenesis). However, as systems they also seek to remain the same (morphostasis). Thus, institutional provisions generally lag in meeting emergent community needs. As Thorstein Veblen wrote in 1899, "institutions are . . . adapted to past circumstances, and are therefore never in full accord with the requirements of the present. . . . This process of selective adaptation can never catch up with the progressively changing situation in which the community finds itself at any given time" (Boguslaw, 1965:150–151). Thus it is that we are always preparing for yesterday, believing it is tomorrow.

   c. Social class and caste.   Another important facet of community structure is social class. Studies of social stratification have substantiated social class or status groupings in most communities. Hollingshead's *Elmtown's Youth* is among the most ingenious of these studies and has been a fountainhead for others (Vidich and Bensman, 1958; Hollingshead, 1969). Some major differentiating characteristics found by researchers are income, lifestyle, and access to services. As noted in Chapter 3, communities differ in their cultures. Diagrams of class structure (or, more accurately, socioeconomic status, usually) vary from a diamond-shaped structure, with most persons in the middle class, to an extreme pyramidal structure, with either very few poor in some wealthy suburban com-

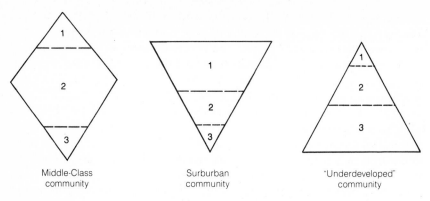

Middle-Class
community

Surburban
community

"Underdeveloped"
community

Figure 7.   Diagrams of class structure (1 = higher socioeconomic class; 2 = middle socioeconomic class; 3 = lower socioeconomic class).

munities or very few wealthy in some Appalachian communities (see Figure 7).

Another differentiation between communities may be that of caste. Most would deny that caste exists in the United States. If it is defined as an impermeable boundary, a status assigned by virtue of some characteristic beyond a person's control (e. g., skin color, gender, national origin, or age), however, it exists for some Mexican-Americans, Asian-Americans, African-Americans, and American Indians.

d. Social networks.   We have placed this discussion of social networks between the sections on structural aspects and behavioral aspects of community systems because in reality it is difficult to describe social networks (see Vaux, 1988: especially pp. 11–15). One set of researchers provided a minimal definition:

> Social networks involve, in principle, the most elementary level of social analysis. Conceptually, social network analysis entails no cultural or psychological prejudgments beyond the minimal ones that there are individuals who have repeated contact with each other, and that there is some cumulative nature to these contacts such that a link may be said to exist between pairs of individuals when these repeated contacts occur. The distributions of these links around an individual or within a population then constitute the networks of social linkages (Salzinger, Antrobus, and Hammer, 1988:3).

There is an active debate among theorists of neighborhoods and urban subunits concerning whether neighborhoods and social networks are the same phenomenon. Some theorists maintain that neighborhoods (and by implication, communities in general) are simply social networks that have a base in a particular locality. Opposing theorists maintain that neighborhoods are not synonymous with social networks and have different dynamics. The opposing positions are similar to the distinctions between place and nonplace communities—that is, must a community (or a social network) be based in a particular location? One test of the answer is whether computer "bulletin boards" or networks through which people exchange information (some of which may be personal) can be considered real networks; the important criteria being the significance, breadth, and duration of the networks for their members.

Social networks have become popular as a vehicle for "consciousness raising" among disadvantaged populations such as women, gays and lesbians, and racial or ethnic minorities. Such networks emphasize awareness of commonality among the members and usually foster awareness of their disadvantaged status and the societal dynamics that underlie it. Further, the network provides support (often the networks are called "mutual support" groups) to members that consists of both emotional support and suggestions for immediate action. Rape support groups and feminist groups in general fit this description (Kleiman, 1980; Welch, 1981). The more organized the groups become and the more specific their goals (e.g., the National Organization for Women, N.O.W.) the less they resemble social networks and the more they become formal organizations. Probably most "movements," including civil rights, antidraft, antinuclear, antiwar, and right-to-life, could best be described as social networks even though many are very large and many are connected somewhat loosely with formal organizations that are dedicated to particular instrumental, limited goals of the movement.

In addition to social causes, networking can be a means of career development, apparently:

> Networking is just another name for making friends. It's contacts building contacts. It's getting yourself known and getting to know people in your field. Networking is exchanging information, exchanging contacts, and exchanging resources. It helps you create your own accidents. . . .
>
> Yippie-turned-yuppie Jerry Rubin, whose first Networking Salons helped, in theory and practice, to pioneer the term networking suggests, "In order to be a successful networker, you'll have to show non-stop assertiveness in a classy and charming way" (Juario, 1989:7).

Networks can be highly useful to professional persons who are seeking support for a client for precisely the reasons previously mentioned. The client may need support, enlightenment, and guidance for specific action and may accept it best from a group with the same problems. Alcoholics Anonymous (A.A.) is probably the most successful of these social networks and one of the most dramatic. In one instance, the then-governor of Iowa, Harold Hughes, himself a recovering alcoholic, responded to late-night calls from other A.A. members. Social networks often cross economic and social lines in their common identification as victims, or people with problems. Clearly, in these instances, social networks function as strong nonplace communities that perform functions for their members and for the environment. For the environment, they function as agents of change and at least as "escape valves" for their members even if they do not accomplish major personal or societal change.

Networks have infiltrated therapeutic services more directly. Alan Vaux examined the efficacy of "network therapy" as an alternative to therapy with individuals, families, or groups:

> the goal of network therapy is to reestablish the individual's network as a functioning unit, in order to enhance closeness, supportiveness, and the helpfulness of members to one another and to the disordered individual. . . . These goals are achieved through convening the network, connecting members, and shifting responsibility and control to the network. Network therapy is a time-limited, goal-oriented approach that focuses on mobilizing the network as a collaborative support system in times of crisis (Vaux, 1988:278).

3. Behavioral Aspects. These systemic characteristics tend to be of shorter duration than the structural characteristics discussed in the preceding section.

a. Social control. The overall purpose of social control is *to maintain the system, not necessarily to maintain the status quo.* Social control may be exerted by the entire community through its network of values and goals, which are embodied in one or several of its institutions. These institutions may act on behalf of the entire community or it may, as sometimes happens, act on behalf of some group or special interest. For example, African-Americans in ghettos sometimes charge that police do not act in their behalf to protect their property or lives but only to enforce order on behalf of white businesses and white property owners or, in south Florida, on behalf of Hispanics. The "web of urban institutions" that operates to enforce racial discrimination has been convincingly described and analyzed (see Knowles and Prewitt, 1969).

In nonplace communities, social control may be exerted by formal or informal sanctions. In a professional community such as nursing or teaching, sanctions may include temporary loss of license or a public notice that the employer is blacklisted, which means that no member of the profession should work for that employer.

Social control is modified (but not necessarily lessened) by the overlapping memberships that community members have. Power structure and decision-making studies have revealed the interlocking positions held by some persons in the community (Domhoff, 1971; Domhoff and Dye, 1987). The same family may be represented on the public library board, the planning and zoning commission, the board of directors of a bank, and also may operate a large business. Such overlapping memberships may lessen the effect of centralized social control or may aggrandize it. The Lynds' Middletown study indicated that whatever the formal arrangements might have been, the commercial leaders of the community exerted a great deal of social control; Caplow found this to continue to be true fifty years later. The same has been found in most communities.

A related aspect of community, and one that has received increasing attention during the past thirty years, is that of "community power." Presthus gave a "social Darwinist" description:

> Simply put, individuals of similar interests combine to achieve their ends, and such combinations of interlaced values and interests form subsystems of power. The community is composed of a congeries of such subsystems, now co-operating, now competing, now engaged, now moribund, in terms of the rise and fall of local issues. Some subsystems are more powerful than others; some are transitory; others persist, one supposes, because the interests which they institutionalize are persistent (Presthus, 1964:6).

The classic and most frequently imitated study is Floyd Hunter's *Community Power Structure* (1953). His basic findings have not been refuted. He found that the most powerful persons in the community were heads of large commercial enterprises, especially banking and finance; and that other leadership was composed of professional men and a few representatives of government and labor. Hunter found that within the group of those who were powerful, a relatively small number were policymakers, or the "power elite" of the community. Other studies with a somewhat different focus by C. Wright Mills (1948, 1951), G. William Domhoff (1967, 1971, 1974), and others largely confirm the existence of a national power elite with bases in various communities. Domhoff detailed the activities of the power elite in the Bohemian Grove, a gathering place north of San Francisco (Domhoff, 1974). The dispute continues between "elite" theorists and "pluralist" theorists as to whether there is any single, dominant power group (Banfield, 1961; Domhoff, 1967; Rose, 1967; Silk and Silk, 1981; Domhoff and Dye, 1987). In part, the question is one of identifying the focal system since some theorists focused on the community and others on the national, societal system. Domhoff attempts to tie the two together with results that have been criticized with regard to methodology. Domhoff and Thomas Dye summarize the three methods by which the networks of community power structures can be constructed—the positional, the reputational, and the decisional. Together, these can be viewed as "naturalistic," or "ethnographic" methods (Lincoln and Guba, 1985:7)

> A Positional analysis uses printed public information available in libraries and other archives to establish the leadership interlocks among profit, nonprofit, and govern-

mental agencies as well as to trace the flows of money, information, and other resources among the same organizations.

A Reputational study, in contrast to the positional method, is based upon the personal opinions of a wide range of people who are interviewed about who the key people and organizations in the power structure are. This method was developed by Hunter, who later characterized it briefly by saying it was equivalent to arriving in a previously unknown tribal society and asking the natives to take you to their leaders.

A Decisional mapping of a power structure is based on case studies of the people, organizations, and pressure groups that become involved in trying to influence the outcome of specific policy initiatives in a range of issue-areas.

In effect all three methods generate a list of people and their connections to each other and to organizations and issues (Domhoff and Dye, 1987:9–12).

Hunter (1953), Dahl (1957), and Banfield (1961) each derived decision-making models that ranged from the bureaucratic, pyramid model in which decisions were made "at the top," to mutual adaptation" models in which decisions were made by consensus in a relatively participatory, decentralized fashion. These two models have some relation, of course, to the argument between the "elite" and "pluralist" power theorists. In these decision-making studies, it was found that the political sub-systems played important, but not necessarily dominant, roles. Decisions were made by informal or private subsystems differentiated by social class, organizational position, or by the kind of institution being represented. The informal decision-making structure was often as influential, or more so, than the formal (including political) structures.

b. Socialization.   Socialization is essential to the life of a community. If new members are not socialized into the community to supply new energy (negentropy), it becomes entropic. Some utopian communities (e.g., the United Society of Believers in Christ's Second Appearing [Shakers]) who were celibate have been unable to maintain themselves as members died, and present-day communes face a constant problem of attracting new members. Kephart (1976) noted an irony that although the commune espouses personal freedom, it must, like all systems, socialize its members to communal values and pursuits.

Enculturating the newcomer is often a community concern. The complaints of urban northerners that some Appalachian immigrants leave junk cars in the yard, throw their garbage out the window, and tie clotheslines to their neighbor's houses point to the difficulty of socialization to an unfamiliar urban setting. Some communities have had to attempt to socialize deviant subcommunities that reject established community values (e.g., the Rajneeshee), specifically norms of productivity, health, and dress. In the face of such deviations, communities attempt to apply social control in the form of jail sentences, compulsory socialization (e.g., enforcing truancy laws or mandatory work programs for relief recipients), or expulsion. Expulsion took the form of "warning out" as early as the sixteenth century in England and was transferred to the United States. Persons likely to become recipients of public assistance were told to leave the county. In 1950, one of the authors was "warned out" of a county in a western state for being in a condition of limited means. The practice continued officially in some states as late as 1959, and one of the authors found people who had previously been warned out when he took over a caseload in 1960.

In the 1960s, *kabouters* (literally, "elves"—equivalent to "hippies") slept in the central plaza of Amsterdam on the steps of a national monument. Their presence and habits disturbed many Dutch citizens, and in some respects presented health hazards (e.g., hepatitis). The law against sleeping on monuments was revived and enforced but to little avail. Eventually force was employed to expel the *kabouters*. Socialization occurred as they became a political party and won seats on the city council, but socialization was incomplete. In order to reinforce the boundary between themselves and the rest of society, some *kabouters* resigned from the council and thus avoided becoming part of "the system." In Beijing, China, in spring, 1989, students occupied Tienamen Square, symbolically the heart of China (and of the world, traditionally), to demonstrate for "democracy and freedom" but were routed by part of the army, and many unarmed students and citizens were killed. In a famous (and inspiring) incident captured by a television camera, a lone man challenged a column of tanks. The question can legitimately be raised, who was being socialized to what values? Whose values and behavior will emerge most powerful? The unarmed protesters or their adversaries in the army and the government? If deviance cannot be reduced or removed, communities may adapt to the deviant values by creating new institutions or empowering different ones. In China, for example, the behavior of the army (or some part of it) perhaps permanently discredited the army and the Communist party, and questioned their legitimacy as the most influential institutions in the society. It is possible that institutions of higher education, and the professionals who are trained in them, will be legitimized as leaders of the society. Apparently something similar has happened in the Soviet Union, in which a "new class" of Soviet managers of industries has exerted increasing power.

New institutions arise to perform new functions, just as public schools were created to socialize millions of European immigrants and Project Headstart to "socialize" racial minorities. In the past decade in Canada, e.g., in Vancouver, new organizations, funded by the Canadian government, have been created to socialize immigrants, particularly refugees, who enter the society.

There are less formal means of socialization; parades and Fourth of July or Victoria Day celebrations socialize citizens into wider patriotic values. Formal ceremonies may mark induction to the community; the Jewish Bar or Bas Mitzvah, Christian baptism, freshman hazing, the "capping" ceremony for new nurses, and naturalization ceremonies are examples. Such rites of passage symbolize the socialization of a person into a new status within the system. One example is drumming and singing in Ojibway (Anishinabe) culture.

> A small boy may grow up standing at the edge of the drum circle. A circle of three or more intense, somber, sweating men. . . . There are times, in the afternoon or early in the evening, when a young boy may be permitted to kneel between the men and beat on the metal edge of the drum with a stick. Then one day when it is time, he will have the courage and the confidence to drum on the white surface, straighten his body, lean forward, and make the sound. It is time to become a man (Brill, 1974:82).

Social networks are probably highly significant in socialization in organizations and communities. Newcomers usually find that the most important task is to join a social network that reliably describes the norms, mores, and sanctions of the system. Everyone who has entered a new school, new job, or new community, or who has changed status within a system can probably remember the process of finding such a network (or failing to find one).

As noted earlier in this chapter, networks function primarily as sources of information and as efficient distributors of information. It has been demonstrated that nonmembers of networks have less information than members of the network about matters that are equally important to both. Networks are typically more fluid and have fewer fixed roles than groups, organizations, or communities; thus, it is easier to fit into a network and both to give and get energy (in the form of information). Networks often serve as "welcome wagons," assisting newcomers to find niches for themselves in new systems and to learn the "lay of the land." Frequently, information exchange is the primary (or sole) reason for the existence of a network, and network members abandon the group, or disband it, when their needs for information are more adequately met in the new system they have joined. Networks are less demanding since they are partial and cannot offer either a full set of roles or complete roles. As illustrated in Chapter 6, "Groups," centrality in the flow of information is often synonymous with leadership roles; thus networks are often the "farm teams" or "out-of-town tryouts" for more established systems. On occasion, a network functions as the embryo of a developing system in which network participants are the charter members.

c. Communication. Communication is a highly important aspect of community system behavior. Institutions such as churches and schools carry on some communication, but the major communications activities occur between persons face-to-face and through public media such as newspapers, television, and radio. In British, early United States', and some Sioux communities, this function was performed by the town crier or its equivalent. Billboards, soapboxes, loudspeakers, sirens, pamphlets, and classified advertisements are all means of communication used and controlled by segments of the community to impart symbols of the community's way of life. In contrast, bumper stickers, T-shirts, stylized hand movements by gang members, and modular telephones in automobiles tend to be communication devices used for individual expression. "The essence of community, as John Dewey suggested, is communication. for without communication there cannot be that interaction by which common meanings, common life, and common values are established" (Ross, 1955). In that communication is one form of energy exchange, it is a vital process, and cannot occur if components are isolated or are unable to interact. The result would be entropy or disintegration.

Social networks, discussed earlier, have communication as their major function. They have both instrumental (goal-oriented) and affective (emotional) functions, but networks perform primarily as conveyors of information, concerning instrumental and affective needs, rather than suppliers or intermediary systems themselves. That is, social networks identify groups, families, neighborhoods, or even communities within which primary needs can be met; but the networks themselves do not meet the needs. However, to the extent that a network evolves a culture in which members meet each others' needs (e.g., a women's group in which members become "family" to each other), it may become a system, better identified as a group, organization, or (in the sense we use it later) family. This distinction may seem petty, but it is necessary to clarify focal systems and whether or not something is a system. In this respect, a social network may be seen as an interlocking set of roles with relatively specific functions compared with groups or communities that are broader in their functions. In other words, social networks resemble groups and communities in some respects while resembling organizations in other respects.

Components of the community system can monitor each other's performance and are provided with directives via feedback linkages such as newspaper reports of governmental meetings, public hearings on controversial issues, and elections. Some communities, such as Synanon, the utopian community of Oneida, and brigades or communities in the People's Republic of China, set aside specific occasions for mutual criticism by members. In some religious denominations and in A.A., testimonials serve a feedback function. Feedback was explicitly and formally sanctioned as part of social welfare programs under Title XX of the Social Security Act, and as part of the Community Development Block Grant through low-income persons' membership on the governing boards. Community groups and client representatives had to be part of the process of program planning and their views had to be acknowledged.

C. Professions as Nonplace Communities

An established profession claims for itself and is recognized by society as responsible for a symbolic territory or domain. Almost by definition, when a group carves out for itself a societal function or some part of the society's stock of ideas, it becomes sanctioned as a profession. When the societal function of instructing the young was delegated to and assumed by teachers, the next logical step was the formation and protection of territory by professional teachers' organizations. The same is true of medicine, law, and the clergy, the three so-called classic professions. It can be said as well of the newer, developing professions of law enforcement, nursing, engineering, and social work. The following is a description of the emergence of a profession:

> A domain of specialized knowledge must develop . . . which will furnish the theoretical underpinnings for the practice skills by which the profession expresses its function. In the absence of specialized knowledge at least the technical means—for example, techniques or skills whereby the professional is characterized and differentiated from the nonprofessional or layman—need to be specified (Boehm, 1965:641).

The major commonality among the professions is that they are formally sanctioned by society to bring about change that is beneficial to the society and its components, as well as to maintain the society. Despite their seeming conservatism on occasion, professions do regulate change as well as maintenance; for a profession to refuse to allow change would be deadly to a society and would probably signal that the profession will lose its societal sanction. Professional licensure symbolizes societal acceptance and sanction for a professional territory: "Each profession has a specific or core function and in a sense holds a monopoly on this function. . . . However each profession shares with all other professions in society what Hiltner has called a village green, a common area that is peripheral to each profession" (Boehm, 1965:642). Clearly, social work, nursing, psychiatry, education and law enforcement, among other professions, share a "village green" that is socialization and social control.

Historically, social work has concerned itself more with change among microsystems (persons, families, and small groups) than with change among macrosystems (organizations, communities, and society). But it has dealt with societal and community change as well, although these have also been the domains of other professional groups such as political scientists and sociologists. There are indications that social work is enlarging its territorial claims, and border disputes between professions within the same institution are common. Examples are social work and law within the juvenile court, social work and psychology in mental health institutions, and social work and educators in the schools. Clearly, there are boundary disputes between home economists and family counselors, between nurses and physicians' assistants, and between teachers, guidance counselors, and school psychologists.

Boehm pointed to other characteristics of community that distinguish a profession: a common system of values and ethics (way of life, or culture); a group identity that holds the allegiance of the members, and social control and socialization within the profession. All of these characterize professions as nonplace communities. However, in practice, professions sometimes fail to meet all of these criteria (e.g., group identity or common values). The most accurate way to define a profession may well be to define it as a social network, that is, a set of interlocking roles organized for relatively specific goals that are set within expressly stated, idealized goals of "service to society" and the sanctity of the persons being served. Professions often lack a sense of "community" that is sufficient to mobilize their members to joint action. The professions usually resemble organizations as much as communities but lack the degree of social control typical of organizations. J. A. Barnes' definition, referred to earlier in this chapter, indicates that social networks may be the best way to describe professions. They are organized for specific purposes, with limited bonds between members, and largely dependent upon affiliations between small numbers of members who are loosely connected to some larger system.

CONCLUSION

Because the term carries many meanings, community is an elusive concept. Meanings range from the territorial community of Robert Park and the Chicago sociologists (Park, 1952) to the almost mystical "mind" community of more recent writers. Three critiques of the concept that are particularly germane to the helping professions are those by Chatterjee and Koleski (1970), Meenaghan (1972), and Gusfield (1975), each of which reviewed the literature of community and concluded that the concept of community continues to evolve. Each critique concluded that community is a perspectivistic idea—that is, it is futile to attempt to understand a total community, but it is worthwhile to select issues or problems and then define community as it is relevant to these particular concerns. This stance is in agreement with our use of the concept of community in this book. We view community as a social system and, as such, perceive it from a particular perspective. To do this, it is necessary to have criteria for classifying patterns of relatedness as a system and then, further, to distinguish the community from family, group, or organization. These criteria come from the composite definition suggested earlier, that a community

1. is a system intermediate between society and "microsystems;"
2. has a consciously identified population characterized by a sense of belonging, that is, it is aware of itself and is part of its members' identities;
3. is organized and engaged in common pursuits;
4. has differentiation of functions;
5. adapts to the environment through energy exchange; and
6. creates and maintains organizations and institutions to fulfill the needs of both subsystems and suprasystems.

Further, its members may or may not occupy common physical space; and its boundaries may or may not coincide with the boundaries of a political subdivision (city, town, or county). Communities can, and do, interlace through overlapping memberships of their significant subsystems. For example, a nurse may be at the same time a Minnesotan, an officer in the Air Force, a Republican, a Roman Catholic, and a member of Right to Life. Each of these may signify a community to which she belongs. Membership in each of them may modify her beliefs and behavior in the others. As stated earlier, community is a vital system to humans, who require some sense of linkage, that is, some sense of community in order to survive and flourish.

SUGGESTED READINGS

Bell, Colin, and Howard Newby.
   1972 *Community Studies: An Introduction to the Sociology of the Local Community.*
   New York: Praeger.
      A comprehensive survey of community theory up to 1972, which suggests promising leads for further theory.
Capelle, Ronald.
   1979 *Changing Human Systems.* Toronto: International Human Systems Institute.
      A generalized overview of change techniques, which is presented by level of system. Chapter 10, "Community Change," suggests a way of selecting among techniques, but in rather sketchy fashion. You may be interested in reading this for ideas rather than as a course text.

Christenson, James A., and Jerry W. Robinson, Jr.
1980 *Community Development in America*. Ames: The Iowa State University Press.

> Beginning with a very brief review of the concept of community, this is a highly useful description of community development themes and techniques. It also examines in some detail the roles performed by community developers.

Christenson, James. A., and Jerry W. Robinson, Jr.
1989 *Community Department in Perspective*. Ames, Iowa: Iowa State University Press.

> This is a companion volume to the earlier book, just listed. Together, those constitute the definitive texts on community development.

Davenport, Judith, and Joseph Davenport III.
1982 "Utilizing the Social Network in Rural Communities," *Social Casework* 63 (2): 106–113.

Dunn, Edgar S.
1980 *The Development of the U. S. Urban System*, Volume I. Baltimore MD: The Johns Hopkins University Press.

> Chapter 2, "An Activity Network Image of Urban System Structure," is an excellent companion to this chapter. The entire book is compatible with the social systems view.

Fellin, Phillip.
1987 *The Community and the Social Worker*. Itasca, IL: Peacock.

> The author uses a systems approach to analyze community and to describe processes within it. The book could be used as a "large-scale" text for this chapter.

Gardner, Hugh.
1978 *The Children of Prosperity: Thirteen Modern American Communes*. New York: St. Martin's Press.

> Insightful and incisive research into communes and their reason for existence. Concluded that failure to transcend individualism doomed many of them.

Vaux, Alan.
1988 *Social Support: Theory, Research, and Intervention*. New York: Praeger.

> An exhaustive review of the theory and literature of social support. The conclusion is that social support is an ecological (systemic) process. Social networks are examined as a specific form of social support.

LITERARY SOURCES

Keillor, Garrison.
1985 *Lake Wobegon Days*. New York: Viking.

> Created in the fertile mind of one of the nation's best humorists, this fictional community embodies "midwestern," small town values, subtly and sometimes hilariously. The community is a vehicle for social criticism and subtle observations about contemporary America.

Lee, Harper.
   1960 *To Kill a Mockingbird*. Philadelphia: Lippincott.
   Now thirty years old, the novel nonetheless portrays the interwoven
   strands of community as seen through the eyes of a young girl. Secrets
   which bind the townspeople together are gradually revealed. The rigid rules
   of racism in the southern town were well portrayed. The movie omitted the
   subtler aspects of community.

FILMS AND VIDEOS

The Amish: Not to Be Modern (1985)
   Rare film of a community that separates itself from the world. Photographed
   over four seasons, capturing the daily life of people who preserve rural traditions. Narrated by Amish themselves, with 400-year old Amish hymns,
   handed down orally, as soundtrack.
Harlan County, U.S.A. (1977)
   This documentary captures accurately the lives of Kentucky miners, their
   community, their working conditions, and their relationship to the mining
   company and union. It won an Oscar for best documentary.
The Hutterites: To Care and Not to Care (1984)
   The Hutterites have preserved a completely communal lifestyle for nearly five
   centuries. While they live simply, they employ modern technology, such as
   computers, but not for personal comfort.
The Last Picture Show (1971)
   Set in a small Texas town in the 1950s, it is very well acted. The lives of the
   residents are interwoven in ways that only gradually reveal themselves. Bit-
   tersweet and poignant. The demise of the movie theater is a metaphor for the
   loss of a *gemeinschaft* way of life in small towns.
Matewan (1988)
   A community of mine workers is entered by a union organizer. His methods
   are a case study of organizing tactics. Portrays elements of community and
   conflict.
Milagro Beanfield War (1988)
   Rituals and binding ties in a Mexican-American community are well portrayed
   in this film, based on the novel. Cultural pride and vitality sustain them in
   their battle with the large landowners who control the water supply.
A World of Difference: B. F. Skinner and the Good Life (1979)
   An intimate, biographical film, which discusses Skinner's theory. He visits
   Twin Oaks cooperative, in which his ideas were put into practice, and ob-
   serves that "his system works better in theory than in practice."

Organizations

Careers in organizations—that is, careers as managers and other professionals—are the principal career opportunities for educated people. Nine out of ten youngsters who receive a college degree can expect to spend all of their working lives as managerial or other professional employees of institutions.

(Drucker, 1982:xii)

After a certain age, most of us are watching television at home or safely hidden away in our cars or offices. The French have a rhymed expression for it: "*Métro. Boulot. Dodo.*" Subway. Job. Sleep.

(Reeves, 1989:26)

INTRODUCTION

The fact that modern societies are organizational societies has been noted by many observers. However, human service professionals have been slow to recognize and take this into account in their appraisals of human behavior.

We tend to concentrate on the interior qualities of those organizations within which we are employed while overlooking the influences of organizations on those we serve. In Western mass societies, organizations are the context of living, the connecting fabric between the individual and society that has, to a significant degree, replaced communities and families as mediating institutions in society. We believe our social systems approach will enable the reader to appraise and evaluate the influences that organizations have on human behavior.

The nature of organizations has been insufficiently understood, and even the most knowledgeable organization theorists readily admit that there is no single definitive theory. Miller wrote:

> Organization theory is a field without a large body of empirically established fact. Like medicine before 1930, management science is based largely upon case studies. . . . Scholars in this area would also profit from an agreement . . . as to what are the basic subsystems common to all organizations. I suggest that comparison with the other levels of living systems can provide this. A generally accepted taxonomy of types of organizations is also desirable, and general systems behavior theory may be able to provide it (Miller, 1972:174).

In his encyclopedic book, *Living Systems,* Miller applied his framework to organizations to prove that

> General living systems theory can provide a unifying conceptual system for organization theory, including a definition which differentiates organizations from living systems at other levels, and identification of the chief subsystems of all organizations with their analogs at other levels. It can provide a basis for understanding how organizations differ and for applying quantitative techniques and formal models to the study of organizations (J. Miller, 1978:597).

We agree with this view, and believe that the systems approach provides the best opportunity to classify organizations and their subsystems. We must begin at the beginning, however, with a workable definition of *organization*. Probably Talcott Parsons' statement is clearer than most:

> Organizations are social units (or human groups) deliberately constructed to seek specific goals. Corporations, armies, schools, hospital, churches, and prisons are included; tribes, classes, ethnic groups, friendship groups, and families are excluded. Organizations are characterized by: (1) divisions of labor, power, and communications responsibilities . . .; (2) the presence of one or more power centers which control the concerted efforts of the organization and direct them toward its goals . . .; (3) substitution of personnel (Parsons, 1960:17).

Each of the characteristics Parsons cited is true to some degree of societies and communities as well. Certainly some organizations are less characterized by these than are some societies and communities. Thus, the differences are not in the absence of these characteristics but rather the degree to which they are present and the form they take. We will expand on this at several points, particularly in the conclusion to this chapter. Consistent with Parsons' view, characteristics to be stressed in Section II of this chapter are goals, differentiation, power, control, leadership, and communication.

Another definition of organization that is concise, albeit cryptic, is by C. Wright Mills: "An organization is a system of roles graded by authority" (Presthus, 1962:4). Persons are not expected to exhibit their full range of behaviors but only those that are necessary or useful to the purposes of the organization, that is, goal achievement. In other words, persons are to perform according to their assigned roles, not according to their personal wishes (unless their personal wishes coincide with the needs of the organization, a situation deliberately sought by many organizations). Further, these roles must be coordinated so that they can combine to achieve the goals, that is, they must be differentiated, hierarchical, and have some functions taking priority over others, although the ranking in the hierarchy can change from one occasion to another.

Taken together, Parsons' and Mills' definitions form a relatively complete description of organizations that includes the following elements: (1) an organization is a social system that has the achievement of specific, explicit goals as its purpose. In order to accomplish this, its members must (2) confine themselves to a relatively narrow range of behaviors intended to fulfill this purpose. The members (3) exercise power over each other in the form of authority and hierarchical control, to (4) assure compliance with the system's goals and adherence to the members' prescribed roles.

I. THEORIES OF ORGANIZATIONS

There are four major types of organization theory, to which we add a fifth—systems.

A. The Classical Model

The classical model is sometimes called the "machine theory" because the organization was viewed as a machine with interchangeable parts and clearly identifiable operations, and members were treated as cogs and gears in that machine. Principles of this formal organization include (1) division of labor, with each unit performing certain tasks; (2) pyramid of control, with each unit subordinate to one above it in the hierarchy; and (3) unity of command, that is centralized control emanating from the top of the pyramid (see Figure 8).

The emphasis is on mechanical regulation, control, and rationality of organization, the latter two being primary characteristics of this model. This has been the most visible model, from the Roman army to the modern bureaucracy. The fact that this form of organization survived thousands of years indicates how effective it can be at achieving goals and ensuring compliance. Henry Ford based his assembly line on the ratio-

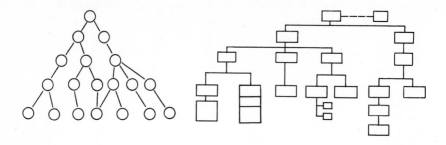

Figure 8.   Diagrams of the classical model.

nality of this model, saying of the giant industrial coporations, "It is clearly up to them now, as trustees, to see what they can do further in the way of making our systems fool-proof, malice-proof, and greed-proof. It is a mere matter of social engineering" (Flink, 1976:82–83). Social–historian Lewis Mumford said that organizations arise from the human need to create regularity in the world (see the discussion in Chapter 3, II,E, "The Human Urge to Explain the World"), which he traced to earliest recorded history:

> Behind every later process of organization and mechanization one must . . . recognize primordial attitudes, deeply engrained in the human organism—indeed, shared with many other species—for ritualizing behavior and finding satisfaction in a repetitive order that establishes a human connection with organic rhythms and cosmic event.
>
>   Organization Man is the common link between the ancient and modern type of megamachine: that is perhaps why the specialized functionaries, with their supporting layer of slaves, conscripts, and subjects—in short, the controllers and the controlled—have changed so little in the last five thousand years (Mumford, 1970:277).

This probably explains the inscription on the Great Pyramid of Egypt, presumably scratched by one of the original workmen, which says, "Khufu is a drunk." Workers apparently resented their bureaucratic supervisors 4500 years ago, too.

B. *The Human Relations Theory*

Human Relations theory arose partly in reaction to "machine" theory. It is exemplified by Elton Mayo, Kurt Lewin, and indirectly the philosopher John Dewey (Etzioni, 1964:32). It stressed the informal structure, and the emotional, nonrational motivations that operate in organizations. It emphasized such processes as communication, participation, and leadership. Japanese organizations' motivational programs for workers, such as saluting the company flag, singing the company song, and other means of encouraging a corporate spirit and corporate identification, and "Theory Z" are variations of Human Relations theory in that they stress increased productivity and decreased alienation due to greater participation and involvement in corporate decisions by workers [see the discussion of Theory Z (Ouchi, 1981b) later in this chapter].

The best known studies issuing from the Human Relations theorists were the Hawthorne studies, including the Bank Wiring Room study (Mayo, 1945; Olmsted, 1959:25–32; Roethlisberger and Dickson, 1947). The results of these studies showed conclusively that machine theory was inadequate to explain behavior in organizations; clearly, other factors besides rational, impersonal calculation determined the workers' production. In these studies, it was found that the highest motivation for one group of workers was neither money nor working conditions but rather what is now known as the "Hawthorne effect"—the fact that they were a special group being researched! The general conclusion that sets this theory apart from the machine model is that workers do not function as separate, distinct units organized in linear chains, but rather as members of groups to whose norms they adhere. The influence of the small group became readily apparent.

Later adaptations of Human Relations theory have employed Maslow's "hierarchy of needs" to explain motivation and behavior in organizations. In this view, needs are hierarchical, with "safety" needs (adequate food and physical protection, e.g.) and "security" needs (medical care, income assurances in case of illness, e.g.) being fundamental. If these needs are filled, one progresses to "higher" wants/needs: "social" needs including contact with others, and membership in groups; "esteem" needs for positive regard by others, and one's own positive feelings about self. If all other needs are satisfied, a person then progresses to the "highest" need, which is self-actualization, the fulfillment of one's potential as an individual person (Maslow, 1968). Herzberg's two-factor "hygiene" theory is another variation. In this view, workers have two hierarchies of needs, one of satisfaction, one of dissatisfaction. The "satisfaction" scale refers to the upper end of Maslow's scale, the worker's need for stimulation and for self-fulfillment (Maslow's "self-actualization"). The "dissatisfaction" scale refers to the lower end of Maslow's scale, including the employee's "security" needs for pay, safety, and health, and for insurance coverage (the so-called fringe benefits). The worker can be "high" on one scale and "low" on the other, "high" on both, or "low" on both. That is, a worker can be highly satisfied and highly dissatisfied at the same time concerning different aspects of the job (Herzberg, Mausner, and Snyderman, 1959). Perhaps the pay and fringe benefits are excellent, yet the employee is frustrated because there is little opportunity for creativity or career advancement, a fre-

quent finding of studies on workers' alienation. Human Relations theory restored human, personal factors to the study of organizations.

C. *Structuralist or Conflict Theory*

The structuralists, who include Karl Marx and Max Weber, represent
in some respects a synthesis of the two theories just discussed in that
they recognize both formal and informal structures, and their interaction, as significant. They agree with the classical theorists that the attempt to achieve goals through rational, impersonal structure is useful
and does not necessarily lead to unhappiness among workers. They also
recognize a necessity for the organization to meet the human, personal
needs of its components, as well.

The structuralist view did not place primary emphasis on the human,
emotive factors, however. It stressed the importance of the work setting
and the influence of the technology used in the industry. This gave rise
to the study of the "sociotechnical" aspects of industry, the interaction
of persons with technology (often called *cybernetics*). Another difference
between the structuralist view and the machine theory is that the former
pictures organizations as open systems; that is, the structure of the organization varies according to the environment and the technology employed (Tausky, 1970:55–62). A pyramidal, bureaucratic structure will
not fit every organization.

The major difference between the structuralist view and the two previous theories is that the structuralists recognize the inevitability of conflict within the organization. Etzioni said, "The structuralist sees the organization as a large, complex social unit in which many social groups
interact. . . . The various groups might cooperate in some spheres and
compete in others, but they hardly are or can become one big happy
family as Human Relations writers often imply" (Etzioni, 1964:41).

The structuralist view can be called a "conflict" or "tension" theory
of organizations. This theory resembles a systems approach in that it
recognizes components within the organization and recognizes that
there is inevitably tension in the interaction between the components
and the larger organizational system. Like systems theory and unlike
the machine and Human Relations theories, structuralist theory does
not view conflict as a problem, the resolution of which will restore equilibrium. Rather, conflict may lead to a new steady state and is thus an
inherent characteristic of organizations. Indeed, one administrative or
organizational development strategy may be to induce conflict deliberately in order to stimulate change. Coser (1964) cited positive effects of
conflict—for example, that it may force a confrontation that leads to a
test of power and the possibility of significant change. The history of
nearly any organization reveals successive tensions and conflicts whose

resolution (or nonresolution) contributed to its present condition. Some of these conflicts can probably be viewed as "healthy" because they restored vitality or resolved issues that had retarded the organization's development. Structuralist theory, then, portrays organizations more realistically than either the classical or the Human Relations theory alone.

D. Neoclassical or Decision Theory

Etzioni called this neoclassical or decision theory because it is concerned with the achievement of rational decision-making *whenever possible.* This theory recognizes that there is, in addition to the horizontal differentiation by task, a vertical hierarchy or differentiation by "levels of decisions" that are made. This differentiation is made on the basis of power (i.e., whose decisions are binding upon whom). This theory distinguishes between policy-making and policy implementation. In this theory, power consists of access to information that is sufficient to formulate policy, and the ability to get others to carry out the actions necessary to implement the policy. Perhaps most important is the qualification *whenever possible.* This school holds that human behavior in organizations is best described as "intendedly rational" (Simon, 1945:196). It recognizes the nonrational aspects of decision-making in organizations. Also emphasized is *search behavior,* the concept that an organization does not seek endlessly for perfectly rational behavior but instead seeks satisfying solutions that are "reasonably good" or "acceptable" (Etzioni, 1964:30–31). If tension or conflict between components and the organization cannot be completely resolved to everyone's satisfaction (and it rarely or never is), the organization must find another "solution." The solution may be to coerce the component into agreement, or to modify the organization's behavior, to accommodate the difference, to arrive at a compromise that does not fully satisfy either but permits continued movement toward a mutual goal.

Neoclassical theory resembles systems theory in that it recognizes the inevitability of tension and conflict. It goes beyond Human Relations theory in stating that tension and conflict occur not only over personal factors but over the actions necessary to achieve the goals. That is, conflict is sometimes nonrational, but it is often rational and concerned with decision-making. Further, it recognizes the necessity for differentiation in order to make decisions that lead to task achievement. This does not imply that a fixed hierarchy is necessary, since the structure can change according to task, nor does it imply that certain components must always be the decision-makers, since leadership may also change according to task. The theory simply recognizes that people will "organize," that is, differentiate their efforts to achieve a task. It also recognizes that people will disagree about how to organize.

E. The Systems Model

Organization theorists have made various observations about organizations as systems. Gouldner described the "natural-system model" including the following characteristics (Gouldner, 1961:394–395).

1. Organizations are "natural wholes"; the underlying model is organismic.
2. Structural changes are cumulative, unplanned, adaptive responses to threats to the equilibrium of the organization rather than purely rational, objective behavior.
3. While goal attainment is the fundamental reason for an organization's existence, it cannot be pursued to the exclusion of other functions of the organization. Goal attainment is only one of the important functions of the system (see Figure 2, p. 15)

March and Simon stressed this organic analogy:

> A biological analogy is apt here, if we do not take it too literally or too seriously. Organizations are assemblages of interacting human beings and they are the largest assemblages in our society that have anything resembling a central coordinative system. Let us grant that these coordinative systems are not developed nearly to the extent of the central nervous system in higher biological organisms—that organizations are more earthworm than ape. Nevertheless, the high specificity of structure and coordination within organizations—as contrasted with the diffuse and variable relations *among* organizations and among unorganized individuals—marks off the individual organization as a sociological unit comparable to the individual organism in biology (March and Simon, 1968:33).

Presthus emphasized that large organizations are similar to society as a system in that they have specialization, hierarchy, and authority, and that they socialize their members in similar fashion (Presthus, 1962:94–95). This systems model, although not without faults, seems to avoid the pitfalls of the preceding models. This systems model of organizations agrees with decision theory that the goal is not perfection. It goes one step further by stating that goal-seeking behavior (GE, GI) is not necessarily the primary behavior of a system at all times since, as earlier stated, exclusive attention to goal attainment leads to neglect of other essential functions of the system. The systems model also stresses a wider context of decision-making and organizational behavior than is pictured in other theories. Like the structuralist theory, it takes into account environmental influences as well as the influences wielded by groups within the organization. Conflict is seemingly better explained by the systems model in that it recognizes the inevitability of conflict within and between components and subsystems, each of which holds to the legitimacy of its own goals. James Miller, a former college president, stated the systems point of view very well:

No decision is entirely rational or satisfactory, a fact which can give administrators some solace. There is no perfect rational solution to most administrative problems. The higher the echelon, the truer this is of the issues which confront it. The dimensions along which many decisions must be made are incommensurable. Human lives are incommensurable with money. Money is incommensurable with time. Time is incommensurable with professional excellence. Yet all of these are in scarce supply to a given organization and trade-offs among them must be decided upon (Miller, 1972:79).

Thus the context and environment of any organization is complex, and is best portrayed by the systems model.

Control is also pictured differently in the systems model. It is, like goal attainment, exclusively pursued only to the detriment of other functions and, at times, other functions do take precedence. The fact that power, control, and the influence of the environment may vary from one time to another requires us to use a flexible model of organization. The systems model has flexibility that allows for understanding variant forms of organization that do not fit the classical model.

II. BEHAVIOR: CHARACTERISTICS OF ORGANIZATIONS

Kahn claimed that it is correct to identify the "job to be done," or goal achievement by organizations, as the function of the organization that takes precedence over any other function. He suggested that other activities that contribute to the overall functioning of the organization should be called "subfunctions" (Kahn, 1969:145). We disagree. Although it is goal achievement that justifies an organization's existence, other functions are necessary and at times take precedence.

A. Goal Direction

What is an organizational goal? Etzioni said that a goal is "a desired state of affairs which the organization attempts to realize" (Etizioni, 1964:6). In this sense, a goal may be expressed by an ideal or myth or by a rational, projected set of specific objectives—that is, it may be "maximum service to the patient" or "caseloads of 50, with short-term crisis intervention allowing attention to 50 percent more clients than at present" (Etzioni, 1964). The goal expressed by either statement is a desired future condition of the organization in which its declared purposes would be fulfilled. These goals guide the organization in its activity; they either legitimate or exclude certain specific actions undertaken or contemplated by the organization.

Etzioni's conception of goal is similar in some regards to the "ego ideal" of the person, and to the self toward which one strives in Sartre's form of existentialism, or Maslow's self-actualization. In fact, Argyris said "research points up quite clearly that the importance of the organization as an organism worthy of self-actualization is now being recognized" (Argyris, 1968:83).

Two aspects of goal attainment should be distinguished. *Effectiveness* refers to the degree to which the organization achieves its goals; *efficiency* refers to the manner in which it is done, specifically the amount of energy and resources necessary to achieve a goal. The former is part of the GE and GI functions of systems; the latter is part of the SE and SI functions. Efficiency in an organization requires reduction of conflict (or "friction," in slang) within the organization; thus some internal control of the utilization of energy is necessary for goal attainment. One example would be the coaches' encouragement of team spirit with its implied reduction of intrasquad animosities in a football team so that points (or goals) may be scored. As several theorists point out, goals are not static. Goals can be *displaced* (i.e., other goals can be substituted for them). The most frequent form of this is making ends of means. For example, efficiency in public welfare is purported to be a means to effective service to clients and society, but all too often efficiency in the form of having to account for every dollar spent becomes an end in itself. When this occurs, the completed forms become more important than the clients they represent—a frequent complaint of human service professionals in most kinds of organizations. Another example is the accusation by many university students, especially undergraduates, that universities have displaced education with publication and research, resulting in lower-quality instruction.

There are other forms of goal change. One is *succession*, in which an organization achieves its initial goals and establishes new ones, or the goal disappears and the organization turns to new goals. Examples of this include those private welfare agencies that began as adoption agencies in an era when there were more children available for adoption than now, and whose goals have become the treatment of emotionally disturbed children or family treatment. This is one result of what Hasenfeld called "the turbulent environment" in which social service agencies exist, and the definition of social problems shift with startling rapidity (Hasenfeld, 1983). Both Christmas Seals and the March of Dimes established new goals after attaining their original goals, the elimination of tuberculosis and polio as major health hazards.

There may also be goal *multiplication*. The Red Cross, which began as a service on the battlefield to soldiers, broadened its goals to include services to soldiers' windows and orphans, disaster relief, and visiting political prisoners. The Boy Scouts have, in recent years, broadened their former goals of camping, crafts, and character development to include ethical leadership for adult leaders, and family supports through family life education. There are, of course, advantages and disadvantages to such goal multiplication. Among possible advantages are that synergy may increase the effectiveness of an organization and that staff recruitment may be easier because they enjoy variety, and because a wider range of contributors may be motivated to support the organization. Disadvantages include shortage of energy and conflict between goals.

B. Differentiation

Differentiation is probably more pronounced in organizations than in other social systems. Differentiation is the prime sociological characteristic of modernization according to Etzioni (1964:106). Modernization means essentially that modern society is a society of differentiated organizations, and these organizations differentiate internally to carry out their purposes more effectively. For example, education has become the domain of organizations grouped under the rubric of "schools." These in turn have differentiated along dimensions of age and function: preschool, elementary, middle, and high school. High schools have differentiated into technical, vocational, college preparatory, and general. Postsecondary education has community colleges to prepare students for specific occupations, colleges for general higher education, and universities for occupations designated as professions. The most recent differentiated form is elder hostel for the elderly.

Durkheim pointed out that differentiation of tasks within an organization may have disadvantages. If workers do not see and understand other activities as parallel to their own and are not horizontally related to them, they each become nothing but "an inert piece of machinery." They must "keep in constant relations with neighboring functions . . . not lose sight of [their] collaborators, that [the worker] acts upon them and reacts to them" (Durkheim, 1968:43); they are, then, not machines. Differentiation may lead to isolation of the components of an organization (e.g., in offices and factories where there is little exchange between clerical and professional staff or between workers and management). Some factories, e.g., Volvo and Saab in Sweden, employ "autonomous work groups" in which a group of workers produces a car, and each worker performs a variety of tasks; the outcome is a shared group product, with less differentiation or specialization. United States industries originated "quality circles" forty years ago; the idea was then adopted by Japanese industry, and reimported to the United States during the 1980s. It is estimated that about one of every nine Japanese workers is involved in a quality circle (Handy, 1985:333).

> The quality circle consists on average of a half-dozen employees, headed by a supervisor, who constitute a natural work group. As group members, they are charged with pinpointing quality problems and developing effective solutions to them. . . .

For example, the fourteen members of a quality circle at the Kariya plant of Nippon Denso examined leaky auto radiators and determined how to produce a 100 percent leak detection rate. Nippon Steel sliced its liquefied petroleum gas consumption by 5.3 percent over a four-year period as a result of quality-circle suggestions each year (Larwood, 1984:402).

As Larwood notes, however, "quality circles depend on circles members' believing that they can make a difference. . . ." (Larwood, 1984:403).

C. Power and Control

In the definition of organizations by Talcott Parsons, discussed earlier, the existence of one or more "power centers" that control the organization's efforts was acknowledged. Bierstedt stated this emphatically: "Power supports the fundamental order of society and the social organization within it, wherever there is order. Power stands behind every organization and sustains its structure. Without power there is no organization and without power there is no order" (Bierstedt, 1961:246).

Organizations must ensure compliance in achieving specific, narrow goals and therefore must apply some kind of control—the use of power. One characteristic of organizations as distinct from other systems is the explicitness of power; it is largely visible and institutionalized.

What is power? Max Weber defined power as "the possibility of imposing one's will upon the behavior of other persons and in this general sense power is an aspect of most, if not all, social relationships" (Bendix, 1960:294) A similar definition of power, widely used in political science, is Robert Dahl's: "A has power over B to the extent that he can get B to do something B would not otherwise do" (Dahl, 1957:201–215). Similarly, Bierstedt said:

Power is the ability to employ force, not its actual employment, the ability to apply sanctions, not their actual application. Power is the ability to introduce force into a social situation; it is the presentation of force. Unlike force, incidentally, power is always successful; when it is not successful, it is not, or ceases to be, power. Power symbolizes the force which may be applied in any social situation and supports the authority which is applied. Power is thus neither force nor authority but, in a sense, their synthesis (Bierstedt, 1961:243).

What we mean by "force," in systems terms, is the application or deprivation of energy in order to affect the functioning of another system. Force should not be taken to mean only physical forces; moral force or Gandhi's Truth Force qualify as well. Since power is an energy function, it is finite; energy expended (through GE or GI functions, for example) to influence the behavior of others may deplete the system's power potential.

We agree with Miller's terse definition: "In my conceptual system I use the word *power* as the ability of a system to elicit compliance from other systems" (Miller, 1972:66). We will define power, then as *the system's potential to achieve its goals by the application or deprivation of energy to another system or component so as to affect the functioning of that system or component.* The degree of effectiveness of power depends upon the extent to which the "target" system is affected and the extent to which the goal is achieved. One example is the use of federal funds for Appalachian development. The stated goal was social and economic change; the result was an improved highway system and some new courthouses, which benefited the residents of the county seat towns and the politicians (in the opinion of one well-informed resident). A great deal of energy (funds and propaganda) was expended, but although there were some substantial achievements, they were not the ones originally intended. In this instance, the federal government's power to achieve its goals was shown to be minimal. If the federal government's covert goal was *political*, its power to achieve its goals through the political system of Appalachia was quite effective. Power must thus be measured by its objectives, not merely the magnitude of its effects.

We consider power and control to be similar except that *control* suggests narrower and more precise goals than does power. Further, power may have effects other than control. The application of power could release control ("the truth shall set you free," e.g., is a good psychoanalytic principle). One example is education, which is the application of the teacher's and school's power so that the student is freer to perform the necessary tasks of adulthood (an idealistic view of education, we admit). Etzioni stated the importance of control:

> The success of an organization is largely dependent upon its ability to maintain control of its participants. All social units control their members, but the problem of control in organizations is especially acute. Organizations as social units that serve specific purposes are artificial units. They are planned, deliberately structured; they constantly and self-consciously review their performance and restructure themselves accordingly (Etzioni, 1964:58).

Control is a central concept in cybernetics, together with related concepts such as "steering" and "regulation." The question, to what extent can social systems be steered? was investigated by Felix Geyer and Johannes van der Zouwen in their book, *Sociocybernetic Paradoxes* (1986). They concluded that systems, in their closed aspects, steer internally and, in their open aspects, are responsive to externally generated control. In other words, internal control is primarily a function of the system as a whole and external control is the system's function as a part of a larger system.

The objective of power and control is *compliance*, the cooperation of a system or component in achieving the goals of the system that applies power and control. Dessler suggested that "there are two basic aspects of organizations (their *structure,* and how *compliance* is ensured) that organization theorists have focused on" (Dessler, 1980:7). Organization theorists and managers of organizations perhaps devote more attention to compliance than to any other aspect of organizations—how to assure the desired results. The problem of compliance is apparent in the following analysis of the destruction of the space shuttle Challenger on January 28, 1986, an analysis worth reading by any serious student of organizational dynamics:

> The Commission concluded that the failure was not in the design of the launch decision structure or in the procedures followed in arriving at a decision, but rather in actions (or nonactions) of key decision makers within the system [who] . . . (1) ignored the warnings of Morton Thiokol and Rockwell engineers regarding the potential dangers presented by the low temperature and ice buildup at the time of the launch, and (2) failed to communicate those concerns to key decision makers. . . .
> . . . it is an over-simplification of the problem to account for the decision strictly in terms of those specifically mentioned . . . a proper accounting of that decision requires us to adopt a more comprehensive and systems-oriented perspective . . . . [This] requires us to examine the interaction and joint influence of various cognitive, psychological, and social factors (Hirokawa, Gouran, and Martz, 1988:414–415).

One powerful factor was the "perceived pressure" from NASA officials, which led the Morton Thiokol engineers to set aside their own misgivings about the launch:

> Another psychological factor that apparently exerted a powerful influence on the decision to launch the *Challenger* concerns the "launch commit criterion" in operation during the deliberation process. Traditionally, NASA decisions involving the launch of manned space vehicles were governed by a very conservative rule that dictated that a launch *should be canceled if there is any doubt of its safety.* . . . In the case of flight 51-L, however, it seems clear that a very different decisional rule was in operation. Specifically, it appears that Level III managers operated under the rule that a scheduled launch *should proceed unless there is conclusive evidence that it is unsafe to do so* (Hirokawa et al., 1988:423).

With whom would the engineers comply? Their own organization and its professional standards, or with what they perceived to be NASA's pressure not to postpone the launch? What did compliance mean in this instance? Compliance with what and with whom?

There are three forms of control, as Etzioni describes them: (1) physical control, (2) material rewards such as goods and services, and (3) symbolic rewards (Etzioni, 1964:47–59). Etzioni describes three kinds of organizations based upon the form of control used by each: (1) coercive organizations, which use threat and punishment, resulting in alienation among members of the organizations; (2) remunerative organizations, which provide material rewards, in which the members calculate the benefits they will receive; and (3) normative organizations, which use moral involvement and social acceptance as means of control, which tend to encourage high levels of commitment to the organization by its members (House, 1975:74–78). The latter, symbolic or normative rewards, are in many ways the most significant because one's sense of identity and what value one has is derived from symbolic interaction with others (as noted in Chapter 3, I, C, "Language"). Symbolic rewards are most likely to be used by the systems with the least physical control or material rewards—religious institutions are the prime examples. In this light, professions such as nursing, social work, or education can be regarded as means of social control; through the deliberate use of symbols, they assist organizations such as schools, hospitals, prisons, or the military in securing compliance (SE and GI functions).

Organizations whose primary purpose is social control are examples of what has come to be called *total institutions,* a phrase coined by Goffman in his classic work, *Asylums* (1973). He described a total institution as an organized agency of society in which a large number of like-situated persons, cut off from the larger society for an appreciable length of time, together lead a formally administered round of life. This is descriptive of such organizations as prisons, mental hospitals, the military, and, in some respects, public and private education. These systems are composed of two groups variously called staff and patients, guards and inmates, keepers and kept, or faculty and students.

Generally, the purpose of a total institution is to socialize or resocialize the population with which it works. This is done by the staff through a two-step process designed to change the "structure of self" of their charges. The process begins by changing the person through external definition, usually by (1) divesting the person of socially defining symbols and characteristics (e.g., the "bald" haircut in army basic training and personal clothing); (2) using clothing to symbolize distinctions between inmates and staff, e.g., separate uniforms for guards and inmates, and "street clothing" for administrators; or hospital gowns for patients, as opposed to the green or white clothing of the medical staff; and (3) severing links with outside systems that tend to support and validate previous identity. Thus, depersonalization and dehumanization are often the initial phase of experience within a total institution. Once a new, imposed definition has been established, the second step in the process is to see that the definition is internalized by the inmate (or patient, prisoner, or student) thus changing that person's "selfhood" or self-image. The objective of power and control, again, is to ensure compliance with the organization's goals.

Lewis Coser coined the term "greedy institutions" to denote organizations that make a totalistic claim on its members' time and energy: "They seek exclusive and individual loyalty and they attempt to reduce the claims of competing roles and status positions on those they wish to encompass within their boundaries" (Coser, 1974:4). Coser differentiated greedy institutions from Goffman's total institutions on the basis of the latter being physically separate, using the device of isolation. Greedy institutions rely on voluntary compliance and loyalty. Status rewards are heavily relied on and the higher the status the higher the personal commitment of time and energy.

D. Leadership

Leadership may be either formal or informal, and it includes power and control used to achieve organizational ends and to make means effective. *Command* is defined as the use of power to ensure compliance, and *leadership* is defined as a "continually creative function involving constant appraisal"; the distinction is really between power and authority, or "authority of position" and "authority of leadership" (Dubin, 1961:350). "Authority of position depended upon centrality in the organization's communications system—it was determined by a structural decision—while authority of leadership was dependent upon the superiority of the leader" (Zaleznik and Jardim, 1967:217). In other words, command derives from the organizational position, from the role and status, while leadership derives from the personal characteristics of the leader. But leadership is not solely dependent upon these personal qualities; it also depends upon the context (the environment) in which it occurs.

Murray Ross and Charles Hendry suggested a simple, yet elegant formulation, which can be adapted to form a typology of leadership (Ross and Hendry, 1957:13–36):

1. The person AHEAD of the system through special accomplishment or creativity, e.g., Gandhi, Einstein, Lenin, Freud.

2. The person who is THE HEAD of the system, given leadership through formal structural procedures such as election or authority delegation, e.g., President Bush or a corporate Chief Executive Officer (CEO).

3. The person who is A HEAD of a system, one who situationally emerges with particular talents or qualities for determining and attaining systemic purposes.

In actuality, most situations of leadership will be some combination of two or three of these aspects. It can be observed that these three roughly conform to the dimensions of systems we use throughout this book, i.e., evolutionary, structural, and behavioral.

It should be added here that leadership, like power, is not only vertically hierarchical but may be horizontal. Leadership occurs at all levels;

groups operate within organizations and leadership emerges from these. In some organizations, such emergence of leadership at lower levels is deliberately cultivated; the usual manner in which this is done is to decentralize decision-making. In essence, this is the concept behind moves to decentralize the decisions of government and return initiatives to lower levels—state, county, and city governments. Presidents Carter and Reagan were the most prominent advocates of such decentralization and of dismantling federal governmental organizations. Mechanisms for accomplishing this included revenue sharing and block grants to the states, which supposedly require leadership by the states and localities.

III. STRUCTURE AND CULTURE OF ORGANIZATIONS

A. *Cultures*

Charles Handy presented four "cultures" of organizations, which are each embodied in a typical structure (Handy, 1985): (1) the role culture, (2) the power culture, (3) the task culture, and (4) the person culture.

1. Role Culture. In Handy's conception, the role culture is a bureaucracy. Its structure is a "Greek temple," with a relatively shallow pyramid of control at the top, and supporting vertical columns (see Figure 9).This culture is based on rationality and specialization. Each "pillar" or department has its assigned function, and reports to the triangle of power at the top. Coordination is performed by the triangle, made up of a relatively small number of people. Role prescription, as described by Weber later here, is more important than individual personalities. The major source of power in this culture is *position* power, the status the person holds. Rules and procedures are the major elements of the culture. As Handy described it, this structure operates well in a stable environment; its role occupants can feel secure within it. However, its adaptability is limited. This culture is clearly compatible with the classi-

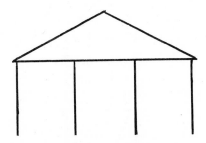

Figure 9. Role culture*.

cal model previously described, and with the "bureaucratic situation" that follows.

2. Power Culture.   Here power derives from a central power source, a powerful person, usually the entrepreneurial founder. Rules and procedures are less important than employees' connections with those who are powerful at the center; in this sense, it is a highly political organization. The organization depends upon trust and face-to-face relationships. Handy pictured this as a web (see Figure 10).This kind of organization is flexible and reacts quickly to threat or opportunity, but it is limited in size, since *gemeinschaft* qualities may be difficult to maintain in a larger organization. Work is accomplished by individuals rather than committees. It is frequently a competitive, "tough" climate, and judgments about effectiveness or worth can issue quickly from the center. Examples include a treatment facility begun by an entrepreneurial social worker to serve developmentally disabled clients, and a clinic founded by a medical specialist to serve Alzheimer's patients. In these instances, staff must be very alert to changes in external resources or clientele.

3. Task Culture.   This culture is exemplified by the development of the space program by the National Aeronautics and Space Administration (NASA), which was accomplished by "modular" work structures and assignments. Units were formed as needed and disbanded as particular subprojects were completed. This can perhaps best be represented by a grid (see Figure 11). The so-called "matrix" organization

Figure 10.   Power culture.*

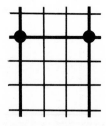

Figure 11.   Task culture.*

embodies this culture. The organization assembles the appropriate resources and expertise at the appropriate intersections of the grid. Expertise is placed at the intersections where projects occur and, since a premium is placed on expertise, power flows from these temporary locations. The organization (and its temporary subunits) are united by specific tasks, in the short term, and by a sequence of tasks accomplished, in the long term. This is a highly adaptable organization. Examples might include an emergency response team in a hospital; a crisis intervention unit in child protective services, or an "external resources" team that writes grants to secure outside funding, with a very short "turnaround time."

4. Person Culture. The person culture is similar to the power culture in that both are based upon personalities, but the person culture is highly decentralized. It is best represented by an aggregation of independent professionals who share a single location, whether law firm, medical practice, or university department. Here each individual is the central point: thus there may be no single center (see Figure 12). Handy said the structure is as "minimal as possible," and that a "cluster" may be the best description, or perhaps "a galaxy of individual stars" (Handy, 1985:195). Control is minimal or nonexistent, except by mutual consent. Individuals have a great deal of autonomy, either because they are protected by their own expertise and the demand for their services elsewhere, or because they are tenured in their position (as with teachers or professors). Handy said.

> The kibbutz, the commune, the cooperative, are all striving after the person culture in organizational form. On the whole, only their original creators achieve any success. Too soon, the organization achieves its own identity and begins to impose on its individuals. It becomes, at best, a task culture, but often a power or a role culture (Handy, 1985:196).

He added that there are many persons who prefer a person culture, but find themselves in other settings. For example, the stereotype of professors is that they are person-oriented, working in a role culture. They do what they must, and teach when they must, to retain their

Figure 12.   Person culture.*

Understanding Organizations by Charles B. Handy (Penguin Books, Third Edition, 1985), copyright © Charles B. Handy, 1976, 1981, 1985. Reproduced by permission of Penguin Books Ltd.

positions in the organization, but essentially they view the organization as a base upon which to build their own careers and carry out their own interests (Handy, 1985:196). This might appear to be increasingly true as universities and colleges rely more heavily on outside resources through research grants secured by faculty members.

B. *The Bureaucratic Situation*

The term *bureaucratic situation* was coined by Presthus, who used it to describe the total environment provided by large organizations (Presthus, 1962:4). This is the same as Handy's role culture; we use it in the same sense, knowing that not all organizations are characterized by what is often derogatorily referred to as "bureaucracy." Bureaucracy is a phenomenon contemporary with industrialization and its primary theorist was Max Weber. Weber's primary concern was power: the distribution of power, control of power, legitimation and uses of power, and the satisfaction derived from membership in the organization. It is clear from Weber's writings that organizational structure is intended to permit and regulate the use of power. The principles of bureaucracy as Weber described them are:

1. division of labor and a high degree of specialization of tasks;
2. a hierarchy of office in which each officeholder or employee is under the control and supervision of a higher one;
3. a consistent system of abstract rules to assure coordination through uniformity of work results, e.g., a manual;
4. impartiality in the conduct of the office;
5. career employment within the organization;
6. machinelike efficiency; and
7. separation of career and personal life, so that the organization's control is limited to work-related matters.

These are, of course, characteristics of the classical or machine model of organizations, as well. To these should be added that,

8. ideally, positions are filled by persons fully trained and experienced to the degree required by that office, and
9. transactions are reported in writing and carefully checked and filed (Washburne, 1964:41–42).

The following memos (Figures 13 and 14) are illustrations of extreme applications of some of these principles, especially the first and the last. Note the use of systems analysis jargon in the second (1982) memo (Figure 14). Note also that one memo is from a governmental organization and one from a private organization; neither the public nor the private sector has a monopoly on bureaucratization.

THE JOINT CHIEFS OF STAFF
WASHINGTON, D.C. 20301

12 July 1985

MEMORANDUM FOR DISTRIBUTION

Subject: OJCS Policy on Split Infinitives

1. Split infinitives are not to be used in OJCS
correspondence. The following information is provided to
help in complying with that policy:

    a. <u>Definition</u>. An infinitive is the form of the verb
    preceded by to: e.g., to write, to do, to be. Splitting
    an infinitive (i.e., inserting an adverb between "to" and
    the "verb") should be avoided because (1) it typically
    produces an awkward construction and (2) the adverb
    usually functions more effectively in another location.

    b. <u>Options</u>
    Instead of: It was impossible to <u>even</u> see a foot ahead.
    Use: It was impossible to see <u>even</u> a foot ahead.
    Instead of: He always tries to <u>carefully</u> do the work.
    Use: He always tries to do the work <u>carefully</u>.

2. Please give this information wide dissemination.

FRANK M. APPLIN
LTC, USA
Chief
Action Management Division

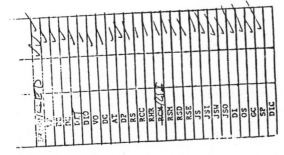

Figure 13.   Reprinted with permission from *The Washington Monthly* July/August
1988 (The Washington Monthly Co., 1611 Connecticut Ave., N.W. Washington, D.C. 20009).

Memo of the Month

[}] BANK of AMERICA

FROM: IOS-Development Support Services #3445
San Francisco Headquarters

TO: IOS Staff

DATE: August 31, 1982

SUBJECT: <u>Pacific Gateway Move Task Force</u>

The attached matrix indicates the Move Task Force Representatives for Pacific
Gateway. The following diagram illustrates the recommended approach for
information/questions to flow in order to ensure all your requirements/needs
are met:

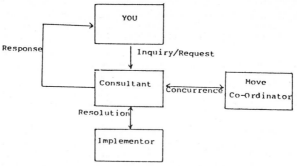

The "Consultant" role is to screen all inquires/requests for feasibility. The
"Implementor" role is to provide back-up to the "Consultant" and to ensure
plans are carried out for day one move in service and thereafter. The "Move
Coordinator" role is to review all updates/concerns and act as primary
interface with all non-IOS departments, e.g. EU-Administration & Premises.

Bruce Lee
Ext. 2-6847
Senior Systems Analyst
(Move Coordinator)

cc: Kathy Stout
Valerie Pinkert
Fran Farmer
Felix Canari
Roger McClure

1v/2116f

Figure 14. Reprinted with permission from *The Washington Monthly,* November,
1982. (The Washington Monthly Co., 2712 Ontario Road, N.W., Washington, D.C. 20009.)

These principles are intended to protect the integrity of the offices and
the officeholders at all levels; like the feudal contract between lord and
vassal which spelled out mutual obligations, these bureaucratic prescriptions detailed the rules for interactions. Blau said that "authority is
strictly circumscribed and confined to those directives that are relevant
for official operations. The use of status prerogatives to extend the
power of control over subordinates beyond these limits does not constitute the legitimate exercise of bureaucratic authority" (Blau, 1956:29). It

is not so easy to limit the power of one's superiors in bureaucracy, however. We have the examples of Nazi Germany, the Soviet Union during Stalinism, Watergate, and the Iran–Contra scandal to remind us of the potential abuses of bureaucratic power. In the Watergate and the Iran–Contra affairs, bureaucratic power was also employed to bring justice; the power of legislative committees and the courts to, e.g., convict Lt. Colonel Oliver North, and to examine the involvement of the president and vice president.

Such rationality as is demanded by rules and regulations is, as the human relations school pointed out, unrealistic. There are limits to rationality. The basic commitment to the organization is only partially rational. It inevitably involves emotive factors such as loyalty and sentiments about the worth of the organization and about oneself as part of it. Such commitments, values, and feelings do not originate with the organization. They must begin in other systems, with the socialization provided by family, school, and community, socialization toward such qualities as reliability, commitment, sacrifice, and the ability to subordinate oneself to larger systems.

Many writers have described the effects of bureaucratic organizations on the personalities of their members. Some have suggested a *bureaucratic personality*. Etzioni described the features of this personality: it (1) is accustomed to shifting between social units, especially the family and the organization, (2) has high tolerance for frustration and the ability to defer gratification, and (3) has the urge to achieve material and symbolic rewards (achievement orientation). Etzioni added this note about the relationship between organizations and other systems:

> The major credit for this convergence of personality and organizational requirements . . . must go to the modern family and the modern educational system, both of which produce the type of person who will make a good organization man. The middle-class stress on the values of punctuality, neatness, integrity, consistency, the accent on conformity, and above all achievement, are the foundation. . . . The organization's effectiveness . . . is due more to the social environment which provides the "right" kind of participants than to any deliberate efforts by the organization to shape personalities according to its needs (Etzioni, 1964:110).

The organization values the kind of personality that puts the organization's goals above its own. To the extent that the organization can enforce this, it has power over its members. Erich Fromm and others have shown that this is unhealthy behavior that encourages alienation because it is manipulative (Fromm, 1962). Presthus says that this may result in "a subtle corrosion of integrity" (Presthus, 1962:18). We refer you to Erikson's conception of integrity (Erikson, 1968:139) discussed in Chapter 8, I,A,1 "Conservation of Identity."

Currently, much attention is being given to the dehumanizing influences of our institutions and organizations. In the effort to structure human interactions in large organizations to conform to criteria of efficiency, objectivity, and merit, the needs of individual persons have been relegated to the background. Alienation, referred to at various points in this book, is an end product of dehumanization. This is also an example of conflict between goals of component and system, and of system and suprasystem. Consequences of such conflict are many, and increasingly visible in shoddy products and inadequate services.

> I can just look at a car and see all kinds of things wrong with it. You can't do that because you didn't see how it was made. I can look at a car underneath the paint. It's like x-ray vision. They put that trim in, they call it. The paint and all those little pretties that you pay for. Whenever we make a mistake, we always say, "Don't worry about it, some dingaling'll buy it" (Laughs.) (Terkel, 1975:229).

Classical organization theory assumes that rational behavior on the part of workers prevents alienation. Human relations theory perceives alienation as inevitable. This is similar to entropy, in that organizations will degenerate into randomness and disorganization if the member's personal needs are not tended to. Both the structuralists and decision system theorists seem to suggest that some degree of alienation is inevitable. The source of alienation is disputed by various writers, however. Robert Agger maintained that alienation is due to attempting to compartmentalize people:

> The conventional wisdom is wrong which implies that when a total person moves from everyday-life into institutional space (say, into working, economic institutional space) the person somehow loses totality by putting on certain clothing or a uniform and becoming known by a job classification or organizational title. For every man and woman the world of work, the week of work, the wages in kind or in other symbolic payment are a vital part of their lives. When at work or anyplace else, the person remains total despite the practices that surround him or her, practices often designed to give people a machinelike sense of identity or even a sense of being components or cogs in a machine (Agger, 1978:100).

One damning indictment of modern organizations is by Scott and Hart, both professors in a school of business administration. They said that "We believe that the most significant source of the subversion of the individual right to 'life, liberty and the pursuit of happiness' is the modern organization, with its supporting technologies and behavioral sciences" (Scott and Hart, 1980:ix). They stated that:

> Outrageous as it may seem, the fact is that a new value system dominates America. The organizational imperative, while originally a subset within the context of the overarching social value system, has now become the dominant force in the homogenization of organizational America, displacing the more individualistic values of the past (Scott and Hart, 1980:52).

They protest the image of the individual person which they believe dominates management's thinking: "It is a vision of individuals who are innately malleable and, thus, completely susceptible to techniques of education, development, and control through the modification of the environment and mind" (Scott and Hart, 1980:59). They point to the theories of B. F. Skinner and other behaviorists as reinforcing this view of compliant workers. Further, they claim that individuals have surrendered their autonomy to the organization. This is consistent with the viewpoint of one of the authors of this book, who labeled corporate domination "the new feudalism" several years ago. Scott and Hart sound the alarm: "What is new is that the organizational imperative does not require the fanaticism so common to mass movements; in the popular parlance, one should be a cool "gamesman." . . . But one central feature of mass movements is present: the substitution of the collective absolute for personal values" (Scott and Hart, 1980:64).

If these authors are to be believed, we face a crisis in the degree to which organizations are responsive to the needs of human beings within them and the degree to which these persons are manipulated for the good of the organization. Further, there is a great deal of concern about whether organizations are responsive to social needs; for example the demonstrations against Exxon's handling of the catastrophic oil spill in Alaska's Prince William Sound in 1989.

C. Burnout

Many theorists and organizational specialists have studied the phenomenon of *burnout* among professionals and members of organizations. Burnout is defined as:

> . . . a debilitating psychological condition brought on by unrelieved work stress, which results in:
> 1. depleted energy reserves;
> 2. lowered resistance to illness;
> 3. increased dissatisfaction and pessimism;
> 4. increased absenteeism and inefficiency at work (Veninga and Spradley, 1981:6–7).

Burnout may be considered a particular form of alienation. Clearly burnout is a serious and, in some extreme cases, life-threatening condition. Studies indicate that such work-related stress affects 80% of business executives, 66% of teachers and secretaries, 44% of garment workers, and 38% of farmers (Veninga and Spradley, 1981:12). Women are highly vulnerable to burnout because they (1) frequently hold tedious jobs with little chance for advancement, (2) often lack leisure time because of family responsibilities, and (3) are sometimes isolated and lonely because of demands on their time, which limit opportunities for other social contacts (Veninga and Spradley, 1981:12–13).

Veninga and Spradley identified five stages of burnout, beginning with an initial period of satisfaction with the job ("the honeymoon"), followed by a second stage in which the characteristics previously listed (energy depletion, etc.) begin to be evident. The worker is not necessarily aware of the symptoms in this stage. In a third stage, the symptoms become chronic and begin to interfere with the person's functioning at work and at home. In a fourth stage, *crisis*, the worker becomes obsessed with the problem and burnout dominates his or her life. If the worker progresses as far as the fifth stage ("hitting the wall"), he or she cannot function on the job and his or her life deteriorates in significant ways (Veninga and Spradley, 1981:38–39). There is no inevitable progression through the stages. People have highly individual patterns, sometimes moving in and out of burnout depending upon their own resources and the resources available to them from the environment and as they find ways to relieve the chronic stress contained in the job. Change can come about, in true systemic fashion, by altering the job, the environment, or the person's perception of the job or themselves. At times, however, the only available course is to exit the job.

One means of altering the job and the environment that Veninga and Spradley do not explicitly mention is *networking*, mentioned in Chapter 4, II,B,2 under "Social Networks." A worker may find other workers experiencing similar problems, and they may be able, through group action, to provide mutual support or, even further, to effect change in the job situation. Certainly, these were the elements that fostered the development of labor unions. Among other benefits of unions, they may combat a sense of isolation and powerlessness. The movie and television series "Nine to Five" showed not only some hilarious means of achieving change (including tying up the boss as a prisoner) but also some serious efforts at reduction of burnout including "flextime" (allowing workers to vary their hours), more individualization of work space ("flexiplace"), and day care for employees' children, an idea that has now become almost commonplace among corporations and federal legislation. Usually, efforts to humanize organizations take the form of decentralization: less emphasis on specialization by workers, reducing units to smaller scale, or restructuring decision-making processes to allow employees to have more influence in determining their own fates and that of the organization. Quality circles, as discussed earlier, may be one means of accomplishing this.

IV. EVOLUTIONARY ASPECTS

Are there realistic alternatives to large-scale bureaucracies? Max Weber thought the apparent alternative was patrimonialism, that is, control by persons (apparently males) rather than laws and regulations. Patrimonial control is one in which judgments are the prerogative of the leader. The leader appoints his friends and loyal supporters to positions of authority and delegates patrimonial powers to them. Although Weber himself favored bureaucracy because of its emphasis on equity and impartiality, he recognized the likelihood of the bureaucratic situation becoming cumbersome and immobile, the tendency of means to become ends, and the self-perpetuating nature of such organizations.

As Weber observed, probably all organizations are, and should be, some combination of bureaucracy and patrimonialism, formal and informal. The Constitution of the United States established ground rules enabling the coexistence of the two. The office of the presidency exemplifies the patrimonial aspect. The president appoints to executive positions those loyal to him and his cause, those who have aided in his attainment of the office. For example, John Kennedy appointed his campaign manager and brother, Robert, to the office of attorney general. Richard Nixon appointed his campaign manager, John Mitchell, to the same office. President Carter appointed loyal Georgians, and President Reagan selected supporters who had been loyal to him during his California governorship. President Bush chose to appoint Texans and Northeasterners who had contributed to his progress toward the presidency. Immediately after the election, President-elect Bush named his campaign manager and long-time friend, James Baker, to be Secretary of State; and Governor Sununu, who made a critical contribution to Bush's success in the presidential primaries, as his Chief of Staff. He also attempted to appoint John Tower, who guided Bush's career as a young Texas politician, as Secretary of Defense.

A strong symbol of the patrimonial position of the elected executive is the presidential pardon (elected state governors have a similar power) which allows the officeholder to make an independent, legally binding decision that does not require legal precedent or any justification. President Ford pardoned Richard Nixon, and President Carter granted amnesty for those of the Vietnam era who fled the country as a means of avoiding conscription. President Reagan, equally patrimonially, withheld pardon from Lt. Col. Oliver North.

The "new entrepreneur" business owner is another example of patrimonial organization. The business is operated with authority remaining firmly in the hands of owner(s). Promotions, bonuses, and status are the vehicles used to foster employee loyalty. The owners employ and discharge employees as they see fit without recourse or appeal (except as a court may find illegalities). This contrasts with the bureaucratic situation wherein procedures for hiring and firing are thoroughly detailed, often complex, and slow; conditions for promotion and salary advancement are carefully spelled out.

Again, most contemporary organizations are mixtures of patrimonial

and bureaucratic, based on both personal factors and structured procedures. The presence or absence of an employee manual is one distinguishing characteristic.

Other alternatives to large-scale bureaucracies have been attempted by
some organizations, with decentralized structures such as autonomous
work groups that allow freedom and control to line workers (Ouchi,
1981b). Such attempts have drawn heavily on research done following
World War II by the Tavistock Institute in England. These studies indicate
that greater productivity and reduced alienation are best achieved by autonomous work groups. Other efforts focus on redesigning jobs ("job en-
richment," "job enlargement") and restructuring to permit greater self-
determination by workers. In rare instances, United States companies
have permitted workers to participate in management decisions. In Europe, this is known as "codetermination" or "industrial democracy."

A popular concept in management has been "Theory Z," an organizational style derived from Japanese corporations. As management expert
Peter Drucker pointed out, the ideas underlying Theory Z were originated by United States companies two or three decades earlier, following the theoretical formulations of Douglas McGregor, and then
subsequently adapted by the Japanese. Theory Z has been used by
Hewlett-Packard, IBM, Dayton-Hudson, Eli Lilly, Rockwell International, Buick, and Westinghouse, among others. Ouchi, who coined the
phrase "Theory Z management," said that there are several lessons to
be learned from this management style:

1. *trust*, between management and workers, which encourages sacrifice in the belief that eventually the employee will receive rewards;
2. *subtlety*, the recognition that human relationships are far too complex and changing to be captured by bureaucratic rules or labor
   contracts;
3. *intimacy*, the expression of caring and support among those at the
   workplace, certainly not a common experience in United States industries.

Ouchi maintained that these qualities lead to greater productivity in
which everyone shares. He said of Americans:

> We resist the idea that there can or should be a close familiarity with people in the
> workplace. "Personal feelings have no place at work," is the common feeling. . . .
> In the Japanese example, we find a successful industrial society in which intimacy
> occurs in the place of work as well as in other settings. The Japanese example forces
> us to reconsider our deeply-held beliefs about the proper sources of intimacy in
> society (Ouchi, 1981b:9).

In the Japanese model, trust is fostered by companies' commitment to
lifetime employment for each employee (although this has been modified slightly in recent years); in case of recession, companies aggres-

sively look for new markets or new products while workers perform other duties (including janitorial services) until the financial situation becomes better, meanwhile keeping their jobs. The "groupness' of the work situation is encouraged by workers sharing space without walls; interaction is not only encouraged, it is demanded. Of course, this is also consistent with Japanese culture, Permanence of employment and group feeling result in absence of (or at least lessened) alienation, since "people committed to long-term relationships with each other have strong commitments to behave responsibly and equitably towards one another" (Ouchi, 1981b:34). Ouchi remarks elsewhere that this kind of organization resembles a clan with a strong sense of community (Ouchi, 1981b:415).

Decision-making is also a group process governed by consensus. It apparently is disturbing to Westerners who are accustomed to more authoritarian decision-making and who perceived the Japanese as slow to decide and their decision process difficult to fathom. The Japanese reply that it may take longer to arrive at consensus, but that once achieved, it is quicker to implement with little dissatisfaction with the decision. Ouchi said:

> Intimacy, trust and understanding grow where individuals are linked to one another through multiple bonds in a wholistic relationship. . . . The Japanese show clear evidence that wholism in industrial life is possible (Ouchi, 1981b:54–55).
>
> It is a consent culture, a community of equals who cooperate with one another to reach common goals. Rather than relying exclusively upon hierarchy and monitoring to direct behavior, it relies also upon commitment and trust (Ouchi, 1981b):83).

Humanization and improving the "quality of work life" are complex undertakings, involving recognition of more facets of the person than simply his or her role as a production unit in the industrial system. Paradoxically, it may well require the person to give up some freedom and independence (randomly distributed energy, tending toward entropy), to assume new obligations of mutuality (negentropy or synergy) with management and other workers. Toffler suggested that we are witnessing the breakdown of bureaucracy and that it will be supplanted by "adhocracy" (Toffler, 1970:124–151). Adhocracy (from *ad hoc*, according to the circumstances) denotes an organizational scheme congruent with an era of accelerated change, wherein people are brought together to accomplish a specific task and disband once that task is completed.

According to one of Miller's hypotheses, increasing size generates greater variety of subsystems: "In general, the more components a system has, the more echelons it has" (Miller, 1978:92). He commented that organizations, unlike organisms or some groups such as a nuclear family, may outlast the lives of the original members. Because organizations can replace components and learn from experience, it may be true that the longer an organization lives, the better its chance for survival. He further commented that old organizations are resistant to change. Bureaucratic structures, whether governmental or corporate, rely on specification of qualifications for employment and advancement. In Mandarin China the major criterion was classical education; in nineteenth century Russia it was performance on merit examinations and "time in grade" and in the United States today it is technical educational credentials, i.e., diplomas and degrees, then time in grade and "merit." By contrast, the patrimonial situation relies upon the judgment and whim of the executive person(s).

Many have observed that the changes previously discussed (decentralization, or humanization of the workplace) are more cosmetic than real. that organizations tend to perpetuate their ways with as little change as possible. When pressed, governmental organizations "re-organize"; industry becomes "lean and mean" through apparent divestiture of organizational layers, but the effects are minimal; the more things change, the more they remain the same. This can be at least partially explained through understanding the systemic properties of organizations, the part/whole characteristics. As Raymond Gastil observed,

> Seen from the outside, an organization exists to provide services or goods to those outside the organization; secondarily it exists to provide employment to those within it so that they in turn may buy the goods and services of others. . . . Seen from the inside, an organization exists to support its owners or administrators and its employees; secondarily it exists to provide goods and services to others (Gastil, 1977:167).

Thus, for significant organizational change to occur, there must be modification in both internal and external aspects, especially goals. The recent contentions over plant closings provide an instructive example. Corporate industry in its pursuit of its profit goal determines that a particular production facility is not contributing to the profit goal and decides to close that facility. Other interests and organizations are strongly affected by the relinquishment of the secondary goal, i.e., the provision of employment that enables the purchase of goods and services. Efforts are made to block the plant closure and/or develop other ways to maintain employment. Similar dynamics operate with the closing of a prison or a hospital, as regards the impact upon the surrounding community or neighborhood.

The pace of change in an organization is nearly always controversial. The last three presidential elections, for example, indicated public dissatisfaction with the speed of change in the federal bureaucracy; racial reforms were occurring too quickly for some, but tax reforms were occurring too slowly. Centralization of power in the executive branch was feared by many, who cited revenue sharing as desirable. Elections since

1976 have been interpreted as "mandates" against centralized federal bureaucracy.

One reason for the mixed nature of organizational change is the rapid diversification and expansion of major corporations during the past generation. Management expert Peter Drucker said of the new multinational corporation that

> It does not fit the traditional organization structure of the multinational corporation, with a central top management to which management of subsidiaries reports. It requires, rather, a systems approach, in which one body coordinates autonomous managements that do not report to one another.
>
> A major requirement is the ability and willingness to adapt to different cultures and to work with people of different habits and traditions. [It] is not only transnational, rather than multinational; it is, above all, transcultural. And it is an idea whose time has come (Drucker, 1982:192).

Thoughtful analyses (including some by science fiction writers, notably Isaac Asimov in the *Foundation* series) suggest that the governments of the future may not be nation-states. Instead, international conglomerates may rule, and in some cases, more rationally. It may well be that unless governments become equally adaptable, other organizations may absorb what we now recognize as "governmental" functions. The United Nations recognizes the insufficiency of information on multinationals and their activities and has attempted to formulate a code of ethics for multinational enterprises.

CONCLUSION

While the future of organizations is unclear and events seem mixed in their implications, it may be correct that organizations increase their potential for survival the longer they exist. The most successful organizations seem to be those that can adapt rapidly to changing environments—altering goals and functions or altering structure. Part of this structural change may be that, in the future, persons may work for more than one organization; part of one's time will be spent at one organization, part at another, or while one's "home" may be in one department, employees (and faculty members) may be "farmed out" to other departments as their specialties are needed, for a specified period in the life of a project. This was the model exemplified best by NASA's development of the space program. Such "plugging in" or "modular" structure permits rapid modification of organizational structures and require greater professional identification beyond the particular organization that employs the professional. In fact, a significant number of professionals are presently related to two or more organizations, serving as consultants or part-time service workers. Many of these are regular employees of one organization and "moonlight" or act in consultant roles with other organizations. It seems likely that this will become more common. Knowledge of organizations and how to work with, or within, them is essential to effective professional practice for all human service professionals.

SUGGESTED READINGS

Barnet, Richard, and Ronald E. Muller.
  1974 *Global Reach.* New York: Simon and Schuster.
    A detailed examination of the extension of corporations throughout the world. The material is useful for large-scale examples of organizational principles, and the trade-offs between increasing size and concern for smaller-scale systems.
Beer, Stafford.
  1981 "Death Is Equifinal," *Behavioral Science,* V 26:185–196.
    A provocative general systems statement about what is amiss with modern organizations. He suggested that only a systems perspective will enable the relinquishing of worthless models of organizational behavior.
Branch, Taylor.
  1988. *Parting the Waters: America in the King Years 1954–1963.* New York: Simon and Schuster.
    This historical account of the roots of the modern civil rights movement exemplifies the transitory shifts between community and organization.
Dessler, Gary.
  1980 *Organization Theory.* Englewood Cliffs, NJ: Prentice-Hall.
    This is an excellent introductory text. Chapters 1, 2, and 3 together make up a thorough review of older and contemporary theories of organization.
Domhoff, G. William.
  1971 *The Higher Circles.* New York: Vintage Books.
    One of the most thought-provoking studies of power structure. It presents a strong argument for the existence of a power elite in the United States.
Giamatti, A. Bartlett.
  1988 *A Free and Ordered Space: The Real World of the University.* New York: Norton.
    A set of incisive and sometimes humorous essays on university policy and traditions. Giamatti was a former president of Yale University and served five months as Commissioner of Major League Baseball before his death in 1989.
Handy, Charles B.
  1985 *Understanding Organizations.* Harmondsworth, England: Penguin.
    "Jam-packed" with information; also entertaining due to Handy's selection of illustrations and excerpts. The "Guide to Further Study" is unique, a selection of the author's comments and musings on the subject. Highly recommended. In paperback.

Hasenfeld, Yeheskel.
    1983 *Human Services Organizations.* Englewood Cliffs, NJ: Prentice-Hall.
    This is the most useful text for a course on human services organizations.
    It is comprehensive and thought-provoking. One of the authors continues
    to use it as a text; it is entirely compatible with our approach.
Hirokawa, Randy Y., Dennis S. Gouran, and Amy E. Martz.
    1988 "Understanding the Sources of Faulty Group Decision Making: A Lesson
    from the *Challenger* Disaster." *Small Group Behavior,* 19 (4): 411–433.
    Excellent, balanced analysis of decisions and processes that led to the de-
    struction of the shuttle and its crew. Despite the objective, scholarly tone,
    the tension of the NASA environment is palpable.
Kesey, Ken. (1962).
    One Flew Over the Cuckoo's Nest. New York: The Viking Press.
    The modern classic story of the round of life in a total institution. Also
    available on video starring Jack Nicholson.
Kimberly, John R., and Robert H. Miles and Associates.
    1981 *The Organizational Life Cycle.* San Francisco: Jossey-Bass.
    This is a seminal book. The authors proposed a biological or systems view
    of organizations while stating its limitations. Ouchi's chapter on organiza-
    tional failure is most relevant. Miles' chapter on research is highly valuable.
Lauffer, Armand, et al.
    1984 *Understanding Your Social Agency,* second edition. Beverly Hills: Sage Publi-
    cations.
    An excellent way to introduce students to a systems view of social agencies.
    It is a slightly different set of systems ideas from ours, but the two books are
    compatible.
Matejko, Alexander J.
    1986 *In Search of New Organizational Paradigms.* New York: Praeger.
    His proposals for alternative organizational cultures, based on his experi-
    ences in Poland, Zambia, and Canada, and ten principles of true participa-
    tion in organizations are incisive.
Miller, James G.
    1978 *Living Systems.* New York: McGraw-Hill.
    Chapter 10, "The Organization," pp. 595–745. Very productive of stimulat-
    ing ideas for the serious student of systems.
Ouchi, William G.
    1981 *Theory Z: How American Business Can Meet the Japanese Challenge.* Reading,
    MA: Addison-Wesley.
    The originator of theory Z makes a compelling case.
Scott, W. Richard.
    1987. *Organizations: Rational, Natural, and Open Systems.* Second edition. Engle-
    wood Cliffs, NJ: Prentice-Hall.
    This text examines theories of organizations in a manner highly compatible
    with a social systems viewpoint. The contrast between the approaches he
    examines is very instructive.
Shilts, Randy.
    1988 *And the Band Played On: Politics, People, and the AIDS Epidemic.* New York:
    Penguin.
    The definitive book on the AIDS crisis, it portrays in rich detail the behavior

of federal, municipal, and gay organizations through mid-1988. One of the authors uses it as a casebook on organizational behavior.

Veninga, Robert L., and James P. Spradley.
1981 *The Work-Stress Connection.* Boston: Little, Brown.
Comprehensive discussion of burnout. Suggests means to reduce or eliminate work-related stress.

FILMS AND VIDEOS

"Norma Rae" (1979)
Based on the real life of a Southern worker who was instrumental in unionizing the plant she worked in. Sally Fields plays the title role well, and Ron Leibman's portrayal of the union organizer is well done.

"One Flew Over The Cuckoo's Nest" (1975)
True to Ken Kesey's novel about a mental hospital. Jack Nicholson plays McMurphy to perfection. A fine example of a totalistic institution.

"Silkwood" (1983)
This film presents the theory that Karen Silkwood was killed for her disclosures of violations at a nuclear-processing plant. Meryl Streep accurately presents Silkwood's complex personality. The interaction of a corporation and a "whistle-blower" within it are portrayed in detail.

"Welfare" (1972)
One of Frederick Weisman's series of documentaries, among the best materials for the study of organizations. This one portrays an unending purgatory for welfare recipients and staff in a Manhattan welfare office. This has been used regularly in an organization course by one of the authors.

Groups

Nothing is harder to stop than a freely and fully united band of human beings.
Milton Mayer, *On Liberty: Man vs. the State*

It is within the group that the power, basic and immense, human beings have over one another occurs; the power of acceptance or rejection.
Gisela Konopka, *Social Group Work*

INTRODUCTION

The social group is a critical system to each person and, in particular, to the helping professions. As an arena of social interaction, the group has potential to provide for a range of human needs that include:

1. a need to belong and to be accepted;
2. a need to be validated through feedback processes;
3. a need to share common experiences with others; and
4. opportunities to work with others on common tasks.

The human group is a social system that has received, and deserves, extensive investigation. The term *group* includes those patterns of association and activity in which persons engage most of their "selves" from day to day. It is a holon composed of individuals and small constellations of persons and it is a component of its environment. A group is more than simply an aggregate of individuals; it has a unique wholeness of its own. As Lewin phrased it, "The whole is *different from* the sum of its parts; it has definite properties of its own" (Marrow, 1969:170 [emphasis ours]). (Note that the words "different from," not "more than,"

133

are used.) Thus the human group is a system distinguishable from its environment, having the characteristics and functions of a system and providing the connectiveness between its components and its environment. Like other social systems, groups are characterized by energy exchange. The term *synergy,* originated by anthropologist Ruth Benedict, was used by psychologist Abraham Maslow to apply to groups; the following passage illustrates Hampden-Turner's use of Maslow's idea and illustrates the diffusion of systems ideas through various disciplines.

> Synergy involves the resolution of the selfish/unselfish dichotomy by making the enhancement of the Other the precondition or result of personal enhancement. . . . Further evidence for synergy came from the supervisors' reports on their work groups. There was a substantial increase in groups which reached decisions by mutual agreement and in reports that "differences in opinion are directly confronted and discussed to productive solutions" (Golembiewski and Blumberg, 1970: 51–52).

Since the discussion of groups in this chapter is from a social systems viewpoint, a cluster of persons can be considered a group only if it fulfills certain specific criteria of systems. Donald Campbell suggests that rather than starting with the assumptions that aggregations are systems, it is advisable to subject such aggregates to empirical examination to see whether they do in fact have the properties of systems. If the subject of such examination is not found to possess such properties, that is, cannot be established to be a holon, then the analysis should properly be carried out at the next lower level (Campbell, 1958). Thus, a group with *a high level* of systems properties might be analyzed largely with group concepts; *a moderate level* with group and individual concepts; and *a low level* with individual concepts. In other words, a gathering together of persons does not make a group. The expression "the group jelled" conveys a point in time or process when an aggregate of persons became an entity, a group, distinguishable from its environment, and different from the sum of its parts.

This leads to the question: What are the significant properties of a group as system or entity? The remainder of this chapter addresses this question.

I. DIMENSIONS OF GROUPS

There are as many kinds of groups as there are group leaders, observers, and therapists (and perhaps members, since each has a unique personal perspective on the group). Rather than attempt a comprehensive taxonomy, we will discuss a few important dimensions that have been used to classify groups. These dimensions are here discussed as polarities. Any given group, at any given time, theoretically could be placed at some point on each continuum.

A. Instrumental versus Expressive

Drawn from Parsons' formulation, this continuum is similar to others that are frequently used: "task vs. sentiment," "goal achievement vs. group maintenance," "task-oriented vs. group-oriented," and "guidance behavior vs. sociable behavior" (Olmsted, 1959:135; Parsons, 1964:79–88). The distinction is usually understood as being between a particular, articulated, time-limited objective and a diffuse, unarticulated, enduring and supportive group climate. Further, the distinction is usually taken to imply that a "goal" or "task" is adaptive, that is, related to the environment, whereas "expressive" or "sentiment" is related to interactions among components of the group. It seems to us that the distinction is best understood as a distinction between two steady states toward which the group could evolve. The first steady state is one in which some fairly clear, specific objective has been accomplished with specific results for "vertical" relations (Warren, 1963:161). The other state is one in which the objectives are fairly diffuse and nonspecific, with the general result of integration of components (i.e., "horizontal" relations) (Warren, 1963:161–162). Consequently, "instrumental versus expressive" activities or orientations are intended to move the group toward one of these two steady states. Probably "adaptive versus integrative" would be more accurate. Bales agreed with this:

> The social system, in its organization . . . tends to swing or falter back and forth between two theoretical poles; optimum adaptation to the outer situation at the cost of internal malintegration, or optimum internal integration at the cost of maladaptation to the situation" (Weisman, 1963:87). Bales identified this as the "equilibrium problem" (Hare, 1976:93).

These are polarities and are not mutually exclusive. The "adaptive" steady state focuses *more* attention on goals and tasks but also deals with integration, although to a lesser extent. The "integrative" steady state, similarly, does not exclude some adaptive activity. For example, the United States Supreme Court must spend some time mediating between the justices' personal feelings at times (Woodward and Armstrong, 1981). A sensitivity group must make decisions about meeting dates and when termination should occur. Reginald Rose's play *Twelve Angry Men* illustrates the successive steady states of a jury as it alternately focuses upon the court's demand for a verdict and the members' needs (Rose, 1955).

It is this variability that makes the group difficult to characterize in contrast to the family, which is predominantly integrative, and the organization, which is predominantly adaptive. The community is largely made up of groups and shares their indeterminate character; indeed, it is sometimes difficult to distinguish between communities and groups. We suggest this guideline: *The greater the breadth of influence upon its members and the more diffuse its goals, the more the group resembles a community.*

To the extent that groups are aimed toward specific goals, they resemble organizations. In fact, many such groups are probably components of organizations and may be accurately considered as such; in fact, they can be called *work groups.* These examples clearly demonstrate that groups range widely in character. Some resemble families or communities and some resemble organizations in their position on the "adaptive vs. integrative" continuum. Northen (1969:189ff.) commented that problem solving in groups is a major emphasis at a certain stage of group development; at that stage, perhaps, all groups move toward the instrumental end of the polarity.

B. Primary vs. Secondary

Olmsted equated this polarity with "instrumental vs. expressive," calling the poles "primary-expressive" vs. "secondary-instrumental" (Olmsted, 1959:133). This is logical, and we agree with this usage, but some further precision is advisable. A group may be essentially expressive or integrative but be of minor significance to the members. The afternoon (or morning) neighborhood coffee klatch is a good example. It is predominantly (if not purely) expressive. If it is important to its members, it is clearly a primary group; but if it has little importance to them, it should be considered secondary. One criterion, then, is the breadth of influence the group has upon its members and particularly its influence upon their affective functioning. Another way of saying this is that if members react to each other more as role occupants than as persons, it is a secondary group. As these roles become more formalized, the group becomes more goal-specific and narrows its range of influence; thus, the closer the secondary group comes to being an organization.

C. Narcissistic vs. Generative

This polarity is similar to Parsons' polarities of "self vs. collectivity" and "particularism vs. universalism" (Parsons, 1964b:58–67). The polarity is self gratification of one or more members versus wider commitment to the group's goals. Mills noted that this dimension is similar to Freud's pleasure and reality principles, and to Erikson's concept of generativity (Mills, 1967:120–122).

The importance of this dimension of groups is that it explains the ability or inability of some groups to survive. In other words, they violate the principle that no function can be concentrated on to the exclusion of other functions. Evolutionary capacity is nullified by inability to change structure (i.e., a closed, morphostatic system results). A "generative" system, like a generative person, is engaged in mutually constructive interchange with its environment.

These dimensions used to classify groups indicate that groups share important properties of systems: adaptation, integration, goal-seeking, structural maintenance, and structural change.

II. ASPECTS OF GROUP AS SYSTEM

A. Evolutionary Aspects

Analysis of any specific group requires much attention to its evolution—more so, perhaps, than with any other system except family. This is true because groups and families are more dependent upon particular persons than are other systems and are thus more likely to be affected by changes in personnel than other systems. Organizations, in fact, are usually deliberately designed to minimize dependence upon individual persons. Because groups are more susceptible to these factors, the formation and disintegration of a group are more likely to occur during a single member's lifetime than are other systems; it is thus more subject to observation and analysis.

Accordingly, in literature about groups, less attention has been given to structure and more to "process" and to problem solving as a significant aspect of process. Because of this, the balance or steady state of the group has received most attention in research. In group work practice, it has been almost a dogma that all aspects of groups are subordinate to the maintenance of steady state. In our discussion of other systems, we have had to establish that they are systems and to establish that *steady state* is a valid term to apply to them. With groups, the problem is the converse; so much has been researched and written on the group as a system and on group "equilibrium" or steady state in particular, that the task is to establish that any other aspect of the system is of equal importance.

1. Steady State

The group is like an organism—a biological organism. It forms, grows, and reaches a state of maturity. It begins with a set of constituent elements—individuals with certain personalities, certain needs, ideas, potentialities, limitations—and in the course of development evolves a particular pattern of behavior, a set of indigenous norms, a body of beliefs, a set of values, and so on. Parts become differentiated, each assuming special functions in relations to other parts and the whole. . . . As a group approaches maturity it becomes more complex, more differentiated, more interdependent, and more integrated (Mills, 1967:13).

This is a detailed way to describe a group's steady state. More general ways are to describe its "identity," or its "culture." Mills described groups as having some of the same qualities that Erikson described in persons. Groups have "personality," similar to the personalities of individuals, according to some writers (Miller, 1978:543; Shaw, 1981:19–20). This personality was labeled "syntality" by Cattell as early as 1948. Syntality was defined as "the personality of the group, or, more precisely, as any effect that the group has as a totality. . . . Syntality traits are inferred from the external behavior of the group and may include such behaviors as decision making, aggressive acts, and the like" (Shaw, 1981:20). It might be more accurate to say that each group possesses its own culture, rather than a personality; a microcosm of the larger culture, without which it would not be a system but merely an aggregate of individual persons.

a. Norms and consensus.   A group establishes norms through consensus. Northen's definition of *norm* is:

> a generalization concerning an expected standard of behavior in any matter of consequence to the group. It incorporates a value judgment. It is a rule or standard to which the members of a group are expected to adhere. . . . A set of norms introduces a certain amount of regularity and predictability into the group's functioning (Northen, 1969:33–34).

"Regularity and predictability" are obviously relevant to steady state. Sherif explored the concept of group norm and found that when individuals are placed in groups, the individual norms tend to converge into a group norm (Cartwright and Zander, 1960:23–25). This was illustrated in the Bank Wiring Observation Room study in which workers had explicit expectations about the production norms and pressured others to conform (Roethlisberger and Dickson, 1947). Another example was Shils' finding that soldiers observed group norms about supporting their "buddies" (Mills, 1967:4n.). As cartoonist Bill Mauldin stated in *Up Front*, combat units "have a sort of family complex."

> New men in outfits have to work their way in slowly, but they are eventually accepted. Sometimes they have to change their way of living. An introvert or recluse is not going to last long in combat without friends, so he learns to come out of his shell. Once he has "arrived" he is pretty proud of his clique, and he in turn is chilly toward outsiders (Cartwright and Zander, 1960:165).

The norm is cooperation; the underlying consensus is survival.

Consensus is "the degree of agreement regarding goals, norms, roles and other aspects of the group" (Shepherd, 1964:25). When such agree-ments and need satisfactions operate to bind members to the group, the group has "attractiveness" or "valence," and the result is *cohesiveness* of the group. Such cohesiveness gives rise to *solidarity*, which is "the stabi-lized mutual responsibility of each toward the other to regard himself as part of the other, as the sharer of a common fate, and as a person who is under obligation to cooperate with the other in the satisfaction of the other's individual needs as if they were one's own" (Bales, 1950:61). The Polish union Solidarity obviously includes this meaning in its name. For a decade after the union was declared illegal, Solidarity's members exhibited sufficient cohesiveness to prevail over the govern-ment of Poland, to be declared legal again, in April, 1989, and to become functionally part of the government. Grace Coyle described group bond as having three levels:

1. conscious purpose, for example sociability or friendship;
2. assumed or unavowed objectives, such as achievement or status, ego expan-sion, courtship (especially among adolescents), and class rise;
3. unconscious purpose, including sanctioned release of aggression, escape from reality, and sublimation of erotic impulses (Coyle, 1948:Chapter 4).

Consensus and cohesiveness, then, are *expressive, integrative*, and *pri-mary* aspects of the group.

b. Goal direction. The other component of steady state that should be discussed is goal direction or goal pursuit. In contrast to consensus and cohesiveness, goal attainment is *instrumental, adaptive*, and *secondary.* Group "purpose" means any ultimate aim, end or intention, or as we define it in the glossary, a desired steady state of the group. Group "ob-jective" or "goal" usually refers to a specific end, that is instrumental to the purpose. We use "goal" to mean both those ends the suprasystem assigns to the group and those ends sought by the group itself.

Locomotion is the name given to group goal pursuit by Kurt Lewin and the Group Dynamics theorists (Olmsted, 1959:115). It means that groups move within an environment or field to achieve goals that are mutually defined by a group and its relevant environment. Goal-directed behav-ior affects group consensus and cohesiveness. It may disrupt earlier ex-pressive, integrative norms and force members to choose between in-strumental and expressive behaviors. In some instances, groups may disband because of the divergence.

2. Stages of Evolution. Several formulations of group evolution have been presented by group theorists. We present here a brief sketch out-lining a highly general evolutionary process in groups. Weisman sum-marized one such evolutionary view:

1. The group adapts to its environment; in response to this adaptive behavior, members develop activities, sentiments, and interactions. These adaptive components are the group's external system.
2. The group develops activities, sentiments and interactions beyond the necessary adaptive behavior, through its goal-oriented behavior; these become the internal system.
3. As the internal system elaborates, it develops bond, cohesiveness, norms, roles and statuses.
4. In feedback fashion, adaptation is affected by the environment and the developing internal system.
5. The group, in turn, modifies the functioning of its members (Weisman, 1963:87).

Homans carried this further and described the development of the internal system as a process of "elaboration." At some point, a countertrend occurs in which members' behaviors and sentiments become more alike. Homans described this as "standardization" and, as we show below in Table 2, this is a form of social control (Homans, 1950:109–110, 119–121). If social control or adaptive and integrative functions fail, the group may disintegrate or merge into other units. For example, a task force may dissolve and members return to their own departments or organizations; or a friendship group may merge into a larger group, such as a church group or fraternal group.

In Table 2, we synthesize a scheme of group evolution from several sources (including Trecker, 1955; Garland, 1965; Mills, 1967; Sarri and Galinsky, 1967; Tropp, 1976; and Shaw, 1981). Our scheme focuses on the internal development of the group; little reference is made to the environment. Thus the scheme is abstracted from reality, since the environment has profound influence on groups.

In our survey of literature on group evolution, three major phases with several subphases seem to emerge. A fourth phase may or may not occur. If it does, the result is a loop back to some earlier stage and subsequent redevelopment of the group, or the result may be disintegration or termination. None of these phases is presented here as discrete or absolute. This is a *highly general synthesis* that—to refer again to the introduction of this book—corresponds to reality of groups in the same way that a map corresponds to mud, rocks, and clear, running water.

a. Phase I: E pluribus unum. During the first major phase exploration of each other occurs among the members. The activity of members in this phase is similar to the "inclusion" stage identified by William Schutz:

> In the inclusion stage, the member confronts questions dealing with his [sic] individual membership in the group. He asks: Do I want to be part of this group and do the other members want me to be part of it? Who else is here? Should I become

intensely involved or marginally involved? Can I trust my real self to the others? (Galper, 1970:72)

Such questions are answered by probing each other. In this phase, each member relates primarily to the leader rather than to one another. Eventually, in successful groups, members agree to tolerate each other's thoughts, feelings, and behaviors although there may be some reluctance initially. Such tolerance permits open discussion of the group's emerging culture, i.e., the way we do things.

Carl Rogers identified and described the phases of encounter groups. His phases are similar to our intentions here. Rogers described "patterns or stages," the first five of which fit within our first major stage. They are (1) "milling around," (2) "resistance to personal expression," (3) "description of past feelings," (4) "expression of negative feelings," and (5) expression of personal feelings (Rogers, 1970:15–20). Discussion of symbols and meanings may take the form of tentative exploration of what structure is possible for the group, what "freedom" means in this group, and how others interpret what the leader says. The interpretation that members arrive at determines the group's *valence* or attractiveness. Members begin to share their *life space* (Lewin's term) to permit others to enter their interactional, personal territory, their "bubbles."

b. Phase II: the control phase. In this second major phase, the emphasis shifts, as Schutz describes it, from "inclusion" to "control" In the control stage he [sic] asks: Now that I have decided to be a member of the group, what power will I have in it? Who is in charge and how do I find this out? What does the group want of me? (Galper, 1970:72)

One text describes a stage following the preliminary testing of each other by members, a stage in which members are engaging in productive, mutual activity. This is called the "working stage" and has the following characteristics: (1) a focus on the immediate interactions; direct and meaningful interaction, including confrontations; (2) free communication among members; the group becomes an "orchestra," listening to each other and working productively together; (3) self-disclosure is the norm; (4) members know each other through feedback and learn to trust the feedback; and (5) group cohesion is increased as they become "a trusting community" (Corey, Corey, Callanan, and Russell; 1982:91–93). Peck described this:

A soft quietness descends. It is a kind of peace. The room is bathed in peace. Then, quietly, a member begins to talk about herself. She is being very vulnerable. She is speaking of the deepest part of herself. The group hangs on each word.

Then the next member speaks. And as it goes on, there will be a great deal of sadness and grief expressed; but there will also be much laughter and joy. . . . And then something almost more singular happens. An extraordinary amount of healing and converting begins to occur—now that no one is trying to convert or heal. And community has been born (Peck, 1987:103–104).

Table 2. Synthesis of Stages of Group Evolution[a]

Phases	Cognitive aspects	Affective aspects	Behavioral aspects
I. E pluribus unum			
Components' goals predominate	Discussion of symbols, meanings	Checking for feelings, values of others; tentative "valence"	Observes behavior of others; tentative participation
Affiliation (approach-avoidance)	Attempt to find common meanings, symbols	Expression of feelings	Interaction and reaction in overt behavior; territory shared
Commitment	Limited agreement on symbols, meanings, norms	Development of group bond; satisfaction of individual's feelings; group values emerge	Beginning of modification of behavior to conform; mutual accommodation; locomotion
II. Control phase			
Group goals predominate	Internalization of developing group culture; accommodation of schemas	Same as cognitive	Roles defined and agreed to
Socialization	Standardization; acceptance of group views; subordination of idiosyncratic views	Subordination of idiosyncratic feelings; reinforcement of those that "match" others'	Group prescription of behavior; reduction of deviance; differentiation of roles and territories
Social control ↳ᵃ			
Stability (internal)	Enforcement of group views, codes and stated purposes; "right thinking" and developed symbol systems	Enforcement of group values; statements expressing solidarity and allegiance; traditions	Rituals, offices, hierarchy
Group goal direction (external) ↳ᵃ	Problem solving; decision making; thought exclusively focused on goal and means to achieve it; "brainstorming"	Elevation of values that support goal; devotion to them, excluding other values, both personal and group	Focus on specific group goal; sacrifice and joint effort
Intimacy; cohesiveness	Exchange with each other to the exclusion of nonmembers; "private" group views, beliefs, actions	Devotion to each other, to exclusion of ties with "outsiders"	Group rituals and culture concretized and protected

Phase			
III. Conflict phase Components' goals predominate	Dissensus on norms, goals, evaluations; selectiveness of evidence used against group members	Disaffection; return (or maintaining) to predominance of individuals' sentiments; "hidden-agendas" predominate	Antagonistic behavior; violation of roles, territories, boundaries; violation of rituals, hierarchy
		Loop to earlier phase or move to terminal phase	
IV. Terminal phase Disintegration (into subgroups or complete disassociation)	Maintenance of divergent views; ideological combat	Hostility; defensiveness; feelings of betrayal, anger	Alliances; power struggles; "splitting" from the group; "betrayal" to outsiders
		OR	
Termination (planned or by agreement)	Reinforcement of belief of worth of group; attempt to analyze "meaning" of the group	Feelings of guilt, rejection because of termination; warmth toward other members	Open communication about termination; displays of sentiment; approach or "flight" behaviors

[a] Arrows indicate that these subphases may be reversed in sequence.

Rogers' stages 6–10 are not applicable to all types of groups but illustrate evolution in encounter groups. In these stages, immediate interpersonal feelings are disclosed; a "healing capacity" develops; members are willing to risk, resulting in self-acceptance and change; "facades" begin to be discarded, and the member receives feedback, both positive and negative. Rogers described in stages 6–10 the elements that we include in the subphase, "socialization," in Table 2. Members have taken the group norms "to heart"—they have internalized them. They have begun to sort out roles of "facilitator" (not always group leader), "conciliator," and so forth. They "heal" each other and restrain other members who violate the group norm of "caring" for each other. Those members who express caring or negative feelings interact with the group's norms of behavior. Intimacy and cohesiveness are achieved as thoughts, feelings, and behavior are expressed among members, which are not expressed to others outside the group. The notable difference between our scheme and Rogers' is that he deals little with group goal direction. This is understandable since his encounter groups were oriented toward relatively diffuse goals, and achievement of goals beyond group process were of minor importance.

c. *Phase III: Conflict phase.*   Phase III can occur at any point in group process. It does not necessarily follow Phases I or II. When it occurs, however, it is a crisis in the life of the group; the group will either loop back to an earlier stage (similar to regression in individual persons) to resolve the issue or resolve the issue in some fashion so that the group can proceed (analogous to Erikson's description of the resolution of growth crises—see Chapter 8). Rogers described well some of the most intense encounters that can take place in groups, in his stages 11–15.

> *Confrontation.* There are times when the term feedback is far too mild to describe the interactions that take place. . . .
> *Norma:* (loud sigh). . . . Any real woman I know wouldn't have acted as you have this week, and particularly what you said this afternoon. That was so *crass!!* It just made me want to puke, right there!!! And—I'm just *shaking* I'm so mad at you—I don't think you've been real once this week! . . . I'm so infuriated that I *want to come over and beat the hell out of you!!* (Rogers, 1970:31–32).

This group could have disintegrated or reverted to an earlier stage. Positive resolution can occur, however. One example is the full expression of negative feeling to another member, which leads to a deeper understanding and acceptance between the two members. Rogers called this "the basic encounter" (Rogers, 1970). This is compatible with Schutz's stage of *affection.*

If such positive outcomes as Rogers and Schutz described are not forthcoming, however, conflict may result in disintegration and termination. Lewis Coser raised the rhetorical question. "If conflict unites, what tears apart?" His answer was that "not all conflicts are positively functional for the relationship, but only those that concern goals, values, or interests that do not contradict the basic assumptions upon which the relation is founded" (Coser, 1964:73,80). It could be assumed, then, that if members of one of the groups Rogers described did not take the healing role or offer mutual support, the conflict would indeed concern the basic function of encounter groups (i.e., to provide an experience of confrontation and caring). The group would terminate, in all likelihood, or break into subgroups as indicated in the disintegration subphase of our Phase III.

Northen described several attempts to resolve conflict that include:

> *elimination,* that is, forcing the withdrawal of the opposing individual or subgroup, sometimes in subtle ways. In *subjugation,* or domination, the strongest members force others to accept their points of view. . . . Through the means of *compromise* . . . each of the factions . . . give up something to safeguard the common area of interest. . . . An individual or subgroup may form an *alliance.* . . . Finally, through *integration,* a group may arrive at a solution that is both satisfying to each member and more productive and creative than any contending suggestion (Northen, 1969:42–43)

The latter is an example of synergy, of course, and of the sense in which we mean *integration* as a basic system function. ØddRamsoy, a Norwegian sociologist, investigated the conflict inherent between system and subsystem in social groups (Ramsoy, 1962). He observed that a group as an entity must be tending toward adaptation and integration. The members thus always face the dilemma of making choices that favor system, subsystem, or suprasystem. He postulated that conflict between part and whole decreases as the integrative problems of the common inclusive system outweigh each subsystem's adaptive problems and goal problems. Ramsoy, as others including Coser (1964), concluded that *conflict can be reduced through concentration on a supraordinate problem.* This occurs most readily when the problem is an external threat. In the presence of a stranger there are no subgroups. Conflict then may provide the occasion for a redressing of the necessary balance between adaptation and integration in a steady state. As an outcome of group process, it means that components (group members individually) and system (the whole group) may both have satisfied needs and goals synergistically. That, indeed, is the height of achievement in the evolution of any system. We do not intend to minimize the existence or functionality of conflict in systems, but no system endures with conflict alone, rather than cooperation (synergy), as its predominant mode of activity.

B. Structural Aspects

1. Boundary and Autonomy. As with all systems, the boundaries of a group are determined by the group and its components through interaction among the members and with the environment. Persons define themselves as members and are defined by others as being members of the group (boundaries are reinforced both internally and externally). For example, segregation by race, age, or gender is usually prescribed by society, whereas separation into religious denominations is largely a matter of individual choice in many societies (though not all, certainly; Iran is an exception, currently).

Groups have greater or lesser degrees of autonomy from their environment. A delinquent group such as Whyte's Norton gang was relatively autonomous from its environment, with few direct controls or supports (Whyte, 1955). In 1987, the Los Angeles city attorney stated concern about the lack of controls on gangs: "In a mood of frustration, you feel like the only effective way to deal with street gangs is with a flame thrower" (Vigil, 1988:x). The group of workers in the Bank Wiring study was much less autonomous, being subject to a high degree of control by the Western Electric company (Roethlisberger and Dickson, 1947). The boundaries of both groups were clear; the Norton gang's boundary was much less permeable. Another example of permeability of boundaries is Mauldin's description of combat units cited earlier in this chapter. A group, as any other system, must have discernible, locatable boundaries in order to exist.

2. Differentiation, Hierarchy, and Role.   As previously noted, differentiation of roles occurs as part of elaboration in the evolution of groups. These roles are ranked by the group according to the roles' utility for adaptation and integration. In addition, the person filling the role is evaluated; members of the group may respond to either the role or the person, or to both. As noted, in secondary groups, members tend to respond more to roles than to persons. When rankings are agreed upon by group members, the group may be said to be stratified (Bales, 1950:77).

Some roles become standardized among groups and persist regardless of the person occupying the role. Some roles are common to most groups: the *scapegoat*, who is the recipient of group hostility; the *clown* or *joker* (Hare, 1976:146), who may be either the butt of humor or the donor, and who serves an important expressive function; the *peacemaker*, to whom the group turns for conflict reduction, an important integrative or social control function; the *idol*, who sets some moral or social standard for the group; and the *critic*, "who is idealistic and argumentative" (Hare, 1976:148).

A recent article cites Fritz Redl's concept of *role suction*, the strong invisible power in a group wherein the group unconsciously selects certain members to fulfill particular functions that meet some of the group's covert needs. The term *suction* indicates that group forces operate in powerful ways to "suck" a given member into an emotionally needed group role (Gemmill and Kraus, 1988:301).

These members perform "covert roles":

> In a covert role, a member functions to absorb or contain the emotion that the remaining members of a group have difficulty expressing or accepting about themselves. Once a covert role is assumed, it is difficult for group members to discuss how the role has been covertly assigned, since it happens outside their awareness (Gemmill and Kraus, 1988:300).

These authors suggest that groups' syntality includes (in Carl Jung's terminology) a "group shadow":

> Like an individual, a group in the process of doing its work develops a shadow of its own, composed of the unexpressed emotional negativity occurring within and between members. Attributes group members find difficult to accept in themselves and in one another constitute the group shadow. . . . These covert fragments form one basis upon which members are differentiated within a group (Gemmill and Kraus, 1988:301).

The subject of most research on groups is leadership in its various forms. The two most commonly identified forms are the *task* (instrumental or adaptive) *leader* and the *social–emotional* (expressive or integrative) *leader*. The latter is sometimes called the sentiment leader. In his study of groups, Homans observed several rules for leadership:

1. The leader will maintain the primary position.
2. The leader will live up to the norms of the group. The higher the degree of conformity, the higher will be the member's rank.
3. The leader will not give orders that will not be obeyed; "losing face" would result.
4. In giving orders, the leader will use established channels.
5. The leader will listen.
6. The leader will be self-aware (Homans, 1950:440).

While this seems to be a recipe for leadership, the rules describe common expectations for the leader role, for example:

> The fact is that leadership in a group may be at one time abrupt, forceful, centralized, with all communications originating with the leader, and another time, slow, relaxed, dispersed, with much communication back and forth between leader and followers. Each mode is acceptable, appropriate and authoritative, but each in different circumstances (Homans, 1950:419).

Gemmill suggested that

> a group, when faced with the inevitable uncertainty and ambiguity regarding its initial direction, creates the role of "leader" in order to avoid confronting feelings such as helplessness and fear of failure. In other words, a group unconsciously colludes to create a leader role upon which its members can collectively project threatening feelings and impulses. . . . Once this role is created, the person occupying it becomes, in the view of other group members and himself [sic], the primary

person responsible for successful accomplishment of group goals (Gemmill and Kraus, 1988:304).

In other words, interaction between the leader and the group members and between the group and its environment determine which form of leadership is most functional for the group at any particular time. The leadership role need not, and usually does not, reside in only one person. Leadership tasks are usually, if not always, distributed among the members. Perhaps leadership is best defined as "the set of functions through which the group coordinates the efforts of individuals" (Katz and Bender, 1976:117).

C. Behavioral Aspects

1. Adaptation. This has been discussed under the section on steady state in this chapter. It remains here only to restate that all group behavior has some bearing upon securing and expending energy externally (SE and GE functions) whether explicitly designed to do so or not. Berrien, in his discussion of groups as systems, stated that adaptation is fundamental in that systems must "produce some service or product acceptable to another social system" (Berrien, 1971:120). Parsons would undoubtedly agree, but we repeat that a system cannot concentrate on adaptation to the exclusion of integration.

An important component of adaptation is leadership, specifically the problem-solving and decision-making activities inherent in the leadership role. These activities have received much attention in research on groups and in research on organizations, in particular. As noted earlier, problem solving has received prime attention in social group work practice. Mills preferred to refer to task leadership and decision-making in the wider context of

> an *executive system;* i.e., the set of executive orientations and processes as they are distributed and organized among and performed by group members. Any member, regardless of position or office, who performs executive functions . . . participates in the executive system. . . .
>
> The executive system is the group's center for assessment of itself and its situations, for arrangement and rearrangement of its internal and external relations, for decision-making and for learning, and for "learning how to learn" through acting and assessing the consequences of action. . . . The executive system is the partly independent, autonomous center where information about the role-systems . . . is processed (Mills, 1967:93).

More accurately, it is an executive *subsystem* that primarily serves the function of goal attainment. This is isomorphic to the ego functions of the personality system, as Freud described them. Miller referred to the "decider" subsystem that must exist in any system (Miller, 1978).

2. Socialization. Socialization, is, of course, integrative behavior within the group intended to furnish energy to the group and to reduce the likelihood of conflict. The use of small groups to facilitate socialization is widespread, e.g., the pledge group in a sorority, basic training in the military, groups to prepare schizophrenic persons for employment (Epstein, 1982:211–212), and to resocialize former cult members (Goldberg and Goldberg, 1982). Much like the family, the small group can readily serve as a transition into wider systems. Socialization into the group itself is based upon some match between the person's needs and the group's offering; a good example is the frequent use of groups by adolescents for security, opportunities to make friends, and to learn the cultures of both youth and adult life stages.

The process of socialization may be of three kinds:

1. Compliance, in which the person conforms, but does not agree with the group's view.
2. Identification, in which members adopt the group's view because the group becomes part of their own identities.
3. Internalization, in which the group's view is adopted because it meets some personal objective, or resolves a member's internal or external conflict. That is, the group's view agrees with the member's view (note the priority is on the member's view here).

In this process, the person may engage in various role strategies aimed at achieving desired ends (Goffman, 1961). The adaptation of the person and the integrative behavior of the system must reach some mutually acceptable bargain, or the process of socialization will fail.

3. Social Control and Social Conflict. The process of standardization is related to social control. A group achieves consensus or steady state by shaping its members' behaviors in certain ways. The application of sanctions in one form or another is social control. As noted earlier, social control is exercised by the entire group through various means. The major means of control is energy applied to, or withheld from, a member. One example is the traditional Roberts' Rules in formal meetings; if members do not conform to its usage, they may not be recognized (i.e., allowed any oral interchange with the entire group) or may be ejected from the group. An extreme example would be forcing group members to accept certain roles such as worker, hunter, or mate in order to survive. A more subtle example is that new members of the United States Senate are expected to "be seen but not heard." The play *Twelve Angry Men* illustrated the various forms that social control can take in a group, from threat of violence to ridicule and "putting down" a member.

An important part of social control in groups is conflict and the management of conflict.

> Group experience *is* conflict . . . a response to the reality that there is a shortage of what people need and want. . . . To organize, a group must coordinate one part with another, and in doing so must limit the freedom of some parts. . . . And further, groups accept and reward some members more fully than others, and this inequality creates yet another type of conflict. . . . Change, which occurs at every moment, is determined both in direction and in quality by the manner in which conflicts are resolved. Response to conflict determines the new state of the system (Mills, 1967:14–15).

As noted earlier, probably the most complete statement of the dimensions and uses of conflict in groups is found in Coser's *The Functions of Social Conflict* (1964).

4. *Communication.* We previously defined communication as "transfer of meaning or energy" by any means. According to this definition, virtually all group activity could be considered communication, rendering the term so broad as to be meaningless. Rather, we mean communication intended to accomplish adaptation, integration, social control, or goal attainment (in other words, the SE, SI, GI and GE functions) for the system.

Bales' interaction process analysis theory of groups (Bales, 1950) is based upon the analysis of units of communication into a few categories, such as "shows solidarity," "shows tension release," "disagrees," and "shows antagonism." Tabulating the number of units exchanged during a given time and their distribution by categories allows some index of group process to be derived. This has been a popular means of group analysis.

Other theorists, especially those with backgrounds in information theory, have focused on communication as the basic process in groups. Satir's conjoint family therapy and Berne's transactional analysis both focused on communication. Small group communication has become a field of study in its own right, with a rapidly increasing body of literature that includes descriptions of communication nets in groups, including the diagrams in Figure 15 (Shaw, 1981:152; also see Handy, 1985, 180).

Groups

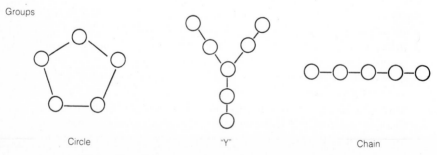

Circle   "Y"   Chain

Figure 15.   Diagrams of communication networks.

> Literally hundreds of studies have been conducted using the communication net approach. The main findings . . . can be summarized rather directly. First, centralized communication nets are more efficient in transmitting messages. Hence, when the task only requires transmission of information (as the tasks used in some of the early studies did), the highly centralized *wheel* is the most efficient net. . . . The *circle*, on the other hand, cannot route all information to any one node as efficiently as the wheel, but the information can be routed to, and the nonroutine aspects of the group's task (e.g., reasoning to a solution) can be done by, *any* group member equally (McGrath, 1984:167).

However, Shaw's view of these studies indicated that the *independence* and *saturation* of the positions in the networks are more important than the central location. Independence refers to the degree of autonomy the person has from others in carrying out tasks; saturation refers to the total load the person must handle, including task and role demands and message transmission, in carrying out tasks. Group members gain satisfaction from high independence, primarily, and from moderate saturation (Shaw, 1978; McGrath, 1984:168). Communication, then, is best carried out when members have significant freedom, and are not overwhelmed by the demands of communication.

One powerful element of leadership is control of communication between members. Sometimes a purpose of communication in groups is to allow the group members to improve their communication skills within the group and then transfer these skills to other systems. An example is a group of single, pregnant young women and their parents. This group provided

> the means whereby families may learn new, more appropriate communication behavior. . . . In some instances, family members learn how to communicate better when the therapists and the group decode messages that are sent and inappropriately received in a family system. In other instances, good communication among the therapists in the group's presence serves as a positive model (Papademetriou, 1971:88).

III. SOME USES OF GROUPS

Small groups are distinctive among social systems examined in this book in that a group system can be created for particular purposes by human service professionals (as could an organization, although this occurs less frequently). Groups can be created for purposes of therapy, self-actualization, support, problem solving, goal achievement, or to influence larger systems as in community organization and social action.

A. Human Potential Groups

Human potential groups are organized to further the purposes of their members, usually personal growth, through provision of "intensive group experience" over a limited time span. Examples include T-groups, sensory awareness groups, encounter groups, sensitivity training groups, and marathon groups.

As compared to the dimensions of groups earlier discussed, human potential groups tend to focus on expressive functions. These groups are structured to emphasize feelings and impersonal transactions. The norms include mutuality of support, openness, and disclosure. The group's powers of acceptance and validation are employed. However, it is essential that group leaders be competent to deal with the hazards of intensive group experience.

> A study by Yalom and Lieberman found that 16 of 130 undergraduates who completed encounter groups (of 209 who began) could be considered "casualties"—defined as enduring significant, negative outcome . . . caused by their participation in the group." This was a careful study, using selected, supposedly competent leaders, representing most major therapeutic ideologies (Kovel, 1976:168)

B. *Therapeutic Groups*

Therapeutic groups are structured to serve as vehicles for persons struggling with intrapsychic concerns. Often the group is open-ended and long-term, with members cycling in and out. In describing the efficacy of therapeutic groups, Kovel says, "in a therapeutic situation an individual's problems often become clearer when expressed in a context of interaction with, or in reaction to, several others. Sometimes behavior in the group stimulates or surfaces problems which an individual has not dealt with in his [sic] interviews with a therapist" (Kovel, 1976:52). Therapeutic groups usually have an expressive focus with leaders clearly differentiated from the group. Socialization and communication are emphasized. Group process may be subordinated at times to the need of an individual.

C. *Self-Help Groups*

Over the past 30 years, there has been a phenomenal increase in the incidence of persons who come together around a common concern. Self-help groups exist for virtually every personal concern. Sharing experiences and ways of coping are the vehicles for mutuality of help—self and other, helping and accepting help. Professional direction is usually not wanted, although in some circumstances, a professional helper may convene a group or sponsor it. The focus is either on participants working on a kind of personal problem they share with the other group members *or* joining together to influence external systems to provide resources or recognize members' needs and rights (e.g., a divorced women's group, or a divorced fathers' group). Although some self-help groups may be largely task-oriented, sentiment is an ever-present factor. Katz and Bender provided this classification of self-help groups:

1. "Groups that are primarily focused on self-fulfillment or personal growth" (therapeutic groups).
2. "Groups that are primarily focused on social advocacy," e.g., welfare rights groups, Gay Rights National Lobby, and AIDS activists;
3. " "Groups whose primary function is to create alternative patterns for living" (e.g., lesbian or gay groups);
4. "Outcast haven" or "rock-bottom" groups (close supervision in a sheltered environment by "peers or persons who have successfully grappled with similar problems") (Katz and Bender, 1976:37–38).

Some self-help groups are spawned locally, whereas others are national organizations with local face-to-face chapters. Alcoholics Anonymous and Weight Watchers fit the cultural penchant for mobility. Members who migrate to different geographic locales can immediately affiliate with a local chapter in their communities. Vattano described self-help groups that "are primarily concerned with the failures and inadequacies of the environment and social institutions" (Vattano, 1972:13). Notable examples are welfare rights groups, gay rights groups, tenant associations, and the Guardian Angels (a "vigilante" group that became a national organization). Such groups evolve their own leadership in order to pursue specific goals, often the protection of civil rights. This includes groups such as Skinheads, survivalists, and white supremacists, whose avowed purposes are to preserve themselves and their values, by violence if necessary, against those whom they define as enemies.

D. Support Groups

These are groups to provide information and mutual support for persons who have a vested interest in others who have a particular condition or problem. These groups differ from self-help groups in the degree of direction provided by the leader or facilitator. They differ from therapeutic groups in that group members are not seeking personal psychological insight or growth. Examples include support groups for family caregivers of patients with Alzheimer's disease (Wasow, 1986) and for family members of persons with AIDS (Kelly and Sykes, 1989).

CONCLUSION

It seems clear from the wealth of research on groups that groups do share the common properties of systems. Furthermore, it is apparent that most group theory is based in systemic thinking. Since group experiences are both natural and essential to social living, purposeful use of groups offers opportunity for people to come together to pursue mutual interests and goals. Those who work in human services must understand group phenomena and develop competence in working with groups in order to use wisely the fundamental and immense power contained in the human group.

SUGGESTED READINGS

Alissi, Albert S.
    1980 *Perspectives on Social Group Work Practice.* New York: The Free Press.
      A reader, this book includes historical, classical material on social group work
      and current critiques. Highly informative regarding social work's use of the
      group.
Durkin, James E.
    1981 *Living Groups: Group Psychotherapy and General System Theory.* New York:
    Brunner/Mazel.
      This is the best example of the attempt to reconcile the systems approach
      and other group treatment theories. Highly useful for the practitioner or
      teacher looking for stimulating ideas. Includes some case examples of the
      fit between the two bodies of thought.
Gemmill, Gary, and George Kraus.
    1988 "Dynamics of Covert Role Analysis: Small Groups." *Small Group Behavior,*
    19(3):299–311.
Glasser, Paul, Rosemary Sarri, and Robert Vinter, eds.
    1974 *Individual Change through Small Groups.* New York: The Free Press.
      Chapter 5, by Sarri and Galinsky, "A Conceptual Framework for Group
      Development," is especially recommended.
Handy, Charles B.
    1985 *Understanding Organizations.* Harmondsworth, England: Penguin.
      Chapter 6, pp. 154–184, "On the Workings of Groups," is a fine, brief sum-
      mary of knowledge about groups in organizations. As noted in Chapter 5,
      this a unique book in its organization and excerpts.
Hare, A. Paul.
    1976 *Handbook of Small Group Research.* New York: The Free Press.
      This is the definitive collection of information regarding small groups. Most
      useful for anyone wishing a mass of detail for formulation of theory.
Johnson, David W., and Frank P. Johnson.
    1982 *Joining Together: Group Theory and Group Skills.* Englewood Cliffs, NJ:
    Prentice-Hall.
      This book is truly impressive in its comprehensiveness and its inclusion of
      examples and exercises. Perhaps too large for a supplementary text, but it
      contains a wealth of material for students. A delight to read.
Marrow, Alfred J.
    1969 *The Practical Theorist: The Life and Work of Kurt Lewin.* New York: Basic
    Books.
      A biography of Lewin written by a former student and colleague. This traces

the evolution of Group Dynamics from its roots in Gestalt holism to the development of training groups.

Miller, James Grier.

1978 *Living Systems*. New York: McGraw-Hill.

We refer here to Chapter 9. "The Group," pp. 515–593. Useful for examples of processes in groups. It is Miller's massive application of systems processes to groups. It is useful as an example of the lengths to which a systems theorist may go in elaborating the ideas. Useful to the serious student of systems ideas.

Roberts, Robert W., and Helen Northen, eds.

1976 *Theories of Social Work with Groups*. New York: Columbia University Press.

Excellent sections on historical development and thoughtful evaluation of current status of group work theories. They demonstrate explicitly that a systems approach is fundamental to virtually all theories of group work.

Shaw, Marvin E.

1981 *Group Dynamics: The Psychology of Small Group Behavior*. New York: Mc-Graw Hill.

A readable and comprehensive text. It includes reviews of the major theories in the field. Perhaps too large to be used as a supplementary text, but it could be used well as the primary text in a course on groups, or students could be assigned selected readings from it. The discussion of "syntality" (pp. 9–12) is valuable.

LITERARY SOURCES

Golding, William.

1959 *Lord of the Flies*. New York: Capricorn Books, Putnam.

Are human beings evil? Are we basically savage? These are Golding's questions in this famous novel, which portrays a Freudian triad of leadership. Provocative and disturbing.

Rose, Reginald.

1955 *Twelve Angry Men*. Chicago: Dramatics Publications Co.

A play about the interactive processes among jurors deliberating a capital case. Dramatically illustrates the shifts between individual and group goals; demonstrates that a group is indeed different from the sum of its parts. Can readily be used for role playing. The film, rated by the late Henry Fonda as his best (and we agree), is also available.

FILM AND VIDEO

The More We Get Together (1986)

This video is primarily about working with very old, disoriented nursing home residents. Part II, "Three Stages of a Validation Group," demonstrates how to form a group with the goals of anxiety reduction, regaining social controls, and recovering a sense of well-being.

Families

> All happy families resemble each other; each un-
> happy family is unhappy in its own way
> Leo Tolstoy, Anna Karenina
>
> As families go, so goes the nation.
> Margaret Mead, United States Senate Hearing

INTRODUCTION

Because the family can and should be viewed as a special instance of the small group, most of Chapter 6 is applicable to family. In every phase of the person's life cycle, family is of central importance in definition of social expectations and in provisions of the resources necessary for growth. A separate chapter is devoted to the family as a social system since the family is the single social unit in human society inextricably interwoven with all other systems. As noted in Chapter 3, I,B, "The Family as a Human Universal," the family assumes, or is delegated, primary responsibility for socialization into the culture and thus is charged with major responsibility to insure the survival of humankind.

> The family is the *primal* group in which *learning how to learn* begins. The child is taught how to learn before anybody is aware of teaching, and the learning of the child how to learn teaches the parents how to teach as well. And all this occurs long before the child has ever learned the word "why?" This nonsequential experience is biologically important. We need to learn new ways of learning, of developing our senses to take in new information (Brodey, 1977:64).

The approach to family in this chapter is consistent with the systems framework presented earlier. We construe the family as holon with attention to the system itself, its components, and its significant environment. Family fulfills the requirements for designation as a human system. The singular "family" is used in this book to designate this level of system. The chapter is entitled "Families" to emphasize the plurality of family forms. Much of the confusion attendant to "family analysis," "family impact," and the study of "family policy" derives from the use of the singular "family" and its implication of a norm or modal form.

I. APPROACHES TO FAMILY ANALYSIS

We will forego until later in this chapter the dubious pleasures of establishing our definition of family in favor of a brief examination of a few selected approaches to understanding the family. Our intent here is to summarize only those approaches which we find most congruent with the purposes of this book.

A. Family as a System of Roles

The family as a system of roles is an important theme in the literature of family analysis. Roles embody cultural expectations for behavior, and the family is the arena wherein these roles are learned and carried out. In psychoanalytic thought, the resolution of the Oedipal conflict is dependent upon the existence of appropriate role models and the assumption by the child of the appropriate roles. Lidz, a psychiatrist, stated:

> The family is recognized as a biologically required social instititution that mediates between the biological and cultural directives of personality formation, and a social system in which the child assimilates the basic instrumentalities, institutions, and role attributions that are essential to his [sic] adaptation and integration (Lidz, 1963:75–76).

Feldman and Scherz, social workers, wrote:

> The family operates through roles that shift and alter during the course of the family's life. Roles can be explicit or instrumental; they can be implicit or emotional. . . . The healthy family carries out explicit roles appropriately according to age, competence, and needs during all the different stages of family life. The disturbed family experiences serious difficulty in the management of roles (Feldman and Scherz, 1967:67).

The family system of roles must be examined, then, both structurally and functionally. Parsons' earlier formulation of the family as a social system differentiated between instrumental and expressive role functions on a sexual axis; that is, the male-father role as breadwinner and adapter to the environment, the female-mother role as social and emotional provider who integrated the family system's components. In their critiques of Parsons' view, many authors stress the fluidity of the distribution of the instrumental and expressive roles within the changing family in the United States. Billingsley (1968) pictured fluidity of roles in Black families as a source of strength. Black families are able to function effectively in a frequently hostile environment by shifting roles (mother and children as breadwinners when father is unable to find work). They also incorporate extended family, neighbors or others (Shug Avery in *The Color Purple*; Erdrich, *Love Medicine*, 1985; Stack, *All Our Kin*, 1974). The role of the "aunt" in Black families is well known (e.g. Ella's role in *The Autobiography of Malcolm X*, 1966).

Rodman (1966) cited evidence from Parsons' writings to support his conclusion that the female role in general has broadened from the "pseudo-occupation" of a domestic pattern to include role choices of "career pattern," "glamour pattern," and "good companion pattern"; and that society sanctions a feminine role combining these role patterns (see Margaret Adams' comment on this later in this chapter). Parsons and others have held that the masculine instrumental role has also shifted because of the changes in occupational roles. The family business or family farm formerly located and consolidated the instrumental functions in the father and reinforced his paternal authority, primarily through inheritance laws passing property from father to son; the modern father's authority derives from his membership in a work organization, which diffuses and dissipates paternal authority. In addition, the majority of married women in the United States are now employed, and the rate of employment increases with the age of the child. When the youngest child is between 2 and 7 years of age, the rate of employment gradually increases as the age of the child increases, to 60%; there is no further increase through age 17 (Sweet and Bumpass, 1987:148).

The family as determinant and perpetuator of role expectations has long been at issue. In 1902, Engels argued that the family is a bourgeois device designed to enslave women: "The Modern individual family is founded on the open or concealed domestic slavery of the wife" (Engels, 1902:65). More recently, C. Wright Mills stated: "In so far as the family as an institution turns women into darling little slaves and men into their chief providers and unweaned dependents, the problem of a satisfactory marriage remains incapable of purely private solution." Far more attention is devoted to adult-family roles as necessary to family integrity and functioning than child family roles, although the purposes of adult-family roles as explicated are largely parental. Popenoe suggested that inattention to children results from their subordination not only in the family but in society as well:

> Individual" means adults and not children; the rights of adults are given considerably more weight in this regard than are any presumed rights of children. One

> wonders how much of this in the modern welfare state . . . is due to the downgrad-
> ing in the political shuffle of the interests of children; children of course do not vote
> or normally even express their opinions. It is often pointed out that in virtually
> every welfare state the growth of benefits for the elderly has far exceeded that for
> children. If children were involved in formulating welfare-state policies, I have little
> doubt that the situation would be different (Popenoe, 1988:336).

Feminist literature is particularly concerned with women's liberation from traditional role constraints, and frequently men's liberation as well (e.g., Thorne and Yalom, 1982).

Viewed from a role perspective, contemporary work provisions such as flextime, flexiplace, maternity/paternity leaves, and day-care at the work site are designed to relieve role stresses and strains and to accommodate shifts in family structure and role allocations.

B. Family as Cause or Effect

The family as cause or effect is a second major approach. The family can be seen either as "dependent" variable or as "independent" variable. In the former instance, the family is responsive to the demands and dictates of the larger social systems. It adapts or, more precisely, accommodates to the goal requirements of the society within which it exists. The nuclear, mobile family emerges because of the requisites of the economy; it relinquishes its functions to other social institutions due to pressures exerted upon it by its environment. Governments influence by prescriptions and proscriptions, for example, compulsory school attendance, abortion laws, Sweden's law against spanking of children (Popenoe, 1988:199), and court decisions that place the "welfare of the child" above the rights of the parents. In this way, society determines the family.

In the opposing view, the family as independent variable, family is seen to be cause rather than effect. The family initiates change, and society accommodates to these changes; in other words, the family determines the society. Examples of this dynamic are infrequently cited in the literature on family. A sociologist, David Popenoe, recently said:

> Among the thorniest and most unresolved of theoretical questions . . . is the degree
> to which certain characteristics of the family-kinship system may be an important
> cause, rather than merely an effect, of such cultural and social phenomena as indi-
> vidualism and industrialization. At the very least, one should be careful not to con-
> clude that industrialization is *the cause* of family change (Popenoe, 1988:47).

Further, Popenoe says that the "classical Western family," the extended family, "died out in portions of Europe well before the Industrial revolution and, indeed . . . the nuclear family is now seen to be as much a cause as a consequence of industrialization" (1988:58). Another example is sociologist Elise Boulding's view that

> the family is a potentially powerful contributor to the generation of alternative images of the future. During the "quiet" period of history—the times of relative stability, when few demands are made on the adaptive capacities of individuals or groups—and also in periods of severe repression, the futures-creating capacities of the family may remain underdeveloped. In periods of rapid social change, when each age group represented in the household has experienced critically different stimuli and pressures from the larger society, the futures-creating family is held together by strong social bonds (Boulding, 1972:188).

In this sense of creating alternatives, the family is independent variable. It generates social change, according to Boulding, in that the family is a "play community"; play may be one means by which culture is created, and thereby alternative societal futures may be imagined. Clearly, the position of the family as holon interfacing between individual and society allows it to perform this function. However, Popenoe notes that in Sweden, which may be the model of the future, families do less together, including play.

The controversy over abortion laws exemplifies the family initiating change that requires social accommodation, in that family planning, in order to liberate the parents and maintain living standards, requires that society provide sanction and means for birth control. The 1973 Supreme Court decision *Roe v. Wade* gave legal sanction to abortion as a means of birth control. In December, 1988, Nancy Klein was pregnant and comatose as the result of an auto accident. Physicians believed abortion might increase her chance of survival. Her husband requested an abortion, but prolife advocates sought to prohibit it. Two weeks later, a court affirmed the husband's right to make the decision, the judge remarking that outsiders had no right to interfere in this family tragedy. One columnist observed that Ms. Klein's situation had restored rationality to the controversy over the control a woman, or someone legally responsible for her, has over her own body (Goodman, 1989c). This is a vivid example of a family as initiator of change. Attempts continue to overturn the *Roe v. Wade* ruling.

Although few family theorists opt for either extreme, dependent or independent variable, most do see the family as determined by societal changes rather than the reverse. but, as noted earlier, this is not a universal opinion. Scholars now increasingly see families as initiating change. Laslett concluded that the nuclear family preceded industrialization in Europe and thus may have "caused" it (Laslett, 1971, 1974). Our opinion is, of course, that the family is *both* independent and dependent variable, since it is a holon. Mutual causal interactions between families and society can be seen in all aspects of living. For example, shifts in family structure and roles that are responsive to changes in employment patterns lead to marketplace accommodations. Both females and males are employed increasingly outside the home. Employment hours vary, influencing time available to shop, prepare, and serve meals, and for family dining. All of the following could be construed as societal adaptations to such family changes:

1. Extension of hours in which commercial and retail establishments conduct their business (particularly shopping malls).
2. "One Stop Full Service" shopping such as gasoline stations which offer groceries, cosmetics, microwaved hot sandwiches, "instant cash" machines, video rentals, tickets to sports or cultural events, and lottery tickets.
3. Marketing of increased varieties of frozen prepared foods.
4. Fast-food restaurants that generally portray workers or families in their advertising ("You deserve a break today").
5. Large-scale development and production of synthetic fabrics marketed as "wash and wear" (the often-maligned polyester sharply reduced the time necessary to maintain clean clothing).
6. The current marketing of "fax" machines as a means to assure accuracy in the delivery of orders from grocery stores or specialty food shops.

C. The Family as Evolving System

The family as evolving system is a dual approach to family inquiry. One focus is on the developmental cycle of *a* family, while the other is a focus on the evolutionary cycle of *the* family as a social institution.

Family life cycle has been adopted as an organizing theme in courses in human behavior for the helping professions. The general direction taken in conceiving of the family life cycle is from the point of marriage, to and through expansion stages, to and through contraction stages. The more thorough formulations of family stages attempt to account for the related growth tasks for all family members, not just the children. These formulations are grounded in assumptions of a nuclear unit, childbearing, and a marriage that will continue until the death of a spouse. Thus, these postulated family stages are, in fact, applicable to only a limited number of actual families. Family evolution comprises a series of changes as family members encounter transition stages in the life cycle. The preschooler may face becoming a kindergartener at the same time the parents are dealing with the recognition that the future is not boundless. The preteen enters puberty while parents are taking stock of their own adult identity and grandparents are moving toward retirement. The television series, "The Wonder Years" presents this from the standpoint of a sensitive youngster. As the young adult seeks a more fully consistent identity, the parents are adapting to the emptying nest and the grandparents cope with diminishing of functions

The events most commonly referred to that signal role changes and new stages of the life cycle are forming a couple, birth of the first child, departure of the children, and dissolution of the couple (by divorce or death of one partner, e.g.). Added to these are educational, residential, and occupational changes. One popular television series portrays the crises of *thirtysomething,* including most of these life cycle events.

Another approach to the evolution of a family is the study of stress, attending to those points at which families make transitions to new steady states, or fail to do so. Little research has been devoted to the stresses that precipitate changes in steady state; most attention has been given to analyzing each steady state (Olson, 1983; Olson, Lavee, and McCubbin 1988:17). Recent research has focused on morphogenesis and morphostasis, attempting to identify the rules by which change does or does not occur.

A related facet of family change that is being studied is resilience, the ability of families to cope successfully with stress. Olson and his colleagues at the University of Minnesota factored out three dimensions of family dynamics that are relevant to stress and change: cohesion, adaptability, and communication. These three are combined in the "circumplex" model of marital and family types, which has demonstrated validity as a predictor of family success (Olson et al., 1983; 1988:22).

Carle Zimmerman is the best known advocate of a cyclical theory of *the* family. He began with the premise that the family and society constantly interact and cause changes, each in the other. Other social institutions (particularly the church and government) vie with the family for control of family members. Drawing on historical data, Zimmerman proposed a three-phase family typology and suggested it is a repetitive cycle (Leslie, 1967:223-230).

1. *Trustee* family—the living members are trustees of the family name, family property, and family blood. The family itself is immortal, there is no conception of individual rights, and individual welfare is ever subordinate to the family group.

2. *Domestic* family—an intermediate type that evolves from the trustee family. As the state gains in power, family control over its members is weakened. The state shares this power and control with the family and creates the concept of individual rights to be maintained against family authority. Popenoe says:

> The modern nuclear family was organized largely to serve the end of child rearing in an environment of stability and love between the married couple. Backed by the unique coercive powers of organized religion, as well as by the laws of the state, the nuclear family unit was culturally held up as the goal of human sexuality combined with romantic love; it was the only acceptable form of adult pair-bond (1988:329).

3. *Atomistic* family—the power and scope of family authority is reduced to an absolute minimum; the family no longer mediates between its members and society. The state becomes essentially an organization. Hospitals and extended care facilities look after the ill family members; foster care and juvenile institutions provide for children needing care or control; domestic courts provide counseling for parents and children; schools educate with little involvement by parents; the nation conscripts youth without consulting families about their beliefs.

Zimmerman judged the present-day American family to be well into the third phase, the "atomic age" in yet another sense. He did not find the "present decay of the family" unique. He documented similar family dissolution just prior to the fall of the Greek and Roman civilizations. Popenoe agrees, labeling "the emerging value system of America as 'bureaucratic consumer capitalism,' in which expressive individualism overtakes moral commitment" (Popenoe 1988:289, citing Bellah et al., 1985). He speculated, "This style of life could be the wave of the future—the new, individualized, and autonomous individual making a suitable adjustment to a rationalized and affluent world (Popenoe, 1988:327). A study of United States census data revealed that

> Marriage and family relationships seem to be occupying a shrinking space in our lives. Marriage rates before 25 have declined markedly. . . . Parenthood is also being delayed. . . . Again, a substantial proportion of today's youth may never become parents at all. The vast majority will marry and have children, but over half of those who do will experience the breakup of that marriage. Persons who are not currently married . . . have progressively chosen to live alone, rather than with other family members (Sweet and Bumpass, 1987:391).

Zimmerman deplored the popular view of the family as ever evolving to higher and better forms:

> [modern] inhumanity lies close, in a basic casual sense to the decay of the family system. Indeed the familial decline may well be the primary causal agent in the sapping of the universal capacity for human sympathy. Juvenal held this opinion when he wrote of "the decline in the capacity to weep.". . . . The consequence then of a declining family system is that controls of society come more into the hands of men who, in the words of Bacon, have no "hostages to fortune," and who do not possess judgments biased by an immersion in fundamental humanism (Zimmerman, 1947:77).

He recommended open recognition and understanding of the current state of family decline and hoped that a "creative minority" would come forward to reassert the values of familism.

D. *The Structural Approach*

The structural approach to the family has received the attention of a host of investigators. It should be noted that any attempt at family analysis addresses itself to certain family forms and excludes others.

The majority of Western observers of the family accept the two-generation nuclear family as the norm. This is particularly true of those interested in the child-rearing aspects of the family. The "normal" family is seen to be composed of two parents and their minor children. Voiland and associates noted "the rise of prominence of the family of procreation—father, mother, children—as an independent unit. This primary family group has, indeed, become the structural norm of our culture. There are many manifestations of this fact" (Voiland and Associates, 1962:46-47). As noted earlier, it has been the norm in some parts of European culture for five or six centuries. It is this family structure that serves as the basis for societal policy in support of the family (e.g., welfare and tax structure). It should be emphasized that this family composition is no longer found in the majority of families in the United States.

Parsons characterized the present-day American family as "the isolated family," isolated especially residentially and economically from the extended family. He saw this as a natural consequence of the specialization and differentiation of the complex social system of America today. He qualified the degree of isolation: "I think it very important indeed, that there is much accumulating evidence that the extended family is an exceedingly important resource to fall back on in case of emergency or trouble, for financial support and for emotional support and help in planning and all sorts of things of that kind" (Parsons, 1964a:17).

More recent evidence confirms that indeed the extended family may well go beyond the bounds of those related by blood or marriage (see Roberts and Northen, 1976:318–319, for a discussion of family network, or Stack, 1974:31ff.). The high cost of living in many areas of the country during the past decade has impelled adult children to return to live with their parents (the "nest" contracts and expands in keeping with the state of the economy).

Billingsley drew on the formulations of Parsons, Bales, and Shils to establish a typology of forms for categorizing Black family structures. The refinements he introduced through his three categories and twelve types have broad applicability (Billingsley, 1968:15–21).

1. The *nuclear* family includes three types: the incipient, consisting only of the marital pair; the simple, consisting of the marital pair and minor children; and the attenuated, containing only one parent and minor children.

2. The *extended* family includes types wherein other relatives are added to the nuclear household.

3. The *augmented* family includes types of family situations wherein unrelated family members are incorporated into the household.

Boulding classified the second and third types, extended and augmented, under the heading "expanded family" in order to "emphasize the commonality between the biologically related extended family and

the household as a voluntary assocation" (1972:188). She placed all family forms on a continuum from one isolated householder to a cluster of
persons either biologically or voluntarily associated. She correctly
pointed out that there is no hard and fast line between the expanded
family and the "intentional community" (i.e., a community organized
for specific social or ideological purposes). Given the present variety of
forms of families and and communities, such an elastic definition is very
useful.

The study of kinship networks and relationships, particularly in the
work of social anthropologists, has yielded additional insights into the
variety of family forms. Kinship responsibilities in the United States is
a neglected dimension in family studies. Cultural guidelines for determination of allegiance to kinsmen are ambiguous and often conflicting.
Although the nuclear family norm would seem to dictate primary kin
responsibility to spouse and children, conflicting claims do arise. The
parent of today in an isolated nuclear family might have been the child
of yesterday in a closely tied extended or nuclear family. For such a
person, the transfer of allegiance and emotional involvement from the
family of orientation to the family of procreation may be a monumental
task, as indicated by frequent letters to "Dear Abby" from wives and
mothers-in-law about the son/husband's responsibilities to each.

Scholars of the family have only recently begun to study kinship relationships in "remarried families," and the perceptions of obligations
and relationships within them. Social worker Constance Ahrons coined
the term "binuclear" to describe families in which a child is part of two
separate nuclear families, formed by the child's divorced parents (Glick,
1989:26; Ahrons and Rodgers, 1987). Children must decide (often with
strong guidance from one or both parents) who are "kin": Does a step-
mother's mother become "Grandma"? Do they invite the absent parent
and the new stepparent to graduation ceremonies? Parents must decide
their relationships to their biological children with whom they no longer
live: Do they attend the children's weddings or the funeral of the former
spouse's parent, who is, after all, the children's grandparent? These are
often painful questions to resolve, and are frequent situations in family
dramas in television and movies.

The unenviable status of the aged in our society and the guilt felt by
their adult children are products of this dilemma. The unenforceable
"relative responsibility" laws in public welfare are another reflection of
this situation. Similarly, the People's Republic of China removed the
responsibility of children for their aged parents following the 1949 revolution, in reaction to traditional Confucian society, but restored it in the
most recent constitutional reform.

Alternative family forms are increasingly being suggested as possible
substitutions for traditional ones, especially to replace the nuclear family
norm. In the present generation, a new family form has emerged, most

easily termed *living together*. Popenoe notes that in the Netherlands, it has been carried one step further, and called "living-apart-together" (Popenoe, 1988:303). In Sweden, he observes, there are separate names for persons with whom you have a sexual bond, and share a household with (a *sämbo*) or do not share a household with (a *särbo*).

Moore (1958), along with others including some feminist authors argued that the family in any of its traditional forms is dysfunctional in modern industrial society.

E. The Functional Approach

This is another dominant theme in family studies. Usually, functions are looked at in tandem with family structures in acknowledgment of the fact that these two aspects cannot readily be separated, not even for purposes of objective study. There are inherent difficulties in functional analysis of the family, like the problems in looking at the functions of any other social system. The pitfall is, of course, to reason circularly that a pattern or value is "functional" to the given system and the proof of functionality is found in the fact of its existence.

The family is generally acknowledged to exist universally to perform certain functions necessary to the survival of the species. Generally, these functions are enumerated as procreation and child rearing, implying that the family has major responsibility for these societal imperatives. Beyond this level of generality, there are divergent ways of describing and explaining family functions and the relationships of these to the broader social systems.

Parsons applied his functional prerequisites of goal attainment, pattern maintenance, integration, and adaptation to the family system. As stated earlier, he stressed the instrumental and expressive role functions within the family constellation and how these are allocated to the family members, especially on the sexual axis. He accounted for the changing functions of the modern family through emphasizing differentiation and specialization. As the macrosystem becomes increasingly complex, the family as a component system becomes increasingly specialized in the functions it performs for both the larger system and the family components. The core functions remaining in the family are the maintenance of the household and the intimate personal relations of the members of the household, including child rearing and socialization into affective networks.

As specialized institutional arrangements evolve to provide for socialization of children into the culture, the family relinquishes functions and becomes increasingly specialized. This relinquishing of family functions particularly affects women. Margaret Adams, a social worker, commented on the transfer of "nurturant" roles for women from the family

to professions. She described the process by which women are channeled into social work, nursing, teaching, secretarial work, and certain
other professions, as "the compassion trap":

> The proliferation of the helping professions into a complex array of welfare services
> took many of the more highly specialized aspects of the nurturing and protective
> functions out of the home. . . . In addition, when one or both parents were out of
> the home for a substantial part of the day, they had to delegate their acculturating
> functions. Thus the synthesizing role traditionally discharged by women in the
> home was translated into a wider sphere and spread its influence through a broader
> range of activities. Instead of (or in addition to) keeping the family intact and maxi
> mally functional, women became involved in housekeeping tasks on behalf of soci
> ety at large and assumed responsibility for keeping its operation viable (Adams,
> 1971:72).

Christopher Lasch deplored the transfer of nurturance and parenting
from the family to the burgeoning professional experts (Lasch, 1979).
He, as Parsons previously, noted the emergence of specialized peer
groupings that evidently have assumed functions previously performed
by the family. Popenoe's studies in Sweden showed that "many of these
youth were lonely and had few, merely superficial, social contacts. The
young people . . . inhabit an "age-stratified world" in which they meet
very few adults other than their parents" (Popenoe, 1988:320–321).
These peer groups of all ages differentiate on the axis of age. Examples
includes the aged, adolescents, and young adults. Keniston proposed a
"new" stage of life which occurs outside either a family of orientation
or a family of procreation, noting

> the emergence on a mass scale of a previously unrecognized stage of life. . . . the
> stage of youth. . . . A growing minority of postadolescents today . . . have not
> settled the questions whose answers once defined adulthood: questions of relation
> ship to the existing society, questions of vocation, questions of social role and life
> style (Keniston, 1970:634–635).

The youthful followers of Reverend Sun Yung Moon (disparagingly referred to as "Moonies") may well be a manifestation of this new life
phase. Those who have received the most notoriety because of their
parents' efforts to regain their allegiance have been in their twenties,
opting for a vocation devoid of any kind of family connection. This organization's mass marriages of hundreds of couples at the same time to
partners selected by the Unification Church is perhaps an example of
deliberate attempts to create "family" within the church.

Another example of youth organization during this life phase is the
neo-Nazi "Skinheads" located in several cities in the United States.
These groups evolved from alienated working class youth in Great Britain who were notorious for their "bashing" of immigrants. Although

not all Skinheads are racist or violent (Minneapolis and Chicago are exceptions, apparently), the unifying themes of most American Skinheads are racism and violence. As with many organizations of alienated youth, historically, they are subject to exploitation by political manipulators (Coplon, 1988).

This "youth" stage is clearly related to Erikson's sixth stage, that of intimacy vs. isolation (see Chapter 8, I,A, "Perpetuation and Sharing of Identity"). If the family is not sufficient in assisting young adults in resolving this crisis, then they must look to other institutions or create new ones, or conceivably simply fail to resolve the crisis in massive numbers. Currently, there are several proposals to create vehicles for "youth service" programs that would reward teenagers and young adults for participation in volunteer programs with vouchers for housing or education, as well as wages. The most obvious objectives are social control, socialization, and integration into the society in the form of roles as workers, students, and consumers. Described another way, its purpose is to structure the "moratorium" (see Erikson's definition in Chapter 8) to reduce the possibility of deviance, when the family is not capable or sufficient to do so.

Lidz found the family performs three sets of discrete but interrelated functions (Lidz, 1963:44–46). For the children, the family provides physical care and nurturance and at the same time directs their personality development. for the spouses, it furnishes the means to personal fulfillment and stability. For society, the family takes responsibility for enculturating new members. Lidz suggests "it is possible that these functions which are fundamental to human adaptation cannot be fulfilled separately at all and must be fused in the family" (1963:45).

Magorah Maruyama found the extent of family function specialization alarming. He coined the term *monopolarization* to describe the state of affairs wherein the child's relationship to adults is confined to a mother or father or, more precisely, to one set of parents (Maruyama 1966:133). Monopolarization is seen as a meta-assumption of theories of personality and of many Western philosophies. The totality of children's relationships to their parents sets narrow parameters for development and invests undue responsibility in the parents.

Maruyama recommended dilution of this relationship through increased interfamily contacts and integration of persons who are not in the family circuit. This could be accomplished through the formation of voluntary adult–child communities without any necessity of major reforms in family structure (Maruyama, 1966:147). However, many communes deliberately attempted to create alternative family structures. On writer reported twenty years ago that "today's communes seek a family warmth and intimacy, to become extended families. A 50-person commune in California, for example, called itself 'The Lynch Family,' a New Mexico commune 'The Chosen Family,' a New York City group simply

'The Family' " (Kanter 1970:54). Kanter also pointed out that exclusivity of parenting was avoided in successful nineteenth-century communes by separating children from their parents, creating a "family of the whole" (Kanter, 1970:55; Kephart, 1976:91ff.). This was also attempted in Israel, the USSR, and the People's Republic of China, but abandoned in each nation.

II. A HUMAN SYSTEMS VIEW OF FAMILIES

The family has come to be viewed as a system by many observers. Perhaps most notable among these in their relevance to this book are family therapists. One of the outstanding researchers of family therapy, Jay Haley, optimistically stated,

> What family therapists most have in common they also share with a number of behavior scientists in the world today: There is an increasing awareness that psychiatric problems are social problems which involve the total ecological system. There is a concern with, and an attempt to change, what happens with the family and also the interlocking systems of the family and the social institutions in which the family is embedded. The fragmentation of the individual into parts, or the family into parts is being abandoned, and there is a growing consensus that a new ecological framework defines problems in new ways and calls for new ways in therapy (Sager and Kaplan, 1972:270).

For purposes of the following discussion, we will treat the family as a social system (holon) possessing the characteristics of a social system but distinguishable from other social systems by its goals, functions, and climate of feeling. The family is defined both by its members and by the culture and community within which it exists. Lidz's functional viewpoint, referred to earlier, points to the functions performed by the family as system, subsystem, and suprasystem. The family provides the opportunity for intimate social interaction for all its members. It is also the base of personal security for all its members.

To begin with, any discussion of family structure must necessarily start from the perspective of some individual. The inclusions and exclusions of the family system must be from some particular perspective. If that perspective is the legal status of a person for inheritance purposes, it is quite different from a perspective for purposes of establishing who are the members of a household.

A family then is to be construed as patterns of relatedness as they converge in a person. These patterns may be identical to those of another family member or they could be unique to this one person. Those relationships of the person that can be classified as family relationships will be delineated within the remainder of this chapter. The characteristics of family will be grouped under the familiar headings of structure, behavior, and evolution. For consistency, we will use the subtopics introduced in Chapter 1.

A. Structural Characteristics

As with any social system, *organization* is of prime concern. Family organization is distinguishable from other systems by its high level of relatedness. Since it is the smallest social and interpersonal system, there is an intensity of interdependence among its components.

The effectiveness of family organization is the extent to which its goals are fulfilled—the goals of its members and the goals of society. If societal goals are not fulfilled, the family may be dissolved by legal decree, as when children are removed or divorces granted. This action does not necessarily dissolve the family as an interacting system. Malcolm X clearly described the difference. After his family was dispersed by the court, "separated though we were, all of us maintained fairly close touch around Lansing—in school and out—whenever we could get together. Despite the artificially created separation and distance between us, we still remained very close in our feelings toward each other" (Malcolm X, 1966:22). Society, the family, and its members may all share familial goals of economic independence, intimacy, and affection but may be in conflict about the priorities to be assigned to each of these goals. These conflicts may occur when people find it necessary to leave familiar territory to find employment. A Kentuckian told this story to one of the authors:

> A man died and was being shown around Heaven by St. Peter. Off in one corner of Heaven they saw a group of people with suitcases. The man asked who these people were and St. Peter replied, "Oh, they're from Kentucky; they go home on weekends."

In the boom times of the 1970s the greatest "reverse migration" in American history took place as Appalachian coal mining revived and people returned home to work.

In order to achieve goals, the family must, through its organization, secure and conserve energy from both internal and external sources. The members of the family must contribute energy for the family system as well as import energy for their individual purposes. The following dialogue between mother and sons (about the husband-father), from the play, *Death of a Salesman*, illustrates this dependence of family upon energy from its members and from the environment.

> LINDA: No, a lot of people think he's lost his—balance. But you don't have to be very smart to know what his trouble is. The man is exhausted.

HAPPY: Sure!
LINDA: A small man can be just as exhausted as a great man. He works for a
company thirty-six years this March, opens up unheard-of territories to their trade-
mark, and now in his old age they take his salary away.
HAPPY: (Indignantly) I didn't know that, Mom.
LINDA: You never asked, my dear! Now that you get your spending money
someplace else you don't trouble your mind with him.
HAPPY: But I gave you money last—
LINDA: Christmas time, fifty dollars! To fix the water heater it cost ninety-seven
fifty! For five weeks he's been on straight commission, like a beginner, an un-
known!
BIFF: Those ungrateful bastards!
LINDA: Are they any worse than his sons? (A. Miller, 1955:56–57)

The *boundary* of a family is behavioral and is evidenced by the intensity and frequency of interaction among its components. The intensity
of sentiment interchanges is especially distinctive as compared to other
small groups. Popenoe states that in the sixteenth century, the boundary was "porous" in that "the family was thoroughly embedded in the
community. . . . The family had little normative structure apart from
that of the community, and the community's scrutiny of family members . . . was a powerful form of social control" (Popenoe, 1988:64). It
is within the interactional boundaries of the family that the member participates in a particularly *close network of feelings, both positive and negative,*
with a minimal sense of needing to put up a front. The common expression, "I feel at home," conveys something of this freedom to be oneself.
    This exchange between Martha and George from the play *Who's Afraid
of Virginia Woolf* illustrates closeness through negative feeling.

MARTHA: You've really screwed up, George
GEORGE: Oh, for God's sake, Martha!
MARTHA: I mean it . . . you really have.
GEORGE: You can sit there in that chair of yours, you can sit there with the gin
running out of your mouth, and you can humiliate me, you can tear me apart . . .
ALL NIGHT . . . and that's perfectly all right . . . , that's O.K. . . . .
MARTHA: YOU CAN STAND IT!
GEORGE: I CANNOT STAND IT!
MARTHA: YOU CAN STAND IT!! YOU MARRIED ME FOR IT!!
GEORGE: That is a desperately sick lie.
MARTHA: DON'T YOU KNOW IT, EVEN YET? (Albee, 1963:152–153)

Family boundaries change as members come and go. Extended kin,
close friends and neighbors, or foster children may be absorbed within
the boundary of a given family. Recent research on "remarried families," especially those with children and stepchildren, discovered the
existence of "boundary ambiguity" (Boss, 1987). Whether stepchildren
living outside the home are members of the family, and whether adolescents still function as members of the family after they leave home, for
example, are important questions for many families. The boundaries are

both physical and psychological, and it is particularly stressful when the two definitions do not coincide, for example, when someone is absent but the mother continues to view the person as present. Boundary ambiguity is found to be highly related to family stress and overall family dysfunction (Pasley and Ihinger-Tallman, 1989).

Even physical presence is not the measure of participation within family boundaries. A person may be related by birth or marriage and living in the same household, yet not be within family boundaries and not part of the interactional network, the bond that coheres. On the other hand, the family member in the hospital, away at school or military service, or incarcerated may well remain within the family boundary as just defined. In the case of families of servicemen who are MIAs (missing in action), the difficulty is particularly poignant. Again a quotation from Malcolm X is illustrative. Malcolm described his activities:

> I'm rarely at home more than half of any week; I have been away as much as five months. I never get a chance to take her anywhere, and I know she likes to be with her husband. She is used to my calling her from airports anywhere from Boston to San Francisco, or Miami to Seattle, or here lately, cabling her from Cairo, Accra, or the Holy City of Mecca. Once on the long-distance telephone, Betty told me in beautiful phrasing the way she thinks. She said, "You are present when you are away" (Malcolm X, 1966:233).

Maintenance of family boundary occurs on both sides of the boundary. The family frequently excludes nonmembers ("It's a family argument," "the family vacation"). Society supports family boundaries through assigning the family priority on occasions highly charged with sentiment such as weddings, funerals, and religious holidays. Cultures decree special occasions to reinforce family sentiment and interchange, such as Mother's Day and Father's Day. Business organizations permit employees leave for illness of immediate family members and for funerals of members of the extended family. Colleges and universities also recognize and support family boundaries of sentiment through allowing students to absent themselves for such family occasions. One recent book suggested that mid-term exams must be dangerous since there is such a high correlation between the date of the exam and the deaths of grandmothers. One student of our acquaintance mourned three grandmothers in the span of one semester!

As is true of all social systems, families require exchanges across boundaries. Monopolarization, referred to earlier in this chapter, expresses concern that the specialized nuclear family tends toward entropy because of insufficient sentiment exchanges with its environment.

Other concepts applicable to the family are *differentiation* and *specialization*. We have already alluded to the fact that the family has become a highly specialized cultural component uniquely responsible for meeting the security and sentiment needs of its members. The narrowing of family functions can be understood as a result of differentiation within modern society. Other institutions such as social welfare services that provide income maintenance, health care, emotional support, and day care have emerged to specialize in functions previously fulfilled by the extended family. In Minnesota,

> The Working Parent Resource Center in downtown St. Paul may be a sign of things to come. Established in 1984 . . . the center is a sort of one-stop shopping center for working parents.
> Videotapes, books and magazines can be checked out in the center's library; private consultation services are available for harried moms and dads; and parent discussion groups are held weekly, centering on topics like "Survi al Skills for Toddler Parents" and "Quick, Easy Suppers to Go."
> The center also sponsors classes on parenting styles, single parents, discipline and self-esteem, fathers, and living with preteens and teens, among others.
> The center's goal . . . is to help working parents feel less alone (*Star Tribune*, 1989:14S).

Within the family, differentiation and specialization are reflected in role allocations. So that the family can meet societal expectations and continue as an economic household, particular family members are breadwinners by mutual consent of the family members. Differential role expectations are commonly determined by age and sex, but these are uniquely refined in each family system. A particular family may reposit much of its unresolved or unacknowledged tensions in one family member, who then specializes as the "problem" family member. The concept of the family scapegoat is a case in point. Vogel and Bell elucidated the conditions that lead to a child becoming the family scapegoat:

> The parents are fraught with internal conflicts and ambivalence but each consciously expressed only one side of the ambivalence thus forming a set of overt polarization and mutual avoidance. A marriage cannot survive under these conditions so an appropriate object is selected to symbolize the conflicts and draw off the tension. The emotional disturbance of the child is simply the effect of internalizing the conflicting demands placed on the child by his [sic] parents. In the short run he receives rewards from his family when he accepts his special role. The scapegoating mechanism may be functional for the family group through enabling its continued existence but be dysfunctional for the child's development and his adaptation outside the family (Vogel and Bell, 1960:382–397).

Another aspect of family structure is its *territoriality*. Family territory has both a spatial and behavioral dimension. The concept of home territory is notably descriptive of family territory since the occupants have a profound sense of "place" and belongingness (Lyman and Scott, 1967). The family consolidates around, and finds its identity through, achieving and maintaining territory. Behavioral territory was earlier described in the discussion of boundary; it is the interactional territory of feeling-closeness. Physically, the family also occupies territory. The architect, the contractor, the city planner, the mail carrier, indeed the garbage collector, all exist as societally supported occupations to serve and maintain the family within its spatial territory. This territory is signified by the house or apartment number; it may be further marked by posts, fences, and hedges.

The family territory may encompass a village, town, or neighborhood. "In ancient imagery, the center of his territory is a man's 'house,' be it a home or a farm, a firm or a family, a dynasty or a church; and his 'city' marks the boundary of all the houses associated with his" (Erikson, 1969:176). Society requests and requires families to be territorially based, to be oriented in space. Society's primary means of establishing social identifications are the answers to the questions: "Name?" "Address?" Or, less formally, "Where are you from?" which actually means, "What was the place of your family of origin?"

The societal concern with family territoriality is clearly expressed in this quotation: "Show me a man who cares no more for one place than another, and I will show you in that same person one who loves nothing but himself. Beware those who are homeless by choice" (Southey, 1959:508). Similarly, groups of people who are not identified with a particular or specified "home territory" (e.g., Gypsies, Bedouins, migrant workers, or the homeless in cities) are viewed with suspicion by others.

B. Behavioral Aspects

Social control and *socialization* are characteristic functions of the family. The family is always a subsystem of its society and, as such, participates in the socialization processes of that society. It would be defensible to classify all socially defined dysfunctional families as failing to meet the requirements for socialization of its members. A central task of the family is to assure that its members are sufficiently acculturated to participate in the other societal subsystems that enable attainment of societal goals. For example, Project Headstart was instituted to supplement families that were not fulfilling this expectation as societally defined—to socialize the children and, if necessary, the parents as well.

Furthermore, the family is expected to control its members in order to prevent them from engaging in deviant behavior, which seriously interferes with attainment of the system's goals. Witness the recurring idea that parents should be accountable for the delinquent behavior of their children and legal efforts to enforce this parental responsibility.

Billingsley emphasized the fact that the responsibility for socialization is doubly difficult for many Black families. Despite the rise of a Black middle class and increasing integration economically, educationally, and socially, the Black family still "must teach its young members not only how to be human, but also how to be black in a white society" (Billingsley, 1968:28). While television's Huxtable family on "The Cosby Show" is successful and middle-class, its star, producer, and writer, Bill Cosby, regularly points out the special demands and constraints placed on Black families. In addition to the pressures that affect all families in America, the Black family must cope with three additional facts of life (Billingsley, 1968:28):

1. a distinctive historical development;
2. the American stratification system which relegates all Blacks to inferior, castelike status; and
3. the social class and economic systems that keep most Blacks in the lower socioeconomic classes.

No doubt the breadth of the socialization job allocated to the family has narrowed as some aspects have been assumed by other social institutions, particularly the school, but the primacy of family influence in personality development remains relatively intact.

Power in families is a topic that has received relatively little attention. Kranichfeld believes that the research has been misguided, concentrating on men's power derived from outside the family, rather than women's power derived from relationships within the family. Also, it has concentrated on power relations between men and women, neglecting women's power relative to other family members. Consistent with Carol Gilligan's theories of women's development, she says:

> In spite of all the mental, emotional, and physical hardships that women appear to have experienced simply by virtue of their membership in the female gender, they appear to be remarkably resilient and constructive in their approach to human relations. As a group, women continue to struggle for greater equality and justice, but as individuals *almost never do so by choosing to sever the bonds that connect them to other people*, from which they derive tremendous sustenance and reward (Kranichfeld, 1988:232–233).

She maintains that since men and women experience "separate social realities," they wield different types of power. If power is (as we define it later) the ability to achieve goals by affecting other systems' functioning, "women do not just change the behavior of others, they shape whole generations of families" (Kranichfeld, 1988:235); in her view, women's power derives (again consistent with Gilligan's views) from *caring* for others in the family, and maintaining deep emotional connections with them. "The message here seems to be that, when it comes to securing the kind of power that exists in the family realm, nothing—not superior physical strength, nor greater economic resources, nor culturally ascribed authority—can substitute for investment, attention, connection, and care" (Kranichfeld, 1988:239).

Communication is increasingly emphasized as both the keystone of family interaction and the key to understanding family dynamics. Every family's behavior is influenced by the style and effectiveness of its communication. Communication is here used to denote the transfer of meaningful symbols, vocal and gestural. It refers to the transfer of energy to accomplish system goals. The discussion of communication in Chapter 2 applies exactly to the family system.

A family can be seen to have a characteristic communication style. These characteristic patterns of interaction operate within the boundaries of the family and in interactions with external systems. Don Jackson emphasized that the "redundancy principle" operates in family life. "The family will interact in repetitious sequences in all areas of its life, though some areas may highlight these repetitions (or patterns) more quickly and systematically than do other areas" (Jackson, 1970:121). Brodey described the *family dance:* "Each family has its own particular game, its rules and regulations. It has its rules of status, its rules of power, its techniques of movement" (Brodey, 1977:41–42). Humberto Maturana employed the concept of *autopoiesis* (meaning self-creation or self-production) to suggest that a family, as any other system, strives to continue its existence; its characteristic processes serve to so maintain itself. Change must also contribute to survival of a system's identity (Maturana and Varela, 1980; see also Adams, 1988:61–64). An individual family then has a unique combination of communication patterns that strongly influence the behavior of its members. Communication practices are crucial to any understanding of family because of the importance and intensity of feeling exchange.

Communication in the family is extremely complex and subtle because of the number of functions served by the family. One energy exchange can convey a number of meanings, not all of them congruent. An example is a parent's directive to a child to do what the teacher says. Included in this could be several messages:

1. You *ought* to obey authority (to meet societal expectations).
2. But you *ought not* to be required to submit to unjust orders (to meet the child's developmental needs).
3. Nevertheless, do what the teacher tells you (to avoid conflict with the environment).
4. Keep out of trouble (and avoid conflict between parent and teacher, that is, between family system and environment).
5. Because if you don't you'll get it from me (meet parents' needs in order to satisfy the child's need for security).

The child is expected to understand and comply with all these messages.

Adaptation is an essential family function. Family is a system of accommodation to social change. Because the family has consistently had the capacity to change its structure and function to adapt to marked changes in its environment, it has survived wars, industrial and technological revolutions, and traumatic disruptions in social conditions that made traditional patterns of coping obsolete. The family calls upon the energies of its components and exchanges energies with its significant environmental systems. The "utilitarianistic" family of Hong Kong is adaptive to its environment (Lau, 1978). It expands to include nonrelatives, or distantly related relatives, as a means of securing external energy (money). These members secure jobs or create businesses, perhaps a new hawker's stand in the streets, or a fish ball stand. The family may send a child to university overseas to assure a means of emigration should Hong Kong experience economic or political difficulties. If Hong Kong's economy falters, these "expanded" or "augmented" families will share the risk, by contracting into less physical space and living on less income.

Another necessary adaptive mode of the family is its assimilation of exterior stress as experienced by its members. Although other social institutions such as religious and fraternal organizations also fulfill the function, the family is expected to be the primary system wherein one can relax (unwind), cast off externally adaptable role behaviors, and "be yourself," or if a person cannot allow this to happen, substitutes must be found. In some cultures, perhaps the coffeehouse, café, or the geisha perform this function for men; it is not clear how this function is performed for women in these societies. Perhaps sensitivity and support groups (as in the Working Parents Resource Center, cited earlier) are replacements for a defunct family function.

A family is considered maladaptive when it cannot adapt to the changing demands placed upon it by its environment and its members. If it is too unchanging (morphostasis) and devotes an undue proportion of its available energies to maintenance of existing structures, it will not be able to cope with external requirements and the individual development of its members. In essence, It maintains its previous functions and is thus dysfunctional. If, on the other hand, it is in a constantly unstable state of transition, it does not furnish the degree of stability its members require for repair of insults to their egos and for the chance to merely be oneself in an atmosphere of feeling-closeness. This leads to the final system aspects of the family.

C. Evolutionary Aspects

Steady state is characteristic of the family system, which needs to be simultaneously changing and remaining the same. The family exists through its life cycle meeting ever-changing requirements from its members and from society. The well-adapted marital pair, for example, must modify its mode of functioning with the advent of the first child. A family may operate to its satisfaction and to that of society while the offspring are dependent, but run aground when the children need emancipation from their family of orientation.

The steady state of a family is maintained in various ways. James Framo described a family in therapy:

> Family therapy observations have revealed how the symptoms of one member often serve useful and necessary functions for the others, how the underlying system reciprocity is revealed by symptoms appearing in a previously asymptomatic member when the symptomatic one improves, and how a marriage may rupture when the symptoms which had been built into the relationship are no longer present (Sager and Kaplan, 1972:288–289).

All that was said about steady state in Chapter 2 applies to the family. Often the family in crisis is in a situation of disruptive transition from one form of steady state to another. At such times, a family may be more open to importing energies, more amenable to interventive efforts. Erikson's definition of crisis applies to families as well as to individuals (see Chapter 8, I, A, "The Idea of Crisis").

A family tends to function so as to eliminate pain rather than change to foster well-being of itself and its members (Friedman, 1971). It is not easy to achieve a sense of family as a system—as an entity in its own right, more than the sum of its members. Our Western cultural emphasis on the individual as the most significant entity makes it difficult to conceive of the family as other than molder, background, or environment. Paradoxically, at the same time we categorize families as good or bad as measured by the social performance of their members. This leads to the pernicious doctrine that all problematic or antisocial behavior is rooted in the family in a cause and effect relationship. Of course, families may to some degree be responsible, but as society blames its families, it denies society's part in personal and social dysfunction. In the past, the "broken home" was especially maligned. This process is similar to family scapegoating, in which a family member is loaded with the responsibility for family pain and dysfunction. Thus is the family both scapegoating and scapegoated.

Human services professions are coming to appreciate the special systemic qualities of family. Tolstoy's observation that all happy families resemble each other and each unhappy family is unhappy in its own way suggests that the resemblance may be more apparent than real. Perhaps each happy family, too, is happy in its own way. Each family is like others in having rules, games (sequences of events governed by rules), secrets, and ghosts. Each family is unique in that its rules, games, secrets, and ghosts are its own.

Often, work with families is best construed as aiding a family to discover what its own unique patterns are and how they operate.

SUMMARY

The family is a critical human system. It serves unique, yet constantly changing, purposes for its subsystems (family members and combinations of family members) and suprasystems (society and parts of society).

We suggest that the family is best defined from the viewpoint of the person within it. The definition should include those relationships that are "family" to that person, i.e., a person's family is those with whom the person interacts and performs the family functions within the given society. In many crucial ways, the family is the principal intersection between the culture and the persons within the culture, the point of most interaction and change. While discrete aspects of the family may each be better explained by one of the family theories we have examined, a systems view best explains the changes the family undergoes and the relationships that are cause and effect of those changes.

In recent years, family issues have largely been perceived as part of women's issues, and this rethinking and redefinition has enabled the broadening of marital and parental role expectations for both women and men. Family issues have also entered more fully into the political arena, making it possible for politicians to insert themselves and their beliefs into family concerns (especially family planning and abortion). Legislating family matters diminishes tolerance for pluralism of family forms and functions. The fiasco of the 1979-1980 White House Conference on Families illustrates the hazards of politicizing the family. As Steiner observed, "diversity of family styles and traditionalism in family style peacefully coexist only as long as neither one gains actual or symbolic advantage over the other. Planning for a White House Conference ruptured the peace between the two" (Steiner, 1981:45).

What does the future hold for families in the United States? Popenoe waves danger flags:

> One of the key ingredients of a strong family is the presence of a rich subculture—a set of norms, symbols, humor and even language that is special to that particular group. . . . Over the course of life the subculture yields what has been called a "community of memory," a special cultural heritage that family members carry with them until death. . . . With the weakening of the family unit, the disinvestment in family life, this subcultural richness is disappearing. For those who have it, the tie to a rich family subculture is one of the most meaningful things in life. For those who do not, the commercially based cultures of mass societies serve as debased substitutes (Popenoe, 1988,312–313).

Since families are interdependent parts of the fabric of society, they will continue to influence and be influenced by changes in other social institutions. We anticipate families will continue to have their unique position at the point where persons and culture meet; but the fate of the family is not assured.

SUGGESTED READINGS

Ackerman, Nathan W.
1958 *The Psychodynamics of Family Living: Diagnosis and Treatment of Family Relationships*. New York: Basic Books.
A classic, readable, psychoanalytic approach to family diagnoses and treatment. Possibly the first attempt to shift focus from the individual to the family.

Berger, Brigitte, and Peter L. Berger.
1983 *The War Over the Family: Capturing the Middle Ground*. Garden City, NY: Doubleday.
A provocative assessment of the range of family ideology. The authors' own position is that the bourgeois family is the necessary social context for the emergence of the autonomous individual required for political democracy.

Billingsley, Andrew.
1968 *Black Families in White America*. Englewood Cliffs, NJ: New York: Simon and Shuster.
A systems approach to the family that has been used as the small-map text for this chapter. Billingsley drew on experience of Blacks to supplement and revise sociological analyses of the family.

Brodey, Warren M.
1977 *Family Dance: Building Positive Relationships through Family Therapy*. Garden City NY: Anchor Books.
A brief, readable explication of a pragmatic approach to working with families. Excellent incorporation of nonverbal material.

Carter, Betty, and Monica McGoldrick.
1989. *The Changing Family Life Cycle*. Boston: Allyn and Bacon. Also: Carter, E. A., and Monica McGoldrick. 1988. Revised edition. *The Family Life Cycle*. New York: Gardner.
Together, these two books are definitive regarding trends in family life cycle theory. Excellent resources.

Elliot, Faith Robertson.
1986 *The Family: Change or Continuity*. London: Macmillan.
Compact, straightforward study which suggests reality is more complex than Parsons', Marxian, and feminist theories suggest; family is "outcome of the complex interplay of contradictory pressures."

Jackson, Don.
1970 "The Study of the Family." In *Family Process*, Nathan Ackerman, New York: Basic Books.
An approach to understanding the family, drawing heavily on social systems concepts.

Pharand, Gisèle R., Maria L. Sudermann, and Ray DeV. Peters.
    1988 "Comprehensive Assessment of Family Functioning." In *Social Learning and Systems* edited by Ray DeV. Peters and Robert J. McMahon, *Approaches to Marriage and the Family*. New York: Brunner/Mazel.
    Comprehensive overview of research methods and instruments.
Popenoe, David.
    1988 *Disturbing the Nest: Family Change and Decline in Modern Societies*. New York: Aldine De Gruyter.
    An excellent comparison of families in the United States, Sweden, Switzerland, and New Zealand, which raises disturbing questions about the future of families in advanced industrial societies, as the efficacy of mediating systems such as family is reduced.
Sennett, Richard.
    1974 *Families Against the City*. New York: Vintage Books.
    A former student of Erik Erikson, Sennett studied the relationship of family and community in the microcosm of a Chicago suburb. This history revealed the intimate relationship in a vivid and detailed way.
Thorne, Barrie, and Marilyn Yalom, eds.
    1982 *Rethinking the Family*. New York: Longman.
    A feminist analysis of the family.
Watzlawick, Paul, Janet Helmick Beavin, and Don D. Jackson.
    1967 *Pragmatics of Human Communication: A Study of Interactional Patterns, Pathologies, and Paradoxes*. New York: Norton.
    An excellent text dealing with systemic communication in a family context. The analysis of communication patterning in the play "Who's Afraid of Virginia Woolf?" is especially interesting.

LITERARY SOURCES

Anderson, Robert Woodruff.
    1968 *I Never Sang for My Father*. New York: Random House.
    Portrays a relatively closed family system and the effects such closure has on the children as they deal with becoming adults. The film version, starring Gene Hackman, is excellent.
Erdrich, Louise.
    1985 *Love Medicine*. Toronto, New York: Bantam Books.
    Sensitively written novel of a Sioux extended family by a Sioux author. The book beautifully illustrates systems aspects of families and tribe, which become apparent as layers of meaning and family history are laid one on top of another.
Guest, Judith.
    1976 *Ordinary People*. New York: Viking.
    A family coping with the aftermath of tragedy. Also available as a movie, directed by Robert Redford.
Olsen, Tillie.
    1976 *Tell Me a Riddle*. New York: Dell/ Laurel Edition.

A small collection of short stories commenting with sensitivity and insight on common human experiences within a context of culture and family.

Pa Chin.

1972 *Family*. Garden City NY: Anchor.

The first novel in the trilogy *Turbulent Stream*, probably China's best known novel previous to the 1949 revolution. Based on the author's own experience, it describes a traditional Chinese family encountering modernization during and after the revolution of 1911.

Zindel, Paul.

1970 *The Effect of Gamma Rays on Man-in-the-Moon Marigolds*. New York: Harper and Row.

A Pulitzer prize–winning play about the daily tribulations of a family with complex rules, games and ghosts. The film version is especially well presented.

FILMS AND VIDEOS

Desert Bloom. (1986)

The "bloom" refers to an adolescent girl coping with her abusive stepfather in 1950s Las Vegas, with atomic bomb tests as symbolic background. Family turmoil and extended family are well described.

Dim Sum: A Little Bit of Heart. (1985)

Tension between Chinese-American mother and daughter in San Francisco. Humor, warmth, and cultural change beautifully portrayed.

Dominick and Eugene. (1988)

Two brothers, one "slow," are a family. Tom Hulce, of "Amadeus," works on a sanitation truck to support his brother in medical school. Fine acting, sensitively written.

Fanny and Alexander. (1983)

Perhaps Ingmar Bergman's happiest film, of his extended family in Uppsala, Sweden, in 1907. In Swedish, with English subtitles.

The Great Santini. (1979)

Robert Duvall is superb as an Air Force pilot and his family who "hang together" despite frequent moves and his dictatorial behavior. Told from the viewpoint of the adolescent son who frequently conflicts with the father, but learns family solidarity from him.

Homecomin'. (1980)

This film is about a separated African-American family, and the effects on family members. The father grapples with his responsibilities to his son. Avoids stereotypes.

I Know Why the Caged Bird Sings. (1979; made for television)

Based on Maya Angelou's biography of the same title, this is a story of survival, child abuse, and the strength of family ties among members of an African-American family.

I Never Sang for My Father. (1970)
   Gene Hackman as a 40-year old still trying to play son to Melvyn Douglas, a tyrannical father. Profoundly moving.
Interiors. (1978)
   Woody Allen's bleak view of a conflictual family, modeled after Ingmar Bergman's films. Interesting view of family dysfunction.
"Marrying." (1986)
   This episode of the series, *Heart of the Dragon,* on contemporary China, pictures the melding of traditional and modern wedding styles in a rural village. Excellent depiction of an actual extended family.
Ordinary People. (1980)
   As noted above, based on Judith Guest's novel. Excellent acting, with direction by Robert Redford. Family's inability to cope with tragedy.
The Schuster/Isaacson Family. (1979)
   A sixteen-minute documentary on a merged lesbian family. Includes interviews with the children. Short, but enough basis for discussion of values and nature of "family."
Sounder. (1972)
   An African-American sharecropper and his family. The father is sent to jail and the mother must raise the children. A moving film, with excellent acting by Cicely Tyson and Paul Winfield as the parents.
The Stone Boy. (1984)
   Robert Duvall is the unforgiving father of a boy who accidentally shot his brother and loses touch with reality. Emotionally powerful.
Too Little, Too Late. (1987)
   Families and friends of AIDS patients are profiled and interviewed. Their pain and isolation are conveyed by a mother whose son died of AIDS, and who is active in AIDS hospice programs.
The Vanishing Family—Crisis in Black America. (1986)
   This video documentary examines the disintegrating Black family structure, and the difficulties in forming stable relationships among Black teenagers.

The Person

You can't kiss a system.
Fred Duhl

I. THEORETICAL APPROACHES

This chapter deals with the individual person as a human system and introduces concepts of human growth and development that are congruent with the central themes of this book. Some theorists have questioned the applicability of social systems concepts to the person. We subscribe to the premise that the individual human's existence is essentially a socially defined one. Without the individual, there would be no society and without the society there would be no individual. The one determines the other. Social systems concepts explain the interactive phenomena.

Our approach to the person as a human system is developmental and cyclical, and we draw from the works of a wide range of theorists, especially Erik H. Erikson and Jean Piaget. Their formulations are particularly congruent with our holonistic approach.

A. Psychosocial Approach to Human Behavior

The psychosocial view of human behavior is introduced first since this is the major theme of the content about the life cycle. From a systems viewpoint, the individual person is a human system who is both cause and effect of social systems. As the cycle of life unfolds, persons broaden their interaction into systems of ever larger magnitude. Figure

16 shows two of the many possible diagrams of this direction. In either diagram, the person's growth and development is in a pattern of expansion, a movement outward. Pragmatically, we employ the life cycle framework of Erikson to organize and describe elements of that growth process—at least in Western culture, where the emphasis is on the individual person.

In examining individual growth and development within a systems context, it is important to make connections between developmental theories and societal provisions, i.e., social programs and institutions. The interaction among research findings, theories, and societal determinants shapes the social provisions that will be made available.

1. Erikson.   Erik H. Erikson was born of Danish parents in Frankfurt, Germany, in 1902. He attended the humanistic gymnasium and began to prepare himself for a career as an artist. As an artist–tutor in Vienna, he became acquainted with persons in the emerging Psychoanalytic Institute. He acquired psychoanalytic training, working most closely with Dorothy Burlingham and Anna Freud. Interestingly, he also earned a certificate from the Maria Montessori School and was one of the few men at that time who held membership in the Montessori Academy. In 1933, he emigrated to the United States, where he still lives (Coles, 1970; Maier, 1988;72ff.).

Erickson's major work has been to create and extend a conceptual framework for the complete life cycle of humans. His scheme was originally set forth in *Childhood and Society* (1950, 1963, 1985). Major revisions, refinements, and expansions were published in *Insight and Responsibility* (1964), *Identity: Youth and Crisis* (1968), *Life History and the Historical Moment* (1975) and *A Way of Looking at Things* (1987; a selection of earlier papers). He also pioneered in the field of psychohistorical biography with two monumental works, *Young Man Luther* (1958) and *Gandhi's Truth* (1969). He was awarded the Pulitzer prize for his work on Gandhi. In recent years, Erikson has written on the latter period of life (Erikson, 1982; Erikson, Erikson, and Kivnick, 1986).

Erikson's eight ages of the human life cycle are used as the organizing theme for this chapter for two reasons. First, his seems to be the only extant theory of human development that encompasses the complete life span. Second, his psychosocial approach to human development is particularly in accord with the human services, with their simultaneous attention to the individual and the environment. A few of the key ideas of the Eriksonian formulation of the life cycle are enumerated to introduce his thinking.

a. Erikson's view of the life cycle.   This is based on the epigenetic principle. *Epigenesis* (epi—"upon," 'genesis'—"emergence") means that one developmental stage occurs on top of, and in relation to, another in

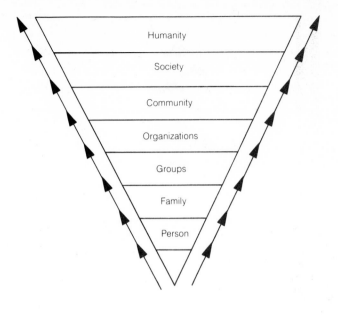

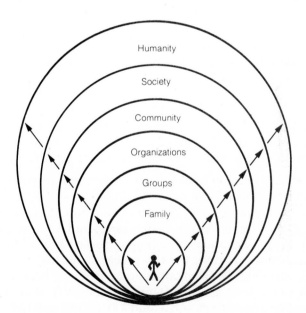

Figure 16.   Diagrams of a person's interactions with systems of increasing scale.

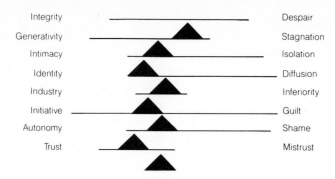

Integrity		Despair
Generativity		Stagnation
Intimacy		Isolation
Identity		Diffusion
Industry		Inferiority
Initiative		Guilt
Autonomy		Shame
Trust		Mistrust

Figure 17.   Stages of life cycle according to Erikson.

space and time (Evans, 1967:21–22). Since this is a hierarchy of stages, not a simple sequence, the potentials for growth and development are all present in the human organism. The parts arise out of the whole, each component having a special time for ascendancy, until all the processes have run their course and have developed into a functioning whole. Thus the human personality is seen as an evolving system comprising potential matrices, which arise according to some sort of ground plan. Correlated with this is the interdependence of the emergent matrices; the development of a subsequent matrix is somewhat dependent upon that which has gone before. Each alters the previously achieved balances. The stages are not discrete, nor are they simply the result of an additive process.

The stages may be pictured simplistically as a set of teeterboards balanced upon each other (see Figure 17). Each level (or stage) depends upon the balance achieved in the previous stage, and an adjustment of any level involves an adjustment of all the others. The point at which each level is balanced is the ratio of polar qualities accompanying each stage.

b. Erikson's life cycle formulation.   This is based in human genetic energy but is totally dependent on social experiences. Three principles of organization and process are: (1) *physical:* constitutional or somatic organization; (2) *ego:* the self as organizing force, and (3) *social:* organizing responsive to the rules and expectations of society and culture. In other words, the somatic process, the ego process, and the societal process equal the human life. The similarities and differences between this triad and the Freudian triad are important. Someone commented that Erikson's is an ego psychology and Freud's is an id psychology. Erikson said, "A human being, thus, is at all times an organism, an ego and a member of society and is involved in all three processes of organization" (Erikson, 1963:36). In our view, of course, these are three systems levels.

Within Erikson's scheme, the unfolding of the human system is seen as a combination of maturation, socialization, and education. The eight stages of the life cycle represent a synthesis of developmental (maturation) and social (learning) tasks. *Maturation* is the predictable course of growth for all members of a species, based upon a shared structure. *Learning* is unpredictable growth, new behavior based upon the individual experience of the organism. The distinction is similar to that between *genotype*, a group of organisms with common heredity, and *phenotype*, the hereditary characteristics that are evident through the organism's interaction with its environment. Growth, then, derives from the constant interaction of maturation and learning. The organism's *readiness* is determined by maturational considerations, while its *learning* is a function of social experiences.

c. The idea of crisis. This is central to Erikson's theory. His use of this term is quite similar to the idea of crisis in *crisis intervention* and refers to a time of necessary change. The crises during growth and development, as Erikson uses the term, connote a heightened potential for development (or change) accompanied by greater vulnerability. Crisis is not necessarily a negative state of affairs but rather an unavoidable occasion requiring some type of coping. This meaning of crisis has existed since antiquity. Hippocrates described crisis as an occasion of imbalance that required the "constitution" of the person to respond (i.e., cope) (Jones, 1923:li–lv).

In Erikson's view, the crises occur at their proper time out of the interaction of the organism's maturation and society's expectations. The outcome (not *resolution,* necessarily) is dependent upon the personality resources the individual has accrued up to that point *and* the opportunities and resources the person has available in the social situation.

Erikson has written extensively and thoroughly on two of the eight crises of development—*basic trust vs. basic mistrust* and *identity vs. diffusion.* Attention to these particular periods of child development is not unique to Erikson, since infancy and adolescence have attracted the attention of much of child development research. His theories about the first critical task of life, trust vs mistrust, are compatible with the work of René Spitz (1965) in his studies of the establishment of an initial object relationship. Erikson's formulation is also consistent with the extensive literature on bonding, maternal deprivation, and even with the work on imprinting. His ideas about adolescence are compatible with a host of theorists including Friedenberg (1962), Keniston (1970), and Goodman (1960). In fact, one gets the impression that infancy and adolescence are indeed the two most critical phases of personality development.

The critical developmental tasks that Erikson enumerated and described are expressed as bipolarities. This formulation is consistent with general systems theory that the dynamism of life derives from the fact of negative and positive charges with tension and, therefore, movement existing between them. It is most important to bear in mind that these bipolarities are not achievement scales to serve as measurable criteria of growth and development. One does not achieve *complete* trust and then move on to the next plateau, autonomy. The outcome of each of the developmental crises is a relative mix of the polar qualities, and the developing person must cope with each subsequent task at its proper time as dictated by maturation and social expectations. In one sense, these critical task of development are present at all times in each person's life and are directly related to one another.

Figure 18 illustrates the interrelatedness of the various crises. This figure focuses on the crisis of adolescence, identity versus identity diffusion, and illustrates how each of the earlier crises contributes to the readiness to cope with this one and how it in turn influences the subsequent crises. Theoretically, it should be possible to take any of the crises represented on the diagonal and fill in the related boxes to show the relationship of that crisis to the preceding and the following steps.

Erikson's worksheet (Figure 19) illustrates his eight stages of the life cycle on five dimensions. The second dimension (B, radius of significant relations) indicates the progression of interrelationships from the dyad of the infant and nurturing persons through the ever-expanding hierarchy of social systems. The eighth stage includes all of humanity. Columns C, D, and E concern social order, psychosocial modalities, and psychosexual stages, and indicate the relatedness of these dimensions.

Erikson's life cycle scheme can validly be described as a systems viewpoint based in the "natural" epigenetic principle. As the individual's life cycle unfolds, it has the maturational potential and the social necessity to be involved in ever-wider social systems and ever-changing social conditions. To fulfill their functional destiny, persons must of necessity be engaged in transactions with these other social systems.

In summary, then, Erikson's eight ages of the human life cycle represent the necessary occasions for the individual to unite biological, psychological, and social forces. He stresses the adaptive and creative power of the person and respects each individual's unique capacity to forge her/his own way of life. His faith in human social creativity is reflected in his optimistic comment, "There is little that cannot be remedied later, there is much that can be prevented from happening at all" (Erikson, 1950:164).

B. Cognitive Theory

1. Piaget.   Phillips begins his book on Piaget by saying,

I hope that you will take from all this a conception of the human brain as a vastly complicated system for the storage and retrieval of information; a system that becomes capable of increasingly complex operations; a system that changes in ways

Figure 18. The adolescent crisis, "Identity vs. identity diffusion."

	1.	2.	3.	4.	5.	6.	7.	8.
I. Infancy	Trust vs. mistrust				Unipolarity vs. prema- ture self- differentiation			
II. Early childhood		Autonomy vs. shame, doubt			Bipolarity vs. autism			
III. Play age			Initiative vs. guilt		Play identifi- cation vs. (oedipal) fantasy identities			
IV. School age				Industry vs. inferiority	Work identi- fication vs. identity foreclosure			
V. Adolescence	Time per- spective vs. time diffusion	Self-certainty vs. identity conscious- ness	Role experi- mentation vs. negative identity	Anticipation of achieve- ment vs. work paralysis	Identity vs. identity diffusion	Sexual identity vs. bisexual diffusion	Leadership polariza- tion vs. au- thority dif- fusion	Ideological polariza- tion vs. dif- fusion of ideals
VI. Young adult					Solidarity vs. social isolation	Intimacy vs. isolation		
VII. Adulthood							Generativity vs. self- absorption	
VIII. Mature age								Integrity vs. disgust, despair

Source: Reprinted with permission from Erik H. Erikson, "Identity and the Life Cycle: Selected Papers," *Psychological Issues* (Monograph). New York: International Universities Press, 1959, Volume 1, p. 120.

Figure 19. Erikson's worksheet.

	A Psychosocial crises	B Radius of significant relations	C Related elements of social order	D Psychosocial modalities	E Psychosexual stages
I.	Trust vs. mistrust	Maternal person	Cosmic order	To get To give in return	Oral–respiratory, sensory–kinesthetic (incorporative modes)
II.	Autonomy vs. shame, doubt	Parental persons	"Law and order"	To hold (on) To let (go)	anal–urethral, muscular (retentive–eliminative)
III.	Initiative vs. guilt	Basic family	Ideal prototypes	To make (= going after) To "make line" (= playing)	Infantile–genital, locomotor (intrusive, inclusive)
IV.	Industry vs. inferiority	"Neighborhood," school	Technological elements	To make things (= completing) To make things together	"Latency"
V.	Identity and repudiation vs. identity diffusion	Peer groups and outgroups; models of leadership	Ideological perspectives	To be oneself (or not to be) To share being oneself	Puberty
VI.	Intimacy and solidarity vs. isolation	Partners in friendship, sex, competition, cooperation	Patterns of cooperation and competition	To lose and find oneself in another	Genitality
VII.	Generativity vs. self-absorption	Divided labor and shared household	Currents of education and tradition	To make be To take care of	
VIII.	Integrity vs. despair	"Mankind" "My kind"	Wisdom	To be, through having been To face not being	

Source: Reprinted with permission from Erik H. Erikson, "Identity and the Life Cycle: Selected Papers," *Psychological Issues* (Monograph). New York: International Universities Press, 1959, Volume 1, p. 164.

that are at least to some degree similar to the constructions that Piaget has given us (Phillips, 1969:xii).

From this suggestion that Piaget was a systems theorist of sorts, we can advance to Maier's statement that

> Piaget believes in universal order and suggests a single unity of all things biological, social, pyschological, and ideational in living as well as nonliving systems. For him, as a biological scientist, "all living forms grow and develop in coherent, logical patterns." . . . All science is interrelated, and a theorem established in one branch of science is directly relevant to the laws and principles of other branches. Altogether, Piaget insists upon cosmic unity (Maier, 1988:19).

Maier goes on to describe how Piaget relates parts to wholes within systems.

Piaget was a systems theorist whose area of concentration was cognitive development. Cognitive theory concentrates on the process of knowing and learning. Much of what has been done in this field can be traced to Piaget and his collaborators. Piaget was born in Switzerland in 1896, and died there in 1980. A precocious child, he published his first scientific paper at the age of 10 and was offered a museum directorship (which he declined). His early interest was in biology, but this broadened to philosophy and psychology during his training at the University of Neuchatel. He sought to combine these three fields in a "psychological and biological epistemology," or theory of knowledge. Piaget only slowly gained a reputation in the United States because he did not fit neatly into any of the established disciplines. Psychology reluctantly acknowledged him, and philosophy hardly recognized his work. Oddly enough, and for reasons we mention later, his greatest impact was on educational theory and practice.

> Piaget has said some pretty important things about children, and anyone who says important things about children ultimately must be important to educators. Teaching is the manipulation of the student's environment in such a way that his [sic] activities will contribute to his development. . . . It should be obvious. . . . that the effect of a given environment on a child is as much as function of the child as of the environment. If a teacher knows that, his behavior will be affected by his conception of what students are like. Indeed, his very definition of teaching will be so determined. Mine was (Phillips, 1969:107–108).

Piaget's emphasis on first-hand involvement, experience, and grappling with problems appropriate to the child's intellectual development was consistent with the view of John Dewey, whose influence on American education has been profound. Phillips said of him and his collaborators:

> The publications of the Geneva school constitute by far the largest repository of knowledge about the cognitive development of children that is available anywhere; students of psychology should be familiar with Piaget's theory even if it turns out

to be basically wrong, because it will undoubtedly serve as a base for many future studies of children's thinking (Phillips, 1969:11).

Piaget's research methods were criticized because they were not always orthodox. He used psychoanalytic and qualitative research interviewing, exploring children's responses, especially their mistakes, to discern the rules by which they made them. Piaget questioned the children while they were doing various tasks and while not doing them and also, on occasion, observed in silence. In his career, he invented over 50 new research techniques. Here is one example: The child was presented with a group of coins and a bunch of flowers. The child was then asked how many flowers could be purchased if each flower cost one coin.

> Gui (four years, four months) put 5 flowers opposite 6 pennies, then made a one-for-one exchange of 6 flowers (taking the extra flower from the reserve supply). The pennies were in a row and the flowers bunched together: "What have we done?— *We've exchanged them.*—Is there the same number of flowers and pennies?—*No.*— Are there more on one side?—*Yes.*—Where?—*There* (pennies). (The exchange was again made, but this time the pennies were put in a pile and the flowers in a row.) Is there the same number of flowers and pennies?—*No.*—Where are there more?— *Here* (flowers).—And here (pennies)—*Less* (Phillips, 1969:5).

This exchange illustrates the flexible interview style and searching for concepts in the child's thinking that was typical of Piaget's methods. In this instance, it appeared to the child that if the objects were spread out there were more of them than if they were bunched up. indicating that the concept of transferability of numbers from one set of objects to another was beyond the knowledge of this four and one-half-year-old child. Piaget also took the "unscholarly" approach of studying his own children and performing small experiments to test their development.

The topics of Piaget's major work include "the construction of reality," "judgment and reason," "language and thought," "logic and psychology," "moral judgment," "the origin of intelligence," and "the psychology of intelligence." His major work is *Genetic Epistemology* (1970).

Piaget is regarded by some theorists as being equal to Freud in his eventual impact on personality theory. He dealt in concrete detail with the major problems of logic, thought, and philosophy that have hindered our understanding of humans in this century. The implications of Piaget's work are important for the human services. He stressed invention and creativity and the ability of the person to grow rather than remain handicapped by past deficiencies or conflicts. His view of teaching was that "every time you teach a child something you keep him from reinventing it" (Phillips, 1969:120).

> The principal goal of education . . . is to create (persons) who are capable of doing new things . . . who are creative, inventive and discoverers. The second goal of

education is to form minds which can be critical, can verify, and not accept anything they are offered . . . we need pupils who are active, who learn early to find out by themselves, partly by their own spontaneous activity and partly through materials we set up for them; who learn early to tell what is verifiable and what is simply the first idea to come to them (Elkind, 1968:80).

The basic ideas of Piaget are relatively easy to understand from a systems viewpoint.

a. Equilibrium. In Piaget's view, equilibrium is a steady state of the cognitive processes. Specifically, he regards equilibrium as a balance between the person and the environment in which the person's knowledge adequately explains what is experienced. Equilibrium as Piaget viewed it may be defined as a state of active compatibility between the needs of the person and the demands and supplies from the environment. That is, there is feedback that confirms and continues to reinforce the person's developing capacity to understand and master the environment. The similarity to Erikson here is obvious.

b. Intelligence. As a biologist, Piaget defined intelligence as a form of biological activity. Intelligence arises from the biological makeup and is always a part of the individual as a biological being. Its function is the same as that of other system processes: to preserve the organism. According to Piaget, intelligence is both the *activity* of coping and the *end state* of "compatibility" of the organism and its environment. Intelligence, by this definition, is the maximum potential of the adaptive capacities; it is never fully realized.

c. Schemas. The structural units that lie at the heart of Piaget's system are *schemata or schemas* (both are plural forms, but we prefer the latter). Schemas function as mediating processes, forming a kind of framework onto which data can, indeed must, fit. But the framework continually changes its shape, the better to accommodate to the new data. Intelligence has a structure and this structure is stable and predictable. It is systematic and orderly. At any particular time it maintains an equilibrium that changes—that is, maintains a steady state.

Since Piaget believed that thought begins as action, he said that thought structures are patterns of internalized actions, ranging from the most elementary reflex pattern to profound philosophical thought. Schemas are organized action sequences and behavior patterns. Schemas arise by association. The reflexes become associated with other experience, and such isolated behaviors as sucking, grasping, looking and hearing become larger and more comprehensive. For example, looking and sucking are coordinated into seeing–grasping–sucking the bottle simultaneously. Progressive refinements of schemas allow the child to see the bottle, hold it, turn it around, tilt it, lay it down, pick it up again, see that it is empty, cry, and so forth.

The later, larger schemas are more highly developed. Eventually the child will be able to think of these operations instead of really perform them—that is, to carry on the action internally, think it through, correct it mentally, and then try it, all without picking up the bottle. Piaget said that thought is precisely such actions and schemas, refined and modified endlessly by intelligence. He carried this a step further by stressing that reality as we know it can only be this structure of associated and coordinated experiences. In other words, reality is structured by the schemas we have built up. Our schemas include time and space and are the frame for our understanding. We are bound by these frameworks except when dreaming or under the influence of drugs or hallucinating, when our usual schemas are loosened and other associations occur. Here the relation to Freudian "associations" seems very close.

There are two fundamental characteristics of schemas, *organization* and *adaptation*. Every act is organized and the dynamic aspect of organization is adaptation" (Phillips, 1969:7). These are the same in all biological processes and are consistent with systems ideas.

Adaptation takes two forms: *assimilation* and *accommodation*. The person attempts to fit new experience into the old schemas, to accept it as similar to previous experience. This is assimilation. Accommodation refers to the person's modification of old schemas to accept the new experience. These are similar, then, to what Buckley called *morphostasis* and *morphogenesis* (see Chapter 1 and glossary), the maintenance or change of a system's structure in order to achieve a new steady state after the input of new energy. These two tendencies, like other polarities, are never mutually exclusive; there is always some balance of the two.

> Piaget's view of the structure of intelligence is quite consistent with the systems view. Just as Freud's concepts of id, ego, and superego came from classical mechanical physics, so Piaget's concept of schema comes from Einstein's theory of relativity and is compatible with Whitehead's and Dewey's philosophies. Piaget specifically refers to physics as being analogous to his own ideas, and many of his experiments deal with children's understanding of such physics concepts as velocity, time, and distance. Piaget has explicitly acknowledged a similarity between his own theories and those of Bertalanffy, the foremost general systems theorist (Koestler and Smythies, 1971:65).

2. The Development of Moral Judgment.   Lawrence Kohlberg, a psychologist, applied Piaget's theory to the development of moral judgments in children and adults. Piaget's studies of this aspect of human development date from the 1920s; Kohlberg's from the late 1950s. Kohlberg's methodology was administration of verbal and written situations that ask children or adults to state what is "right" in each situation. For example, in the "Heinz" case, Heinz's wife is dying and the pharmacist has the rare medicine to cure her but will sell it only at an exorbitant price, which Heinz cannot afford. The respondent must decide what is "right," and why. Should Heinz steal the medicine? If not, why not? If so, why? Because he loves his wife or simply because she is a human being in jeopardy? What are the rights of the pharmacist? Should he be able to set any price he wishes? What of the pharmacist's right to private property that he created? Should Heinz or the pharmacist act according to the "golden rule?" or act according to some other universal rule? The answers given in this and other situations indicate the stage of moral development that the respondent has achieved.

Kohlberg identified six stages (and later a seventh that seems highly speculative) the first four of which emerge from his research. The fifth and sixth stages are logical extensions of the preceding stages, but they are criticized by other investigators for the lack of empirical evidence to substantiate them. The stages are grouped in pairs under three major headings.

a. Preconventional. Kohlberg identified the majority of the population, which fall in stages 3 and 4, as being "conventional" in their moral judgments. Accordingly, stages 1 and 2 are "preconventional," centering upon self, and stages 5 and 6 are "postconventional," centering upon wider social systems, either societal or universal (all of humanity), in making moral judgments.

Stage 1. In this earliest stage, judgments are based upon the direct consequences the child is likely to suffer. "Will I be punished for this or rewarded?" The calculation is simple and straightforward. Clearly, this stage corresponds with the earliest, egocentric stages identified by Piaget.

> Stage 1 represents the moral reasoning of the child who has taken [the] first step beyond egocentrism. If the egocentric child cannot take the role or perspective of any other person, the next step in development is the ability to take the perspective of one other person at a time (Hersh, Paolitto, and Reimer, 1979:65).

Stage 2. In this stage, the child incorporates the desire to please those who provide nurturance. Judgments are based upon the anticipated pleasure or displeasure of these "significant others." The child has now, as in Piaget's stages, differentiated self from other and views self in relation to other.

> The child's conception of right at stage 2 is essentially one of stark reciprocity. An exactly equal exchange of goods or favors seems to be the guiding light of this stage. . . . Reciprocity at this stage does not flow from a respect for the rights or dignity of the other, but merely from a pragmatic expectation of receiving similar treatment (Rosen, 1980:75–76).

The child begins to understand that the will or desires of the other person can change—that they can be changed by the child's actions, and that there is some standard of "fairness" or reciprocity used by the other and to which the child can appeal.

b. Conventional. According to Kohlberg, stages 3 and 4 comprise the levels of development of most of the population. One can, supposedly, assume that the distribution of the general population falls within a classic bell-shaped curve. However, the shape of the "bell" would be quite high and quite narrow, since Kohlberg and his fellow researchers estimate that no more than 5% of the population have progressed as far as stage 6.

Stage 3. This stage is characterized by an advance beyond strict reciprocity. The child now takes the role of the other, and can see the situation (and self) from the other's perspective.

> A desire to receive praise and avoid blame will influence the judgment of what constitutes right and wrong action. Kohlberg refers to this sometimes as the "Good-boy/Nice-girl" stage. One is motivated to observe rules in order to maintain relationships. The individual's conception of right at this stage is limited to people within his own circle and does not extend to a broad societal level. . . . This new role-taking ability will enable [the child] to modify . . . intended behavior on the basis of how [it] anticipates the other might respond to it (Rosen, 1980:76).

Stage 4. This stage can be called "social system and conscience" (Rosen, 1980:77).

> The scope of this stage encompasses the complete network of the entire society. There is a sense of obligation to obey laws and perform duties. Laws are construed as necessary to maintain society. The allegiance to following laws now springs from a conception of a moral order which goes beyond one's own circle of friends and relatives (Rosen, 1980:77).

Judgments in this stage are based upon the rights of society. Vengeance, for example, is the right of society and is interpreted as "paying your debt to society." In a cogent sentence, Kohlberg suggests what underlies the attitude of the general public toward welfare and those who receive it: "Social inequality is allowed where it is reciprocal to effort, moral conformity, and talent, but unequal favoring of the 'idle' and 'immoral,' poor, students, etc., is strongly rejected" (Rosen, 1980:77). This, then, is the stage of conventional morality, and is carried out in such programs as "workfare."

Kohlberg and his collaborators identified a substage (cleverly labeled stage 4B), which is a "moratorium" (borrowed from Erik Erikson) or period of limbo. During this substage, the person is in transition from stage 4 to stage 5 and, in confusion, alternates between relativism and absolutism in moral judgments. Apparently, this period falls between high school graduation (i.e., age eighteen) and the midtwenties. Kohlberg says that there are periods of "disequilibrium" between stages (similar to Piaget) and that the person in substage 4B is in such a disequilibrium, having lost the stability (we would say steady state, of course) of stage 4 without yet achieving stability in stage 5. Kohlberg believes that stage 5, if it is achieved, occurs during the midtwenties, and that stage 6 does not occur before the late twenties (Rosen, 1980:93). If these stages were substantiated by further research, they would tend to confirm Erikson's stages of adulthood as well as Kohlberg's.

c. *Postconventional.* Stages 5 and 6 are the most controversial of Kohlberg's stages, since there is less supporting evidence for them. Kohlberg is accused of deriving these from philosophical premises, rather than psychological, empirical research.

Stage 5. In stage 4, the person accepts and maintains the status quo, for the most part. In stage 5, the person entertains the possibility of changing unjust laws. The person looks beyond the laws to the principles that they embody and can question whether the laws adequately fulfill those principles. Kohlberg's opinion is that the logical outcome of stage 5 is a democratic society. The person becomes aware that there may be two or more valid moral or legal choices and must choose between them. In this sense, the person in stage 5 seeks justice as a principle rather than simply obedience to the law. Equity is preferred over equality; it is clear that Kohlberg has been influenced by philosopher John Rawls. Kohlberg uses capital punishment as an example. If there is no proof that capital punishment deters crime, then the person in stage 5 would conclude that this law does not protect society and would oppose capital punishment. If, on the other hand, there is evidence that it deters crime, the person in stage 5 could conclude that capital punishement serves a valid purpose in protecting society and be in favor of it. The primary criterion in this stage, then, is the social utility of the particular law.

Stage 6. Rosen identified the characteristics of the person who has attained stage 6:

> The rare person whose sociocognitive moral development has brought him [sic] to this stage of moral reasoning is fully autonomous. He is completely decentered from society's expectations and bases his resolutions to ethical conflicts upon universal principles of justice which are prescriptively consistent without exception. Universality, consistency and logical comprehensiveness are the central attributes. . . . Conscience, in this sense, does not connote guilt, but the purely rational quality of his justice structure. Respect for the dignity of each individual, regardless of station in life, has reached a zenith (Rosen, 1980:80–81).

Kohlberg cited a philosopher's solution to the "Heinz" situation as an example of stage 6 moral judgments:

> IF THE HUSBAND DOES NOT FEEL VERY CLOSE TO OR AFFECTIONATE WITH HIS WIFE, SHOULD HE STEAL THE DRUG? Yes. *The value of her life is independent of any personal ties.*

The value of human life is based upon the fact that it offers the only possible source of a categorical moral "ought" to a rational being acting in the role of a moral agent.
SUPPOSE IT WERE A FRIEND OR AN ACQUAINTANCE? *Yes, the value of a human life remains the same* (Hersh et al., 1979:80).

Kohlberg identified a seventh stage, which Rosen called "The Cosmic Perspective," which supersedes the humanistic sixth stage. Kohlberg readily acknowledged that there was no research data to support this, as yet. His speculation in the absence of evidence tends to support his critics, who do no find convincing evidence for stages 5 or 6 either. Kohlberg acknowledged being influenced by Erikson and believes that this seventh stage occurs in aged persons who experience despair and doubt about life's meaning. The person finds meaning by "identifying the self with cosmic perspective of the infinite" (Rosen, 1980:88). Kohlberg does not claim that this is a verifiable stage similar to the earlier ones, but does believe that spiritual growth occurs among the aging that is qualitatively different from earlier moral judgments.

Kohlberg's theories receive thorough and frequently harsh reviews (Hersh et al., 1979; Rosen, 1980), but he is acknowledged to have created the largest body of research literature on moral judgments and for that reason alone is significant.

Some observations on his scheme may be useful here. Persons do not inevitably progress through Kohlberg's stages, as contrasted to Erikson's stages. Kohlberg stated that most of the population remains in stage 4. A serious criticism of Kohlberg's theory is that his idealized persons in stages 5 and 6 (and certainly stage 7) are conceived to be "beyond culture" or "culture-free." This contradicts what we have said earlier regarding the pervasiveness of culture. Socrates, Lincoln, Martin Luther King, Jr., and—one could add—Gandhi, were certainly not free of their respective cultures. One could maintain (as Erikson did of Luther, Jefferson, and Gandhi) that they transformed their cultures through exemplifying certain principles that, in each case, underlay the law, but one cannot accurately maintain that they were culture-free.

3. Gender and Moral Development. Carol Gilligan, a collaborator of Kohlberg, might take issue with Kohlberg's conception of the morally autonomous person in stage 6, on the ground that the person's separation from human attachment is more a characteristic of male development than of female development. In her book, *Another Voice*, Gilligan maintains that the child's relationship to the primary nurturer (usually mother) is crucial to the child's style of moral judgment and to the child's style of relating to others. Gilligan stated that because males typically must separate from the primary nurturing person in order to identify with their own sex, and females do not, males employ a mode of relating that is oppositional, separatist, and places more importance upon principles than upon relationships with others.

II. THE CRITICAL PHASES OF THE LIFE CYCLE

A. Establishment of Primary Attachment (Dependency and Trust) in the Parent–Child Dyad

The newborn infant enters the world in a totally dependent state. The major part of the first year is devoted to the effort to survive and to the formation and elaboration of the adaptation devices directed toward survival. During this early period, the infant is helpless and incapable of surviving by its own efforts. The nurturing person (or persons) compensates for and supplies what the newborn lacks. The newborn is initially in a state of undifferentiation. Physiological organization is rudimentary, and there is no demonstrated psychic organization (in the sense of ego or superego). In the world of the newborn, there is no object or object relation; the infant is profoundly egocentric. Object relations will develop during the first year (Spitz, 1965).

1. Trust vs. Mistrust. Erikson described the first critical social task as a sense of basic trust vs. a sense of basic mistrust. By this, he meant the necessity for the development of a *feeling* of trust in others and in one's self and for healthy mistrust of one's environment (and of oneself, perhaps). Spitz refers to this first task as the initiation of an object relationship. In the Erikson formulation of the dimension of trust, the following elements are important.

1. The nurturing person(s) become an inner certainty as well as an outer predictablity. This is a state that includes the qualities of consistency, continuity, and sameness of experience. These experiences and qualities become part of the child's identity.
2. The infant develops a sense of being able to trust self and the capacity of its own organs to cope with urges.
3. This sense of trust in self and others forms the foundation for the later development of a sense of identity.
4. Since the sense of trust/mistrust is essentially social, it is based in communication (particularly tactile, nutritive, and emotional) between the infant and the caring person(s).

Ever since Spitz's work in the 1930s on the effects of maternal deprivation, controversy in the literature was focused on whether the primary social attachment must be formed between mother and infant. It is fairly well accepted that the mother in this sense does not necessarily mean the biological mother. Some authors refer to the caring person, rather than mother, holding to the necessity for continuity, consistency, and predictability but not seeing this necessarily embodied in any one particular person. Consequently, there is fairly general agreement that the climate within which an infant can adapt to the first social task is of utmost importance, but the question of who the person or persons must be in order to establish this climate remains controversial. This has been a central question in the recent development of infant day-care centers.

The infant's primary needs that must be met are the oral, nutritive needs. The mouth is the initial receptor; it is the most sensitive and demanding tissue in the body at this time. Sensitive tissues develop in other erotogenic zones later, and these form the basis of Freud's stages of oral, anal, and genital. Erikson also employed the idea of zones and refers to the zonal sensitivity of the sense of basic trust vs. sense of basic mistrust as *oral-respiratory* and *sensory-kinesthetic*. He stressed that these are incorporative modes, that is, taking in. The first social activities, then, are concerned with incorporation: getting and learning to get. During the later portion of the first critical stage, the infant begins to give in return.

Formation of the primary social attachment is accomplished in a dyadic field wherein the infant and caring person(s) "are one." Contemporary birthing practices that foster "bonding" strive to highlight the immediacy of mutual attachment between infant and parent(s). Initially, at least, we should not refer to the infant as an autonomous entity in itself. It is helpless, dependent, and must be cared for; it is as one with the other party to the dyad. It is now primarily a component, a component of a system—a two-person system—something that cannot be said at any later time. It is possible to think of the "connectiveness" of the human organism to other humans. In the prenatal environment, the developing organism is connected through the umbilical cord; in the first months of life, it is connected by a psychological "cord" that must be stretched, and later severed, to permit movement to wider social connections. To paraphrase Erikson, the child in the first months of life could well say, "I am what I am given," next say, "I am what I can get," and finally say, "I am what I can give."

Within the dyad, the infant does not long remain a passive recipient. In her definitive theoretical review of object relations, dependency, and attachment, Mary Ainsworth emphasized the important role of infant behaviors both in eliciting parental responses and in active proximity-seeking (Ainsworth, 1969:981). Quite early in life, the infant must respond and interact through the formation of a primary social attachment. From a systems stance, it can be said that the transactions between the human system and the social environment are a necessary condition for the definition of boundary of self. In other words, it is through the recognition of and interaction with "other" that the boundaries of self can be defined. If this process is not sufficiently engaged in, the boundaries of self do not become defined, which may result in the condition known as infantile autism. If the latter part of this process does not occur, that is, the differentiation of self within social attachments, the resulting condition is referred to as symbiosis (see Section 4b).

a. Maternal deprivation. A number of dysfunctional dyadic forms were identified and grouped under the rubric of maternal deprivation (Bowlby, 1962). Maternal deprivation can be described in both quantitative and qualitative aspects. The term usually refers to an insufficiency of interaction between the child and the nurturing person(s) and the conditions in which the insufficiency seems to develop. The term *maternal deprivation* should not be taken literally (that it is not only a mother, and not necessarily literally deprivation). Rather, it is an expression of the effect upon the child. Some of the conditions in which it becomes apparent are:

1. Institutionalization or hospitalization of the infant with no provision for substitute parenting. The danger of this was documented by Spitz in his writings and films (1965).

2. Circumstances in which the child is with a mother or mother substitute who provides insufficient opportunity for interaction.

3. Sufficient care is available to the child, but the child is unable to interact because of previous deprivations, maturational deficiencies, or unknown causes. Not infrequently, parents of disturbed preschool children report that almost from birth, an infant was not responsive to cuddling and "gentling." Frequently a neurological deficit is suspected.

4. Distorted relationships:

a. Situations where the child is not differentiated from the parent. The parent does not distinguish between self and child; the boundary is not clear.

b. Interlocking dependency, a symbiotic relationship wherein the parent "needs" a totally dependent infant and the child requires total mothering. This is the normal circumstance of the neonatal infant, but to prolong it distorts development.

c. The parent may assimilate the child as being certain aspects of himself (or herself) or identify the child completely with the qualities of another person. Again, a measure of this is normal and desirable, e.g., seeing the child as having the father's eyes or Aunt Clara's hair, but when the total child is viewed as possessing the qualities of another, there is little opportunity to differentiate self and establish self as a separate person.

d. The parent(s) perceives the child as the embodiment of a single quality, such as stupid, evil, or totally demanding.

5. Insufficient relationships:
   a. The parenting person is unable to give emotionally because of his/her own isolation or coldness as a person.
   b. The parent may be narcissistic and involved with self so that no more than physical care is provided. The parent's system is so closed toward the child that little or no transaction of feeling is permitted.
   c. Situational factors exhaust the caring person's energies, and little love is available for nurturance of the child. These demands may come from within the family system (parental illness, e.g.) or from the environment (e.g., conditions of poverty).

One or more of the distorted or insufficient relationships listed above are usually found in situations of child abuse.

b. Separation. Another form of defective dyad that complicates the child's efforts to establish a basic sense of trust is labeled *separation.* Whereas deprivation refers to insufficiency of relationship, separation refers to interruption of an already established relationship. It has to do with the need for continuity and predictability.

John Bowlby was appointed by the World Health Organization to study the effects of separation (Bowlby, 1962:205–214). In his own studies, he found that juvenile delinquency was highly correlated with separation experiences in the preschool years. His review of other research yielded similar results. He suggested that early childhood separation is a causal factor for some delinquents. Although this causal relationship has been questioned by critics, his general findings have been accepted and incorporated into the body of knowledge of child development. He concluded that a separation in the first three months of life is not disturbing if an adequate parent substitute is provided. By the age of three months, the child has begun to form a social attachment or dyad with the parenting person(s) and separation begins to present problems to the infant's efforts to cope with this first developmental task. Prolonged separation between the ages of six and twelve months is most deleterious and may not be reversible (Bowlby, 1966:117–119). Bowlby described the character development that results from such harmful separation as the "affectionless character," meaning a shallow and untrusting person who is unable to enter into intimate emotional transactions with other persons.

2. Conclusion. As the first major task of the life cycle, the first foundation in psychological development, the cornerstone of social functioning, the child must engage in striving to establish an essential, primary, social relationship. The interrelatedness of the physical, psychological, and social are most observable in this stage. The infant must survive as an organism and begin to evolve as a self, a person. The social resources available are largely centralized in the parenting person(s), and these resources must be provided to the infant to begin with; later, the child will seek them out. Inputs must be offered and must be accepted—nutritive inputs for physical survival and emotional inputs for psychological survival. The child will emerge from this interaction with a sense of being able or unable to count on others and self, a mixture of trust and mistrust, hope and hopelessness. It should be noted that this outcome is a blending, not necessarily of equal parts, of a basic sense of trust and a basic sense of mistrust.

B. Differentiation of Self within the Family System

The family system is the scene of the second and third of Erikson's crises of psychosocial growth. The mother–child dyad of the earlier task becomes a three-or-more-person system for these tasks. We review these crises as Erikson presents them.

1. Autonomy vs. Shame and Doubt. This psychosocial crisis carries the special requirement for the establishment of a sense of self as an entity distinguished from the environment. This social expectation is congruent with the maturational development wherein the child is beginning to have the physical capacity to manage certain of its functions (e.g., ambulation and elimination). Conflicting desires to assert self as an autonomous being and to be uncertain of its capacity to do so compete within the child, who must risk relinquishing some of the comfortable dependency of the primary dyad.

The first assertion of self as separate is through communicating, "No, I can *will* not to do what you want me to do." The well-known negativism of the two-year-old child expresses this assertion of the will. In the dominant culture of the United States, this has become attached to the cultural dictates about toilet habits, neatness, and respect for property. In other cultures, such negative behavior responds to themes important to those cultures. The corollary of negative assertion is self-control and independence. If the family environment does not provide limits for assertive behavior, the child may be stranded out on a limb beyond the capacity for self-management and direction. If the family environment overly restricts the available opportunities to test the capacity of its own behavior, the child will not have the chance to experience itself as a separate and sovereign entity. In case of either extreme, the child will develop a sense of shame and doubt about the capacity to be a self-determining human system.

These preschool years are, for the most part, centered in the family system, the primary social unit of the culture. It is within this social climate that the child becomes a person, a social being. The autonomy crisis occurs in a field of experience with certain characteristics.

a. Sense of self. It is necessary for the developing person to differentiate self within the nurturer–nurtured dyad. There must develop an awareness of existence separate from the sources of nurturance. The question must be dealt with, "Where do they end and where do I begin?" is a question that arises again in adolescence.

b. Order. Sensitivity to order is characteristic of this age. Children frequently insist on sameness in their environment and become distraught when important objects are relocated. Predictability, continuity, and consistency of the physical environment assume a special meaning, analogous to these same qualities of the nurturing person in the first stage. The environment must be trustworthy because the child, partly at least, self-constructs from the environment. Learning to name objects provides a degree of control over them (Brown, 1965:267–276). Organization of the energies of the self-system is possible only when the suprasystem (immediate environment, in this instance) is organized sufficiently.

c. Assertion of will. This occurs first in negation and then in positive ways. The child diligently attempts to experience being a self-directing entity. First physiologically, then psychologically, and finally socially, children find they can will to hold on or let go. Physiologically, there develops the capacity to hold on to, or let go, of sphincter musculature.

If toilet habits are of sensitive importance to the culture, a major battle may develop over this socializing task. Often toilet training is referred to as "breaking" the child, training in the same sense as breaking a wild mustang. To persuade the child to submit its will to that of the culture as represented by the family becomes crucially important. The child then is encouraged to feel a willing capacity (a capacity to *will*) through self-control, according to cultural dictates.

Psychologically, a child can hold on to or let go of feelings. There is the choice of expressing frustration and anger directly through behavior or controlling it to please "others." If others communicate that these feelings are too dangerous to let out, the child may doubt its capacity to deal with them, or have a feeling of omnipotent power. If others are unable or unwilling to provide any ground rules, the child may feel internal anarchy and shame.

Socially, one can hold on to, or let go of, self in relation to other systems. In holding on, the child may not engage in enough transactions with others and have insufficient feedback to enable the establishment of self within a social context. In letting go, self-boundaries may not be established, and the environment continues to be indistinguishable from self.

d. Ambivalences. Dichotomies of feeling (ambivalences) are a characteristic of this crisis. Polarities are a part of a process of differentiation.

A child may alternately express a sense of love and hate, a sense of independence and total dependence, or a sense of pleasure and displeasure. This proximity of opposites must now be coped with for the first time, and how this is resolved will serve as the prototype for later life tasks. Erikson stated that the cultural solution for this dilemma is embodied in the culture's approach to law and order.

e. Communication. Although language development has begun, much communication continues to be nonverbal. Approval and disapproval are more important reinforcers of behavior and are conveyed by feeling, more than by word. The prohibitive "no-no" may convey prohibition or permission, approval or disapproval, challenge or censure. The sensitive two or three-year-old may well be more responsive to parental feeling than to word meaning. Piaget finds the child's thought processes to be concrete and fragmentary; the concepts grasped are specific and often literal in their interpretation. At any one time, the child may feel all "good" or all "bad." It is essential at these times that the parents not view the child as either all "bad" or all "good."

The child who does not develop a sufficient sense of autonomy may have little or no sense of self. Manifestations of this include cloying dependency, general anxiety, foolhardy behavior, expecting others always to be in control, and severe withdrawal. Severe and pervasive negativism may also indicate lack of sufficient autonomy. A sense of autonomy is manifest in a measure of self-regulation and a capacity to enter into social transactions as a discrete entity.

In the latter preschool years, the child's primary social system continues to be the family, but he or she is beginning to establish linkages outside the family, such as playmates, neighbors, and extended family or family friends, and increasingly, adults and peers in organizational settings such as Headstart, day-care, and preschool.

2. Initiative vs. Guilt. This is the second psychosocial crisis that occurs in the arena of the family system and through dealing with the family system. The child must now be concerned with who she or he is, qualitatively. With the accrued sense of autonomy, shame, and doubt as to the capacity to self-will its own behavior, the child must next explore who he or she is. The Oedipal conflict is central, as is the introjection of right and wrong. As Erikson views this task, the modalities are "to make" (to get) and "to make like" (to play). The bisexuality of the child, which has been apparent up to this time, is directed toward a gender as the culture defines it. The masculine "making" is intrusive, the insertion of self into the social world to accomplish purposes. The feminine form of "making" is inclusion of the social world to accomplish purposes. The genital tissue is hypersensitive at this stage, consistent with Freud's phallic stage.

Active insertion of self or inclusive behavior brings anticipated rivalry and threat of punishment. Identification, in the sense of imitation, is a frequent method of coping with the child's inner compulsion to define self as a person and the culture's expectations that the boy will be like his father and the girl will be like her mother. Erikson stated that the child could say to himself or herself, "I am what I can imagine I will be" (Erikson, 1968:122). The outcome of this crisis will be a mixture of a sense of initiative and a sense of guilt. The person with a goodly measure of sense of initiative will have purpose and direction as part of her/his character, will be self-motivating, and will be able to initiate social behavior and transactions.

This "initiative" crisis has certain common characteristics:

a. Self. The essential psychosocial task now is to create a qualitative sense of self. This exploration begins in the family and then expands outward into other social systems. Because of the arousal of awareness of genital sensations and the cultural expectations of sex differentiation, much of this is played out in the Oedipal context. The child of each sex is expected to identify with the cultural role for that sex as represented by the parent of the same sex. Furthermore, each relates sexually to the parent of the opposite sex. The outcome of the Oedipal complex ("complex" refers to the sets of relationships) is, ideally, the child's relinquishment of the sexual interest in the parent of the opposite sex and identification with the parent of the same sex. This situation is complicated by the absence of cultural clarity about sex-differentiated behaviors in our society, which affects the parents as well as the child. Sometimes the child identifies with the "stronger" parent regardless of sex, and sometimes the child does not know whom to identify with. Sometimes the child continues to wallow in the complexities of this task during later crises. Energies are preempted and the later crises are inadequately dealt with. Ideally, however, an accommodation is reached, and the child expands the field of activity beyond the family and becomes occupied somewhat in other social transactions.

b. Play. Play becomes an important mode of behavior during the initiative crises. Cognitive development has progressed to the extent that imagination can be controlled and used in various ways. Erikson considers play as "autotherapeutic" in the sense that it is a rudimentary form of the adult capacity to create models and experiment with alternative behaviors without committing onself to those behaviors. There are three stages in the hierarchical forms of play:

(1) *autocosmic:* the child's play begins with and centers on its own body;
(2) *microspheric:* the small world of manageable toys; and
(3) *macrospheric:* the sharing of play with others, first in parallel fashion and then in concert (Erikson, 1963:220–221).

In this phase, two kinds of play are important. One is the solitary, day-dreaming variety in which the child can experiment with its fantasies and try out imaginings of what he or she would like to do and be. The second is peer play, wherein children together can work on solving their common concerns. Occasionally, play may carry fantasy beyond control or comfort and be very frightening. Pretending is a reassuring way to help establish the boundaries of reality, especially when adults occasionally enter into the "let's pretend" activities.

c. Consolidation and integration. The initiative crisis is a time of transitional consolidation and integration. The exertion of self into environment with hope and expectation of influencing environment involves a measure of trust in the predictability of environment and one's own predictability, as well as a measure of control or will. To be able to do this enables children to imagine how they might eventually influence the world. Because they are concerned about their intactness and bodily integrity, they may be sensitive to anything that threatens this. They may be frightened by their own fantasies of power and hold themselves responsible for any calamity that befalls others close to them.

Again it is well to mention that the outcome of this particular crisis is a balance between initiative and guilt. This is the critical time for the development of conscience, which can be a tolerant guide or a punitive slavemaster, but a conscience there will be. It is hoped that the initiative will be directed toward "making" things work, people and objects, in the sense of integrated behaviors. But it can be "making" things and people in the exploitative sense. If the child can emerge from these family-centered growth tasks with a degree of trust in others and self, a sense of separateness as a person linked to others, and a sense of purpose, the child is well on the way to a fulfilling life plan congruent with her or his nature as a human being.

C. Definition of Self within Secondary Social Systems

1. Industry vs. Inferiority. The next of Erikson's psychosocial crises occurs in interaction with the organized components of the community: formal organizations (such as the school and the church) and informal organizations (such as the neighborhood and the peer group). Physiological and cognitive maturation provide the capacities, and the culture furnishes the expectations. This is the period of development that Freud labeled *latency* and that Piaget called the phase of *concrete operations.* Erikson described this fourth polarity as a sense of "industry vs. inferiority." "Industry" is used here in the sense of "being industrious," productive or competent. There are certain dominant characteristics of this particular crisis.

a. The theme is mastery. Mastery is sought over physical objects, one's physical self, social transactions, and ideas and concepts. It is the time to learn the technology and ways of one's culture. Institutionalized means are supplied by the culture, whose investment is its own survival. The school is an institution charged with transmission of the cultural technology. The Future Farmers of America and 4-H are organizations for communicating the culture of agricultural communities (and for 4-H, increasingly, urban culture as well). The "block gang"exists to transmit the ways of another specialized, local culture, often without "official," societal recognition. Games, contests, and athletics are also examples of institutionalized culture carriers. The school-aged child participates in various of these organizations and in the process creates a sense of self as competent and incompetent.

b. Peer group experience is a necessary element in the crucible of testing mastery. It provides a social system parallel to the adult society (and intersecting with it on some occasions), with its own organization, rules, purposes, and activities. It is with the peer group that the child can test self and grow to mastery in social relationships with equals.

c. The outcome is again a mixture or balance of the two polar feelings. A dominant sense of inferiority may result from a lack of ability, but most frequently it derives from either insufficient accrual from previous crises or unclear or unreasonable adult or peer expectations and criteria of mastery. The idea of *sense* of industry or inferiority is important. It is the *feeling* the child has about his or her own competence that is crucial, not *actual* competence as measured by parental or adult standards. The person who embarks into adolescence with a feeling that he or she can do at least one thing very well is in a favorable position indeed.

a. Mastery.   Entry into school is an important step to the child, to the parents, and to the culture. One of the very few clearly demarked way stations on the long trail to adulthood, it is the occasion when society insures that each of its young members becomes a participant in an organized, institutionalized culture. In the Midwest, the phrase "kindergarten roundup" well conveys the cultural investment in collecting the mavericks and commencing the long process of "breaking" them, of acculturation to technological society. An arbitrary age is set for such entry, two years younger than the legal requirement for compulsory school attendance in most states, and there exists the social expectation that the child will be readied by the family. If children are indeed ready, they are eagerly looking forward to entry into this new world. If unready because energies are lacking, the child will have "problems." The child and parent(s) may not be ready for separation. The kindergartener may not be able to distinguish teacher from parent, or may not have self sufficiently organized to comply with the expectations for settled and cooperative behavior.

If the culture transmitted by the school is alien or oppositional to the culture of the child's family (as American Indians often experience, for

example), the young child is in a difficult, indeed untenable, posiu.
The technology and ways of doing things the child has become familiar
with and the development of an emerging sense of self and other within
that culture have, by this time, been incorporated as a part of self. To
accept a differing way or culture may be felt as an act of betrayal of self,
family, or tribe. If so, efforts toward mastery may well be invested outside of the school, seeking mastery of their own culture, not that of
others. The lack of participation in school by significant numbers of
American Indian youth by the time they reach high school may, in large
part, be explained this way.

Various writers have documented the existence of this dilemma as
experienced by racial minorities in the United States: ghetto blacks (Baratz and Baratz, 1971), American Indians (Cahn 1969:175–185), and Chi-
canos (Acuña, 1972). Acuña explained how the educational system
serves to socialize the student into accepting and supporting the way
things are in the majority culture. He stated that is accomplished by
"erasing the Chicano's culture, language and values and replacing them
with Anglo-American culture, language and values" (Acuña, 1972:146).
Such socialization is clearly a means of social control. This places the
child in the extremely difficult position of having to choose between
cultures: between family (and tribe, perhaps) and school.

The school has evolved as an overinvested carrier of culture as
changes in technology and family functions have occurred (that is, too
much is expected of the schools, and some expectations are inappropri-
ate). As society has been bureaucratized, so has the school. On the one
hand, the school has become a bureaucratic organization, being a highly
complex institution. On the other hand, the school has the charge of
preparing the young for participation in the existing cultural ways. The
child in the school experiences self as functioning participant in a bureaucratic organization. The child's success in school is seen as predict-
ing later success in adult life, and lack of success is seen as predictive of
adult failure. All of the current "preventive program planning" is based
upon this premise and is aimed at earlier identification of difficulty,
even though there is minimal evidence to support this belief. Many persons who are successful in schooling are unsuccessful in other aspects
of living, and the obverse is also true.

Society, then, expects the child to demonstrate mastery and competence primarily in the single institution of the school. This includes not
only the technology of literacy but also physical mastery (Phys Ed, intra-
murals, and athletic teams), arts and music, social mastery (social dancing, family life education), domestic skills (now often required of both
sexes), and such other technological competencies as driving an automobile and operating a computer. There can be little wonder that the
public schools find it very difficult to fulfill all the assignments the culture delegates to them. The school has even been required to deal with

this society's primary problems: racism, sexism, poverty, and the use of illegal drugs.

   b. Peer group.   The culture expects the child to proceed with the construction of a sense of competence primarily in the school. The other available secondary social system is the peer group. During latency, the child's primary connections continue to be within the family system; it is later in adolescence that the peer group may well take precedence over the family. The peer group of latency is modeled after the culture within which it exists. At its best, it is not very visible to the adult world and has its own parallel culture passed from generation to generation (two or three years to a generation) with continuity, but frequent innovations, as well. The peer group is likely to be strongest in direct relation to the stability of the population it draws from. The peer group of suburbia is likely to be weak and transitory, whereas the peer group in the small town or city neighborhood may be stronger. Increasingly, adults have taken over the peer groups of the latency period. In much of the United States, peer activities are organized and conducted by adults. The wider scope of school functions is part of this; Little League baseball exemplifies another part; the day camp and "away camp" are others. The attention to individual fulfillment manifested by lessons in swimming, driving, tennis, golf, dancing, music, skiing, and so on, has served to diminish the availability of the child-controlled peer group. Other factors are the geographic separation of children from their parents who work elsewhere, in another community, and are not available to transport them, or to be nearby as resources if needed. These adult-managed and -supervised activities undoubtedly enable children to develop competence in a range of skills, but in the process they minimize the child's opportunities to find out about self through interacting freely in a peer culture. This might explain, in part, the phenomenon of "living together" (see Popenoe, 1988:303) within a wider peer culture of young adults who are exploring their selves before fully committing to adulthood.

   c. Outcome.   Mastery of the ground rules of life seems important to the latency-age child. Piaget found that children of this age are quite occupied with justice and accept arbitrary or expiatory punishment as sometimes warranted (Piaget, 1932). As they grow older, they favor the idea of retribution connected to the offending act and its natural consequences. Grasp of the schema for moral judgment forms the basis for organized social relations.

   Problems of latency-age children can be grouped under three general headings. The one-word description most often heard is "immaturity." The largest portion of children referred to child guidance clinics and school special services are aged 8–11. The reasons for referral are:

(1) *Poor school performance.* Achievement of mastery of cultural technology does not measure up to the standards of school and/or parents. The child's school behavior disrupts learning by self or others.

(2) *Symptoms* not expected at this age, but not unusual in a younger child. Some of these are incontinence, fears, short attention span, hyperactivity, daydreaming, and not assuming expected responsibilities.

(3) *Social inferiority* in Erikson's sense. This may be the isolated child or the child who consistently associates only with younger children. A sense of social inferiority may be manifested by over compensatory behavior (e.g., bullying or braggadocio). In the event societal expectations are excessive or opportunities for development of competence are too limited, a kind of cultural inferiority may result.

(4) *Cultural incongruence.* As noted earlier, some children are placed in the difficult position of reconciling or rejecting one of two cultures. If social systems in the child's environment (e.g., family, school, or peer group) recognize this and support the child (by emotional support, counseling, providing opportunity to vent frustration, playing out resentments against authority in a safe situation), the child may be able to reconcile conflicting demands. Often, however, the experience of racial minority children is lack of understanding and support by their environments.

2. *Conclusion.* The middle years of childhood ("the wonder years") are the years for development of a sense of competence—to master self, social relationships, and the technology of the culture. The human system is relatively open to inputs from and transactions with the institutions of the community beyond the family system while retaining a primary linkage to the family. The growing person emerges from this with a sense of being somewhere on the continuum from industry to inferiority. Erikson opines that the child's expression of a sense of competence could be stated, "I am what I can learn to make work" (Erikson, 1968:127).

D. Transitional Self: Identity beyond Social Systems (Adolescenthood and Youth)

This is the transitional growth crisis in Erikson's formulation. It is the time when the biological and social imperatives demand that the evolving person pull herself or himself together and create an identity that goes beyond the accumulation of social roles. In our culture, this more or less coincides with that period of life referred to as adolescence. We prefer to use the term *adolescenthood* to convey the idea of more than a transitory hiatus. The adolescent span of life has become a distinct life phase with its own culture, role expectations, and style.

The concept of identity has entered into the conventional wisdom, and references are replete to individual identity, group identity, and even national identity. Erikson used the term precisely, and applied it primarily to the individual person. He saw the social–psychological task at this age as one of integration, or more precisely reintegration, of the various components of the person into a whole. It is a process of ego synthesis that culminates in ego identity, meaning an internal consistency and continuity of meaning to others. This goes beyond the sum of childhood identifications and is not merely a synthesis of social roles.

Again the concept is that of *sense* of identity. It is not a state of being that can be objectively evaluated by others.

> An optimal sense of identity . . . is experienced merely as a sense of psychosocial well being. Its most obvious concomitants are a feeling of being at home in one's body, a 'sense of knowing where one is going' and an inner assuredness of anticipated recognition from those who count" (Erikson, 1968:165).

Erikson first labeled the opposite pole *identity diffusion,* later *role confusion,* and in later writings (Erikson, 1968) he settled on *identity confusion.* The term conveys the antithesis of integration, the dispersion of selves, the alienation of the self. From a systems viewpoint, one could say that internal and external tensions press the human system to reintegrate its component parts to undertake new purposes and responsibilities. If the components of personality are not brought together, the person is fragmented and has no solid sense of self. The person is not capable of putting energy to concerted use—the person is entropic. Schizophrenia, with its disorganization of personality components and particular disparity between thought and feeling, is the extreme form of such fragmentation. Interestingly, the earlier term for schizophrenia was *dementia praecox,* meaning "insanity of the young." Some theorists, Erikson among them, hold that true schizophrenia cannot appear until adolescence, since it is foremost a condition of pathology of identity and identification. A sensitive expression of this condition is:

> I am learning peacefulness, lying by myself quietly
> As the light lies on these white walls, this bed, these hands.
> I am nobody; I have nothing to do with explosions.
> I have given my name and my day-clothes up to the nurses
> And my history to the anesthetist and my body to the surgeons.
>
> (Plath, 1966:10)

Erikson focused much of his study and writing on the adolescent crisis, including *Identity: Youth and Crisis* (1968), *Childhood and Society* (1965), or "The Problem of Ego Identity" (1959). Two of the characteristics of adolescence he identified, the moratorium and negative identity, are particularly worthy of emphasis here.

The idea of *moratorium* refers to a socially sanctioned period of delay wherein the person is allowed to, or forced to, postpone assumption of the full responsibilities of adult commitments. The culture relaxes its expectations and is more permissive. It is, then, a time when the person can try out a variety of identifications, modes of behavior, and roles without a total commitment to see them through. The moratorium is both necessary and desirable to allow for integration, regrouping of forces, and the setting of life goals, in a culture that places a high value on individuality. The extension of adolescence in the United States can be viewed as a socially imposed moratorium that may be unnecessarily long for some. Moratoria may occur at times other than adolescenthood for some individuals. Often, they are part of the making of decisions or major changes in life goals. If the individually determined moratorium is more prolonged than societal expectations allow, there is reason for concern, for example, Biff in *Death of a Salesman*.

> HAPPY: Well, you really enjoy it on a farm? Are you content out there?
> BIFF: *With rising agitation:* Hap, I've had twenty or thirty different kinds of jobs since I left home before the war, and it always turns out the same. . . . And whenever Spring comes to where I am, I suddenly get the feeling, my God, I'm not gettin' anywhere! . . . I'm thirty-four years old, I ought to be makin' my future. That's when I come running home. And now, I get here, and I don't know what to do with myself. *After a pause:* I've always made a point of not wasting my life, and everytime I come back here I know that all I've done is to waste my life.
> HAPPY: You're a poet, you know that, Biff? You're a—you're an idealist!
> BIFF: No, I'm mixed up very bad. Maybe I ought to get married. Maybe I oughta get stuck into something. Maybe that's my trouble. I'm like a boy. I'm not married, I'm not in business, I just—I'm like a boy. (A. Miller, 1955:18–19)

Negative identity is another important Eriksonian concept. Negative identity is an identity that occurs in a situation in which available positive identity elements cancel each other out. This can occur because any identity is better than no identity at all. Negative identity is "an identity perversely based on all those identifications and roles which, at critical stages of development, had been presented to them as most undesirable or dangerous and yet also as most real" (Erikson, 1968:174). The confirmation of the person's identity come from within ("this is what I feel like") and from without ("this is what you say I am"). This confirming feedback cycle operates in like manner for any identity. Although one's sense of identity can and does change subsequent to adolescence, this is the crucial time for initial identity formulation, the greatest opportunity for such development, and the time of greatest vulnerability.

1. Adolescenthood. There are more definitions of adolescence than there are definers. For a time, adolescence was synonymous with the teen years, but that is no longer an adequate definition. The idea of the "between years" is frequently encountered, but that has an implication of "floating." For our purposes here, we will employ the following definition, recognizing that it, too, is open to dispute: "Adolescence is probably in all societies that period which comes after the biological and hormonal changes of puberty have set in but before the individual's incorporation into society as an independent adult" (Ktsanes, 1965:17). *Adolescence then begins with biology and ends by social definition.* The commencement is organism, the process is organism interacting with culture, and the termination is culturally determined. The seemingly unique element in adolescenthood in the society of the United States is the increasing evidence of adolescence becoming a distinct cultural phase of life in the same sense as childhood and adulthood.

Rather than reviewing all the elements of this Eriksonian crisis, we will approach it from one angle. Freud is widely quoted as believing that the two elements of a successful life were the capacities to love and work. The task of identity formulation can be viewed as the prerequisite for loving and working. We will discuss briefly some of the characteristics of the adolescent and the culture that are important to development of these capacities.

a. The peer group.   The associations of the adolescent with peers are extremely necessary experiences. The peer groups take over some of the parental roles of support and value-giving. Peers absorb much of the available social energy of the youth and become a primary reference group. The person can use peers to find self by projecting his/her ego fragments onto others. The person can experience and express feelings of tenderness toward others, beyond the family system, on new planes. Various roles are available to be tried and either accepted or discarded. Friedenberg found an attitude of respect for competence developing in the peer group (1962:59). In the peer society, the adolescent can begin to be a lover and a worker in close interaction with others. This experience occurred within the family system but only in the role of the child. Adulthood requires more of the person than continuance as a loving, working child within the primary family system. For some youths, the peer group becomes of overriding importance, totally replacing the family. Such substitution of one kind of childlike dependency for another does not suffice for the creation of a unique identity. Some youths remain largely separated from a peer group and still manage to pull together an identity. Peers are, however, an essential part of adolescents' struggles to find out who they are, what they value, and what they want to become.

b. Education.   The school continues to be the primary social institution as it was during latency. Increasingly, occupational choices are centered in the school experience. As occupational choice has become broader and minimally determined by parents' occupations, it also has become more embedded in the school. Curricula are constructed to expose the youth to a range of potential occupations, performance is self-evaluated and judged by peers, parents, teachers, and guidance counselors, and the youth is guided in certain directions. A number of factors enter in determining the "real" possibilities for any given youth. Some of these are race, sex, socioeconomic status, and "intelligence." In a society where persons are signified by what they do rather than by who they are, one's choice of work role or, more precisely, occupational aspiration becomes central to one's sense of who one is and what one may become (see the discussion of bureaucracy and personality in Chapter 5, III "Structure"). While many theorists comment on the absurdity of this institutionalization of identity development, it continues to be, for most youth, the sole societally approved means to acquire a sense of self as a worker and a potential worker.

2. *Adolescenthood and Culture.*   The adolescent (a person between puberty and full status in matters of love and work) is an important person in our culture. There are certain clear manifestations of this importance.

Economically, the adolescent has the status of a part-time worker and a full-time consumer. The jobs allotted to youth are service rather than production and often are substitutes for parental role performance (e.g., babysitting, food preparation and serving, carrying grocery bags, and home maintenance). This age group is a primary target of advertising and merchandising (and has at least one cable television channel, MTV, devoted to its musical tastes). Whole industries in fashion and leisure-time facilities cater to an adolescent market. Pop culture, fashion, food, and music styles originate in the youth culture and permeate the broader culture through the impetus of the advertising and distribution industries. Allan Bloom, in his controversial book, *The Closing of the American Mind*, emphasizes the pervasive influence of rock music in youth culture, stating, "Nothing is more singular about this generation than its addiction to music" (Bloom, 1987:68).

There is a dual ambivalence that exists between the world of adulthood and the world of adolescenthood. This manifests itself in the family system, where parents and youths are both torn between wanting the youths to grow up and wanting them to remain children. The ambivalence appears in the community and broader culture as the adult envies the vitality of youth, whereas youth envies the power and control possessed by adults. Adults may covet youthfulness as a denial of death as increasing evidences of age cause this denial to be more difficult to maintain. Similarly, youth may covet power and control because of the prolonged dependence the culture dictates. This dual ambivalence complicates the forming of a sense of identity because the separation into camps may also contribute to the foreclosure of adolescent identity rather than adult identity. Such identity foreclosure is problematic in a society where choices are many and increasing in scope. The person who made an early commitment to a total, foreclosed identity may later find it necessary to engage in a moratorium in order to experiment with possibilities for change. This may be highly problematic if others are expecting this person to continue with the foreclosed identity. One expression of this is the movie title, "Middle Aged Crazy." As Erikson viewed this, adolescenthood requires the culture to make adjustments because the generation coming up has absorbed the past, lives in present, and must confront the future with new forms of living constructed of material not available to their parents. Margaret Mead (1970) pointed out that youth in fact is the arbiter of modern cultures. Youth finds this construction both of its own lifestyles and those of the culture a bewildering task. Mead helped to explain why youth experiments widely in lifestyles.

As many writers conclude, each generation has a wide range of characteristics from which the culture can select those best suited to cultural survival. Considering culture as a social system, youth can be considered a component of that system and, as such, a source of energy and tension. As the culture system seeks steady state, the youth component must stand in working relationship to other components. In order for this to happen, the system will change (accommodate) or seek to maintain the status quo (assimilate). Within this dynamic interaction, the individual must seek an identity, and the culture is its survival.

Ideology is a special concern of persons in the throes of the identity crisis. The adolescent has a special sensitivity toward, as well as a particular vulnerability about, ideology. As Erikson puts it so clearly, "It is through their ideology that social systems enter into the fiber of the next generation and attempt to absorb into their lifeblood the rejuvenative power of youth" (Erikson, 1968:134). Erikson's psychohistorical studies of Martin Luther and Gandhi demonstrate how individual solution of ideological aspects of their personal identity crises provided creative innovations that profoundly affected the total culture. Certainly Malcolm X and Martin Luther King may be more recent examples of personal identity crises transmuted into the ideology of a subculture (Malcolm X, 1966; Garrow, 1986; Branch, 1988).

The special virtue that Erikson attached to identity is *fidelity*. The proclivity of youth to invest self and substance in a belief, an idea, or a person with total commitment and faith is generally acknowledged. The search for the Holy Grail, the Crusades, the willingness to follow the knight in shining armor be he Arthur Pendragon or Jesse Jackson are examples. To experience total and complete volitional commitment seems a necessary element of an emerging identity.

The characteristic troubles of the adolescent identity crisis are legion. For convenience they may be grouped under the following headings:

1. *Psychosis* usually appears in the form of schizophrenia. This is a condition of identity diffusion in the extreme. The traits may be considered exaggerations of "normal" traits:
   a. feelings of dislocation and estrangement;
   b. total docility or exaggerated rebelliousness;
   c. emotional lability, rapid mood swings;
   d. feelings of everyone being against one;
   e. idealism that seems to be a denial of reality; or
   f. confused body image and sexual identification.
2. *Neurosis* can also be described as identity confusion in that there is a conflict between the ideal self and other selves. Neurosis is a conflict between antagonistic ideas, wishes, desires or impulses that lead to entropy and disrupts psychological functioning. The alternating excitability and lethargy of adolescents might be examples of this tendency, if they are extreme.
3. *Delinquency* is a socially defined adaptation to inner demands and outer expectations. It may be the result of particular internal conflicts ("acting out" behavior), or it may be an individual or group rejection of cultural values of a larger system. The negative identity previously referred to may be manifested by delinquent behavior. While delinquency may be pathological, it may, as said earlier, be better than no identity at all. One view of delinquency holds that some antisocial behavior may represent a striving for growth. This "opportunity theory" formulated in 1960 by Cloward and Ohlin formed the basis for many of the antipoverty programs directed toward youth. This theory hypothesized that juvenile delinquency was a consequence of the paucity of socially acceptable opportunities available to ghetto youth (Cloward and Ohlin, 1960).

In summary, it can be said that the growth crisis of adolescence is the necessity of trying to pull together who one is. All subsystems of the adolescent personality, cognitive, organic, and emotional, are in rapid flux leading to overall upheaval of previous steady state, at precisely the time that the environment demands new linkages and energy exchanges with this newly emergent personality system. "To be or not to be, that is the question" states part of the issue confronting the adolescent. *What* to be or *what not* to be is the second part of the question. The later tasks of adulthood are to a large degree dependent upon the outcome of this crisis. A person must be fairly certain and comfortable with self before entering into a sustained intimate relationship with another.

E. Perpetuation and Sharing of Identity (Adulthood)

This is the phase of the life span generally referred to as the adult years. Adulthood as a period of life development (personality growth) has seldom been dealt with in theories of personality development. Erikson is notable for his attempt to conceptualize the adult "productive" period as an integral part of his life cycle formulation. Pertinent here are the sixth and seventh growth crises, "intimacy vs. isolation," and "generativity vs. self-absorption."

The critical task of "intimacy vs. isolation" is to enter in an involved, reciprocal way with others sexually, occupationally, and socially. One's sense of identity is merged with another to form a new primary social system. To put it another way, the person completes the transition from the family of origin to the family of procreation. This social crisis addresses itself to the activities of love and work. If one is unable to merge an intact sense of self with others, the outcome is a sense of isolation and polarization of affect. The concept of alienation (discussed later in this section) is another expression of a sense of isolation. The theme of love, genital and reciprocal, is central to this crisis.

The two adult crises Erikson delineates are closely related, and the second describes the task of "generativity vs. self-absorption." This involves the task of active participation in establishing the next generation. In his discussion of this crisis, Erikson explains why he chose to express the quality of feeling as *generativity* rather than creativity or productivity (Erikson, 1959:97). He saw the term *generativity* as being derived from "genitality" and "genes." This particularly emphasizes responsibility for perpetuation of the species and the culture. The theme of this task is caring, caring in the sense of nurturance and caring in the sense of concern for others. In his 1973 Jefferson Lecture, Erikson further elaborated his notion of the adult virtue of caring (Erikson, 1974). The polar sense of stagnation refers to caring primarily and essentially for one's self, with pseudointimacy with others and indulgence of one's self. Stagnation can be viewed as the "closed" human system, defending its equilibrium and minimally engaging in transactions of feelings with others.

The adult period, then, requires persons to perpetuate their own ego identities while sharing this sense of identity with others. The culture establishes social institutions, particularly procreative and child-rearing, through which this task can be accomplished. At stake is a sense of well-being for the person, continuity for the culture, and survival for the species.

Other approaches to describing personality development in the mature years generally take one of two forms; either an idealized definition of maturity or a listing of the problems to be overcome. A popular book, *Passages,* by Gail Sheehy (1976) used Erikson's adult stages and the research of Daniel Levinson (cited below) as vehicles for commenting on the experiences of the many adults she interviewed. Her findings supported Erikson's contention that a person can, and does, "go back again," in the sense of redressing the balances of earlier stages.

Levinson's view of adult development follows Erikson, and is highly compatible with a systems view, in that it stresses integration of "self-in-world." He describes a "life structure" whose major components are the person's relationships with others.

> There are both external and internal aspects in the total life structure and in every component within it. The external aspects deal with the persons, social systems, and other realities with which the individual is involved. The internal aspects are values, desires, conflicts, and skills—those multiple parts of the self that are lived out in one's relationships (Herbert, 1989:55)

Levinson identifies distinct periods (Herbert, 1989:57–63):

> A. The *novice phase of early adulthood*, ages 17–33: this phase has four tasks: (a) forming a dream, (b) forming mentor relationships, (c) forming an occupation, and (d) forming a marriage and family. Its sub-phases are:
>
> (1) Early adult transition, ages 17–22, the boundary between adolescence and adulthood. Its primary tasks are to terminate preadulthood, to modify previous relationships, and to make steps into the adult world.
>
> (2) Entry life structure, ages 22–28; the major task now is to establish a provisional life structure between self and society, involving occupation, love, peer relationships, values, and life style.
>
> (3) Age thirty transition, ages 28–33; building a more satisfactory life structure.
>
> B. Culminating life structure, ages 33–40; the two major tasks are to find a place in society and to strive to "make it."
>
> Becoming One's Own Man—"BOOM" (ages 36–40) is a distinctive phase of the Culminating Life Structure period. The major developmental tasks of this phase are to accomplish . . . goals . . . to become a senior member in one's world, to speak more strongly with one's own voice, and to have a greater measure of authority.
>
> C. Mid-life transition, ages 40–45, and Entering Middle Adulthood, ages 45–50, include the tasks of (a) reappraisal of one's life, (b) individuation, and (c) modifying the life structure yet again. Levinson did not study men older than their 40's.

Levinson and his colleagues researched only men. Similar research on women might yield rather different results, as Gilligan's work might indicate.

Following Erikson and Levinson, it is possible to group the central social expectations for adults under four related headings:

1. Sexuality. Adult sexuality is an important part of intimacy and the sharing of identity. Genitality, in the sense of the capacity for full and mutual consummation of sexual potential, is only characteristic of adulthood. Sexual mutuality forms the foundation of the procreative family system. Erikson says, "love, then, is mutuality of devotion forever subduing the antagonisms inherent in divided function" (Erikson, 1964:129). Sexuality is not confined to sexual activities, but includes generativity and child rearing.

2. Generativity and Child Rearing. The assumption of responsibility for transfer of the culture and nurturance of the young fulfills the destiny of the adult of a species. This requirement is particularly stressful for those without a firm sexual identity and the capacity to merge self-interest with the interest of others. This, of course, is not simply being a biological and rearing parent. It includes a participatory, generative role that is gratifying to self and others, such as child care, teaching, or a role that benefits future generations. This is one form of participation in social processes.

3. Participation in Social Processes. To further the purposes of society and culture requires a measure of subordination of personal needs to the others. This is particularly stressful to those who isolate and retain a primarily self-indulgent orientation. An additional complicating factor here is the omnipresent dilemma of the conflict between the values of individualism and social responsibility. One of the most important aspects of social participation is work.

4. Work. A work function is required that is gratifying to self and to society. In our culture, work has become an organizing theme, and we construct our life styles around it. The usual response of the adult to a "Who are you?" question is more often than not an occupational response. When we meet a person who does not work, it is often difficult to relate to him or her until it is determined *why* she or he does not work. Something must be "wrong." Writings on the rehabilitation of schizophrenics have emphasized the necessity of employment if there is to be hope of continued remission. Work provides an identification, represents social usefulness, and is the means of organizing a life. A classic study of unemployed workers in Great Britain concluded:

> According to the findings, a prolonged and fruitless search for work is, in general, accompanied by the following emotions in sequence: first, shock at being out of a job; second, optimism, during search for work; third, when the search fails, pessimism, anxiety and distress follow; and finally, a fatalistic attitude toward life ensues (World of Work Report, 1977:24).

Certain work identifications are still tied to the place of work ("I work in the mines" or "I work in the quarry") but other designations are also used. Now most people express work identification as either "I do" or "I am." Traditionally, the "I am" designation belonged to the classic professions of law, the clergy, and medicine, including nursing. The "I do" description is usually a shorthand job description ("I sell shoes" or "I wire circuit boards"). The press toward professionalization in a wide variety of occupations is an attempt to establish a work identification of the "I am" type, such as "I am a social worker," I am a teacher," "I am a computer programmer," or "I am a stock analyst." There are still symbolic workplace territories such as "They're in the navy," "He's in bonds and securities," "I'm in government," or "She's in politics."

The escalation of occupational titles is another indication of the significance of work as a determinant of status and position. The farmer is now in agribusiness; the undertaker is a mortician or funeral counselor; the barber or beautician is now a hair stylist, and the salesperson is an account executive.

Erich Fromm presented a clear and concise exposition of the idea that the marketplace orientation of our society determines and maintains work identity (Fromm, 1962). Fromm suggested that one is valued not for what one is but for what one seems to be; this is then related to supply and demand. "Image" becomes crucial and the person must project the "right" image to be successful; the resumé becomes the person. Advertisers are concerned with product image, National Association of Social Workers with social workers' image, and National Education Association with teachers' image. One's value as a person, said Fromm, is not self-defined but dependent upon value definitions by others using the criteria of the marketplace. Fromm describes how this has led to the cult of adaptability, with the prime value invested in changeability. Work, then, has permeated our social systems to an extent we seldom recognize. The "problem" segments of our society are defined and labeled by work status:

a. *The nonworkers.* These include the age groups of youth and the aged. These are not unemployed persons; they are clearly identified as nonworkers, not eligible for work identification. The aged are in a worse plight than the young, since school is viewed as a kind of work and "student" serves as a work status (and is accepted on application forms as a proper answer to "occupation?"). It is likely that organizations of, and in support of, the elderly, will be successful in redefining their status to allow them to continue to be active workers (e.g., Social Security recipients may now continue to work, earning up to a set amount before it affects their monthly benefit). This may be acceptable not only because of the difficulty of elders in finding useful roles, but also because of the financial burden upon the active work-force in supporting the rapidly increasing numbers of retired workers.

b. *Waste persons.* As Carse said, "Waste persons are those no longer useful as resources to a society for whatever reason, and have become *apatrides,* or noncitizens. Waste persons must be placed out of view—in ghettos, slums, reservations, camps, retirement villages, mass graves, remote territories, strategic hamlets—all places of desolation, and uninhabitable" (Carse, 1986:133). The same could be said, of course, of society's frequent opinion regarding prisoners, Downs syndrome children, and sufferers of Hansen's disease (more commonly known as lepers, and in some countries still confined to colonies).

c. *The unemployed.* These are society's greatest concern. Proposed welfare programs such as workfare place primary emphasis upon putting the unemployed to work and rewarding persons who make the effort to seek and sustain work. The able-bodied unemployed person violates social prescriptions. That person is without a work identification—in fact, the primary social identity may well be *unemployed*. Since the idea of "right to work" holds sway, such unemployment is attributed either to lack of opportunity or to individual deficiency.

  d. The unemployable. These people present a particular problem because of the humanitarian values held by society. Changing the ground rules and expectations of the worker, as Goodwill Industries (note the use of "Industries") and sheltered workshops do, makes it possible to remove some people from this classification. The "Works" programs of the Roosevelt New Deal gave hundreds of thousands of people a job, an occupation; they were no longer merely "unemployables." The Youth Service programs now being considered in Congress, and the various "Compacts" between the business communities in cities such as Boston and St. Paul, will serve the same function, in converting untrained (and therefore unemployable) youth into apprentices preparing for careers. This fulfills the promise of the right to work and provides opportunity structures in which this right can be realized. Although they are "pitied rather than censured," the lack of work identification is judged to be an important personality deficiency by unemployed persons and their significant environments.

  Unemployment is a significant source of alienation. Alienation is a phenomenon of adulthood, since it is a condition of one's identity. It is, in some respects, the adult counterpart of maternal deprivation. Alienation means the absence or insufficiency of those vital, intimate connections with one's social environment that call forth and sustain one's identity. "Structural unemployment" itself fosters alienation as it breaks the connection between the person and the work environment, and between the person and the society. In most definitions, alienation also includes the feelings and perceptions that accompany these lacks, including the following:

  1. There may be lowered self-esteem, a gulf between societal expectations and perceived self. The person may also experience *self-estrangement* and *self-alienation*, a gulf between ideal and actual self, as though one were someone (or something) other than oneself.

  2. *Anomie* is a term coined by Emile Durkheim to convey what, in systems terminology, may be viewed as absent or faulty linkage with larger social systems. This is experienced as "rootlessness," "normlessness" (the literal meaning of *anomie*), or "meaninglessness." The person does not experience a culture of shared meanings, or a sense of shared norms of behavior. Thoughtful observers have identified the existence of a new, permanent *underclass* of those excluded from opportunities for achievement, particularly victims of racism and discrimination. A prime

characteristic of this underclass is the abandonment of any expectation of social mobility or approved achievement within the "legitimate" social classes or structures. In such situations, persons may create or join alternative subcultures, e.g., criminal organizations, including the Mafia, Chinese Triads, or organized sectors of the illegal drug culture.

3. These persons may perceive, correctly or not, that their deeply held values are not shared or supported by their social environments, and the converse, that one does not share society's (or family's) values.

One of the most frequently examined forms of alienation is *work alienation*. The federal study, *Work in America* (1973) reported a high proportion of workers who found their work to be stifling and unrewarding. Reactions to the publication of these findings were mixed; some questioned their validity, but others, such as Studs Terkel, saw the findings as congruent with their own observations and studies. Terkel described alienating work as a "Monday through Friday kind of dying" (Terkel, 1975:xiii). *Work in America* noted three particularly alienating conditions: lack of autonomy, in the sense of freedom to perform assignments without close, arbitrary supervision; lack of advancement and opportunity for personal growth; and lack of opportunity to make decisions.

The largest group of alienated workers is probably female. In addition to the reasons already mentioned, women face other alienating circumstances. They frequently are not taken seriously as career-minded workers. "Career women" who are mothers with young children currently are being described as being in the "mommy track" (Goodman, 1989a; Ehrlich, 1989:98–99) an alternative career line in which flexible schedules are a necessity, but in which advancement is slower. Whether this is fair, and whether it promotes or detracts from women's rights at the workplace, is currently being debated. Women are usually not paid as much as men for performing the same jobs (women's wages are approximately two thirds those of men). They are underutilized, less frequently advanced, and less frequently chosen for specialized training.

In conclusion, the crises of adulthood are focused in the socially defined expectations for the person to intimately involve herself or himself with others in the creation and maintenance of the social systems that enable the culture and species to survive. An adult who does not do this will be isolated, self-serving, and stagnant. To paraphrase Erikson, the adult may say, "I am what I can love and care for and about."

F. Conservation of Identity (Elderhood)

This is the concluding task of the life cycle and, as such, can be characterized as the crisis of aging. *Conservation* refers to consolidation, protection, and holding on to the ego integrity one has accrued over a lifetime in the midst of loss and divestment of usual roles and functions. The positive sense of conservatism is that identity passes from one social context to another and yet remains the same. The self maintains its continuity and consistency from one social system to another.

Erikson's polarity during the waning years of life is "ego integrity vs. disgust and despair." This is the culmination of the previous seven crises. Integrity refers to "the ego's accrued assurance of its proclivity for order and meaning—an emotional integration faithful to the image-bearers of the past and ready to take, and eventually to renounce, leadership in the present" (Erikson, 1968:139). It is the capacity of persons to accept their life histories, to see the effect they have had upon their world through their relationships, and to accept their mortality. The other pole, the sense of disgust, is characterized by bitterness and refusal to accept death as the finite boundary of the personal life cycle. A positive resolution was expressed by Max Robinson, former ABC television "news anchor," the first African-American to hold such a position. Robinson died of AIDS in December, 1988.

> In his last public appearance, Robinson offered this advice to students at Howard University: "Try to keep your integrity, because you're going to find out in life, at the end, that's all you've got" (*Iowa City Press Citizen*, Dec. 21, 1988).

A definition of "aging" or "age" is difficult to formulate to everyone's satisfaction. In one sense, the aging process begins at birth. Socially, age is defined by function, usually work-related. For example, most professional athletes are "old" by the time they are 35 (coincidentally, the same as the minimal age qualification for president), while a Supreme Court Justice is thought to be still functional at 80, and comedian and actor George Burns is still going strong in his 90's. Some industries consider the 40-year-old worker as too old to be hired, and 42-year-old baseball player Tommy Johns is a marvel. Social security currently sets the age of retirement at 65, although this is planned to increase in the next century, as the average age of the workforce increases, and as elders maintain health increasingly longer. The "old elderly," age 80 and older, are the fastest growing segment of the population of the United States. Birren suggested a utilitarian definition:

> A person is "old" or, better perhaps, "aging" when [the person] is so regarded and treated by . . . contemporaries and by the younger generation and when [the person] has read the culturally recognized individual and social signs symbolic of membership in the generation of elders. The only matter of individual choice open to the old person has to do with whether [the person] wishes to accept or postpone belief in [the] new identity and act accordingly (Birren, 1959:280).

Erikson commented, "it is perfectly obvious that if we live long enough, we all face a renewal of infantile tendencies—a certain childlike quality, if we're lucky, and senile childishness, if we're not. The main point is again a developmental one: only in old age can true wisdom develop in those who are thus 'gifted' " (Evans, 1967:53–54). The tasks of aging in our culture were nicely summarized by Birren in quoting Simmons' cross-cultural studies:

1. To live as long as possible, at least until life-satisfaction no longer compensates for its privation, or until the advantages of death seem to outweigh the burden of life.
2. To get more rest, relief from the necessity of wearisome exertion at humdrum tasks, and protection from too great exposure to physical hazards—opportunities, in other words, to safeguard and preserve the waning energies of a physical existence.
3. To remain active participants in personal and group affairs in either operational or supervisory roles—any participation, in fact, being preferable to complete idleness and indifference.
4. To safeguard or even strengthen any prerogatives acquired in long life, i.e., skills, possessions, rights, authorities, prestige, etc.
5. Finally, to withdraw from life, when necessity requires it, as honorably as possible, without too much suffering, and with maximum prospects for an attractive hereafter (Birren, 1959:864–865).

As earlier stated, aging is characterized by the theme of conservation. It involves relinquishment of certain patterned investments of self. The nature of transactions with other human systems is necessarily modified. The elements of identity involved can be discussed under a few general headings.

1. Work Role and Occupational Identification. This probably has a more profound effect upon those with the "I do" work identification than upon those with an "I am" identification. The retired doctor continues to be seen as a doctor, but the retired shoe salesman is no longer a salesman. Willy Loman in *Death of a Salesman* is an example of a person faced with such a loss of work identity. The relinquishment of the work role is particularly difficult for such a person because so much feedback about one's worth is tied to this role. Loss of work role usually is accompanied by a marked reduction in income and the necessity of readjustment in standard of living. Such persons are deprived of membership in their former work system. Women may face losses (or at least changes) of role earlier when children leave home or their husbands die, in addition to their employment-related changes. On the other hand, many of both sexes who retire from their work roles easily make the transition to a more leisurely pace of living. The time is available to pursue other interests; the economic means may or may not be. In view of the large percentage of people who opt for early retirement, it is conceivable that the work identification of "retired" substitutes for an identification as active worker.

2. Intimate Ties. As the person's friends, acquaintances, and spouse die, that person is again faced with separation experiences faced as a child or young adult. Those who were part of one's personality system are gone. One must undergo the painful process of withdrawing (decathecting) attachments to them at a time when it is most difficult to establish new linkages to replace the former ones. One may not be able to modify one's own personality structure sufficiently to accommodate new attachments. One's environment narrows, and perhaps the intensity of the remaining attachments is increased. Such attachments may become "overinvested"; for example, a pet or a formerly casual acquaintance may suddenly become all important. If no replacements or investments are accomplished, the person may turn inward, seeking energy internally, or may "bank the fires," attempting less and seeking equilibrium on a lower level of interaction with the environment.

3. Sexual Interests. Although little research has been done on the sexual activity of the aged, the findings indicate a gradual decline in frequency over the entire adult period. There is no sharp decline at any particular age. As overt sexual engagement declines, the aged may find if difficult to express or receive tenderness or affection in other ways; grandchildren frequently serve the function of being recipients of affection from grandparents. Because socially our stereotype of the aged indicates that such needs somehow disappear, we are often unrealistic about the behavior of the aged.

Unfortunately, society's understanding of this is blocked by our tendency to deny sexuality in elderly persons. For example, some residences for the elderly prohibit physical manifestations of affection, do not allow the closing of doors when one has a visitor of the opposite sex, and in a few reported instances, prohibit holding hands. The available evidence indicates that sexual companionship (with or without sexual activity) is as important to most elderly persons as it is to those of earlier adult years.

4. Physical Abilities, Particularly Sensory and Motor. Physiologically, the number of taste buds declines with age, eyesight and hearing may suffer impairment, and walking may become more difficult. These limitations necessarily handicap the aged person in maintaining contact with the accustomed social environment. The person's world may be narrowed to the walls of his or her own home, and to the television set.

The older person's self-concept may be threatened by these losses. An example is the 60-year-old man who refuses to be beaten at tennis. The person's reaction may be to deny the losses and demand performance characteristic of an earlier age, or the reaction may be depression and unrealistic refusal to do what one is still capable of. It is common among the aged to make reasonable adjustments to less acute faculties—in other words, to make the best of one's abilities. Such realistic adjustments are part of the person's integrity and maintenance of self.

5. *Intellectual Abilities.*   Borrowing from Piaget, it could be concluded that as one's schemas multiply and more adequately account for one's experience, they become progressively less modifiable. Accommodation declines, while assimilation increases. The aged may exclude stimuli from awareness, to limit the energy exchange with those in their environment. The aged person may become less concerned with interpreting and storing new information and more concerned with preserving previous information, sometimes literally in the form of scrapbooks, possessions of a deceased spouse, or a house that was the family dwelling. Either of these intellectual patterns, becoming more closed or remaining open, may be performed to allow integrity. Erikson's "wisdom" implies, in one's past, the accrued identity of a lifetime. "Despair and disgust" implies closure but may well include feedback that indicates the person's alienation from the environment. Thus it implies openness as well.

6. *Life Review.*   A review of one's life might include the feeling that time is running out, that there are no alternatives possible "at this late date." In *Death of a Salesman*, Willy depends upon his son Biff to reassure him of his own integrity, but Biff has neglected to write to his father:

> BIFF: I was on the move. But you know I thought of you all the time. You know that, don't you pal?
> LINDA: I know, dear, I know. But he likes to have a letter. Just to know that there's still a possibility for better things (Miller, 1955:55).

With the United States' cultural emphases on youth, external appearance, and robust health, to the neglect of wisdom, experience, and the ability to cope with travail, the frail elderly may find themselves in a disadvantaged state and their integrity unnoticed.

Aged persons as human systems must find their steady state, their identity, among the social systems with which they are linked. Erikson said that a person "as a psychosocial creature will face, toward the end of . . . life, a new edition of an identity crisis which we may state in the words, 'I am what survives of me' " (Erikson, 1968:141). What survives are the human systems one has been related to and part of: persons, families, groups, organizations, communities, societies, cultures. These human systems in turn affect other persons who are being born and who are developing. This is why Erikson calls it a *life*cycle—not the life of an individual, alone, but the cycle of life itself: the human system.

Webster's Dictionary is kind enough to help us complete this outline in circular fashion. Trust (the first of our ego values) is here defined as "the assured reliance

on another's integrity," the last of our values. . . . It seems possible to further paraphrase the relation of adult integrity to infantile trust by saying that healthy children will not fear life if their elders have integrity enough not to fear death (Erikson,
1963:269).

In this book, we examine and speculate upon social systems—human
systems. We state in the chapter on families that "a family, then, is to
be construed as patterns of relatedness as they converge in a person."
We can now say the same about all social systems; systems are patterns
of relatedness as they converge in individual persons. Systems do not
exist without persons; persons can exist only because of social systems
of which they are, or have been at some time in their life, a part. Understanding of the implications of this, and applying that understanding to
one's life and practice, are the highest wisdom to which a systems approach can contribute.

SUGGESTED READINGS

Ainsworth, Mary D. Salter.
   1969 "Object Relations, Dependency and Attachments: A Theoretical Review
   of the Infant-Mother Relationship," *Child Development*, 40(4):969–1025.
      The definitive review of early attachment; grouped under headings of Psy-
      choanalytic, Social Learning, and Ethological.
Bringuier, Jean-Claude.
   1980 *Conversations with Jean Piaget.* Chicago: The University of Chicago Press.
      Covering the years 1969–1976, these conversations were first published in
      France in 1977. Not for the novice student of Piaget since it presumes some
      knowledge of Piaget's theory.
Butler, Robert N.
   1975 *Why Survive? Being Old in America.* New York: Harper and Row.
      A landmark work on the plight of the aged in United States society. Dr.
      Butler, a psychiatrist, was the first director of the National Institute on
      Aging. This book was awarded a Pulitzer prize in 1976.
Erikson, Erik.
   1968 *Identity: Youth and Crisis.* New York: Norton.
      In this book Erikson expands on the critical task of identity formation in the
      context of contemporary issues. It is also one of many of his writings to
      discuss the total life cycle. This book has been used as the small-map text
      for this chapter. For a thorough explanation of his life cycle formulation see
      Childhood and Society, second edition. (New York: Norton, 1963).
Fennell, Graham, Chris Phillipson, and Helen Evers.
   1988 *The Sociology of Old Age.* Milton Keynes: Open University Press.
      An excellent, comprehensive examination of old age as a social phenome-
      non. "Our priority has been to demonstrate both the 'normality' and diver-

sity of older people and to encourage more wide-ranging perspectives," said the authors.

Freud, Sigmund.

1949 *An Outline of Psychoanalysis.* New York: Norton.

The last book that Freud wrote, and published ten years after his death, it is a concise explanation of the principles derived from his life's work. It is *strongly* recommended that the reader be familiar with Freud's expression of his ideas rather than relying on the interpretations of latter-day critics. A small book, it can be used in its entirety as supplementary to this systems text.

Group for the Advancement of Psychiatry.

1989 *How Old is Old Enough?* Report No. 126. New York: Brunner/Mazel.

This interesting little book attempts to provide psychiatrists with guidelines for assessment of psychological maturation, examining "historical, psycho-analytic, Piagetian, phenomenologic, and biological" evidence. Chapter 2 is a review of Piaget's theory.

Levinson, Daniel J.

1986 "A Conception of Adult Development," *American Psychologist,* 41:3–13.

Levinson's scheme of adult development has been widely adopted. It is highly compatible with systems ideas, and with the "person-in-situation" view of most helping professions. His original contributions are the periods of "forming a dream," "forming mentor relationships," and "culminating life structure."

Maier, Henry W.

1988 *Three Theories of Child Development,* forth edition, New York: Harper and Row.

The author, a social worker, examines, compares, and contrasts the theories of Erikson, Piaget, and Sears. He further looks at them as bases for social work practice. An excellent resource.

Newman, Barbara, M., and Philip R. Newman.

1979 *Development Through Life: A Psychosocial Approach.* Homewood, Ill.: Dorsey Press.

An excellent text for any student who has not studied human development from a life cycle perspective. It is comprehensive and thorough.

Phillips, John L., Jr.

1969 *The Origins of Intellect: Piaget's Theory.* San Francisco: Freeman.

Perhaps the best source for anyone wishing to read further about the contri-butions of Piaget. Especially good are the Preface, Chapter 1, and Chapter 5.

Rosen, Hugh.

1980. *The Development of Sociomoral Knowledge.* New York: Columbia University Press.

While this is largely a presentation, review and critique of Kohlberg's work, it briefly summaarized the work of Piaget and others who preceded Kohl-berg. Thorough and impartial.

Saxon, Sue V., and Mary Jean Etten.

1987 *Physical Change and Aging: A Guide for the Helping Professions.* New York: The Tiresias Press.

Thorough review of biological theories of aging, the effects of aging on or-gan systems, and such aspects as exercise, nutrition, and death and grief.

LITERARY SOURCES

Bergman, Ingmar.
   1960 "Wild Strawberries." In *Four Screenplays*. New York: Simon and Schuster.
   An elderly man reminisces about the past as a means of dealing with the
   present. The film is sensitively done.
McCullers, Carson.
   1940 *The Heart Is a Lonely Hunter*. Boston: Houghton Mifflin.
   The story of a man with a severe hearing loss who cares for and about
   others. The movie version is beautifully done.
Miller, Arthur.
   1949 *Death of a Salesman*. New York: Bantam Books.
   Miller's classic play of Everyman caught up in a world of change and attempting to live in the past.
Thompson, Ernest.
   1979 *On Golden Pond*. New York: Dodd, Mead.
   Two elders struggling to maintain their integrity. The interaction between
   them and the youngster well illustrates Erikson's comment at the conclusion of this chapter, i.e., healthy children will not fear life if their elders
   have integrity enough not to fear death.

FILMS AND VIDEOS

An Alzheimer's Story (1985)
   This documentary follows a family whose wife/mother is deteriorating, and
   their decision about a nursing home.
Bill (1981; made for television)
   Based on the true story of our friend Bill Sackter, a retarded man who spent
   most of his life in an institution, but blossomed with the help of his friends
   Bev and Barry Morrow. Barry Marrow wrote the story, which won an Emmy,
   and the screenplay for the sequel, *Bill On His Own* (1983). Morrow later wrote
   the screenplay for *Rain Man*, for which he won an Oscar. All three are highly
   recommended for this chapter.
Birth of a Brain (1982)
   Genetic origins of the brain and its development are illustrated through micro-
   photography, computer graphics, and a birth sequence. Brain development is
   shown in parallel with physiological and behavioral changes.
Clotheslines (1982)
   Billed as a "poetic documentary," this film is about the pragmatic, symbolic
   and artistic role of laundry in women's lives. It touches on social roles, traditions, folklore, generations, and the aesthetics of "women's work."
The Color Purple (1985)
   From Alice Walker's poignant novel, this illustrates Erikson's principle that
   much can be remedied later in life. Celie, an African-American girl, is viewed
   as unattractive and is mistreated by those about her. She finds support from

her sister and from her husband's girl friend, and becomes a strong, self-determining woman who cares for others. Beautifully acted.

The Cutting Edge (1983)

This film depicts the adaptation of Southeast Asian youth and families to the United States. Successes and difficulties are openly discussed.

First Dance (1984)

A young man wants to choose his date to the prom; he is gay. What are his rights as a person?

400 Blows (1952)

Francois Truffaut's early film illustrates the process by which a young boy is rejected by family and others, and survives by adopting deviant behavior. A fine film.

Freud. (1962)

Starring Montgomery Clift, this is a credible attempt to present the main tenets of Freud's thought and his life, primarily through his work with one female patient. Well acted and directed. The television series "Freud," aired on cable television in several hour-long episodes, is well worth watching.

Just Because of Who We Are (1986)

The daily physical and psychological harassment suffered by lesbians, and violence against them, is shown in this documentary. Personal stories of rejection, arrest, and attempts at "cures" are related.

Lila (1980)

Lila Bonner-Miller, a psychiatrist, artist, church leader, and independent woman, is 80 years old in this film. Her vitality and involvement with her family and community, as well as her past accomplishments, mark her as an extraordinary person.

Luther Metke at 94 (1980)

Metke homesteaded in Oregon's Cascade mountains in 1907. He was a labor organizer, contractor, painter, carpenter, and Oregon's last ambulatory survivor of Spanish-American War. He exemplifies folk wisdom, folk artistry, and human warmth.

Personal Best (1982)

A plausible story of a young female athlete finding her identity through her achievements, her sexual relationship with another female athlete, and through her anger at feeling exploited. Well acted.

Pixote (Brazilian, 1980)

Described as a "shattering" film about a 10-year-old street kid surviving in Sao Paulo. Fine performances by both professional actors and amateurs.

Something About Amelia (1984; made for television)

Stark, provocative film about incest, with strong performances by Ted Danson and Glenn Close.

Summer Solstice (1983)

An elderly couple (Henry Fonda and Myrna Loy) return to the beach where they met a half-century earlier. They remember and relive the events of those fifty years.

Sybil (1976)

Sally Fields gives a brilliant performance as several of the multiple personalities encountered by psychiatrist Joanne Woodward. Fields is entirely believable, and the dynamics of the case are plausible.

The Three Faces of Eve (1957)

The real patient in this case has identified herself in recent years, and has told her own story. Joanne Woodward is credible as a tormented woman with multiple personalities who finds a self with the help of a psychiatrist.

To Live Until You Die: The Work of Elizabeth Kubler-Ross (1983)

This video shows Dr. Ross working with dying patients, and illustrates the five stages of reaction to dying which she identified.

Epilogue

He laughed because he thought they could not hit
him
He did not imagine that they were practicing how
to miss him.

Berthold Brecht

Chamberlain's law:
Everything tastes more or less like chicken.

This chapter addresses some of the implications of a social systems view
of the world. Does it make a difference what we perceive and believe?
Unequivocally and emphatically, yes! Within each of the realms in
which helping professions operate (either literally or figuratively), there
exists divergence of opinions regarding the most efficacious means to
accomplish change. In the health fields, for example, which will be more
effective, basic research into the physiology of disease processes or
greater concentration on environmental conditions that affect public
health? Which will improve patient care more, intensified training of the
nurse practitioner or restructuring the organizations that deliver health
care services? In the field of social services, should there be expansion
of clinical training of social workers or should efforts be directed toward
the training of welfare administrators and policy analysts?

The listing of such choices could be an inexhaustible exercise. The
relevant point here is that the practitioner, or student, often chooses her
or his means of intervention on the basis of beliefs and values that have
not been articulated, examined, analyzed, and evaluated.

The "helping professions" and professional disciplines that are oriented toward practical application of theory are often accused of shal-
lowness and lack of philosophical clarity. Those who practice these pro-

fessions are condemned by both external and internal critics for failure to be explicit about their assumptions and suppositions, their definition of their competencies, the nature of their helping processes and the goals of their activities. "And I would argue that tacit (and therefore unquestioned) false assumptions have led to at least as many grievous mistakes as explicitly affirmed wrong conclusions" (Andreski, 1973:6). There is, beyond a doubt, some truth to these charges. We in the helping professions share idealism, impatience, and dissatisfaction with the world as it is, and we seek pragmatic approaches to action. Frequently, our desire for change outdistances our willingness to thoughtfully examine the philosophical and intellectual structures that are the foundations of our practice. In this chapter, we comment briefly on these intellectual and ethical foundations.

I. HOLONISTIC THOUGHT

A. Part–Whole Relatedness

You have noted a number of concepts, introduced in the first two chapters and developed in subsequent chapters, dealing with the dimensions of partness and wholeness; of oppositeness, duality, and polarities. Whether we are examining the idea of holon (Chapter 1, "The Social Systems Approach") or seeking the locus of change in the individual or society, we remain in the realm of part–whole relatedness, examining how the one is interdependent with the other. Systems thinking provides a means to appraise, understand, and accept the inevitable unity and separateness of part and whole. As Ronald Jones succinctly stated the "problem":

> From approximately 3,000 B.C. in the East when Emperor Fu Hsi is believed to have discovered the idea of Yin and Yan as they are embodied in T'ai Chi, and since about 400 B.C. in the West when Heraclitus and Plato struggled with the problem of opposites, scholars have tried to resolve the mystery of how many parts come to be a unified whole. This adds up to a 5,000 year problem. Throughout the history of ideas the problem of One and the Many, of part-whole relations, of order and structure has appeared over and over again. Names we are all familiar with identify this as the *pons asinorum*. Nicholas of Cusa (15th Century), Giambattista Vico (17th Century), and more recently Cassirer, Whitehead, von Bertalanffy, Koestler, Sorokin, and Polanyi have made this problem *the* problem. The problem of the integration of differentiated parts, of harmony in diversity, is not merely a problem for idle, remote, and academic speculation.
>
> To make certain that this connection is clearly before us, let me elaborate a bit. It seems to me that the *sine qua non* of man's knowledge, happiness, and existence is to be found in the idea of the reconciliation of differences. It matters little whether we talk about mental health and personality structure or whether we talk in the

context of society. It matters little what the size of the society is. It makes little difference whether the society is a marriage, a small group, a large industrial organization, a community, a nation, or many nations, the basic issue is that of the reconciliation of the individual with the group, the organization, the integration of parts into a unified whole. These issues are all matters of totality, wholeness, completeness, unity, order, structure (Whyte, Wilson, and Wilson, 1960:284).

But this is not a "problem" in the sense of solving, curing, or otherwise having done with it. It is rather a perplexing mystery of human existence. Systemic thinking is a means toward perceiving the issue of the one and the many as a foundation for systems well-being. In fact, the one cannot exist without the many and the many cannot exist without the one.

Alfred North Whitehead described existence as part/whole activity. By that I mean that every actual thing is something by reason of its activity; whereby its nature consists in its relevance to other things, and its individually consists in its synthesis of other things so far as they are relevant to it (Curtis and Greenslet, 1962:61).

B. Qualities and Polarities

The question of differences and opposites has always puzzled humankind. Aristotle dealt with it by holding that an entity, quality, or phenomenon must be one thing or another. A contemporary statement of that belief is, "If you aren't part of the solution, then you are part of the problem."

Earlier Greek philosophers, Anaximander and Heraclitus, postulated that differences must be merged or balanced into a state of wholeness. Hippocrates drew from the thought of Anaximander in developing the doctrine of "coction." According to the Hippocratic formulation, in the course of each disease, there occurs a "crisis" when either coction occurs or the patient dies. Strictly speaking, coction is the action that combines the opposing humors so that there results a perfect fusion of them all. According to Hippocrates, "a disease was supposed to result when the equilibrium of the humours, from 'some exciting cause' or other was disturbed, and then nature, that is the constitution of the individual, made every effort through coction to restore the necessary balance" (Jones, 1923:lii). "Balance" is equivalent to steady state.

In Warmington's and Rouse's translation of *Phaedo*, Plato reports a passage wherein Socrates insists that the Hippocratic method is right and then discourses on the nature of opposites.

Then don't consider it as regards men only," he said; "if you wish to understand more easily, think of all animals and vegetables, and, in a word, everything that was birth, let us see if everything comes into being like that, always opposite from opposite and from nowhere else; whenever there happens to be a pair of opposites, such as beautiful and ugly, just and unjust, and thousands of others like these. So let us enquire whether everything that has an opposite must come from its opposite and from nowhere else. For example, when anything becomes bigger, it must, I suppose, become bigger from being smaller before.

'Yes.'

'And if it becomes smaller, it was bigger before and became smaller after that?'

'True,' he said.

'And again, weaker from stronger, and slower from quicker?'

'Certainly.'

'Very well, if a thing becomes worse, is it from being better, and more just from more unjust?'

'Of course.'

'Have we established that sufficiently, then, that everything comes into being in this way, opposite from opposite?'

'Certainly.'

'Again, is there not the same sort of thing in them all, between the two opposites two becomings, from the first to the second, and back from the second to the first; between greater and lesser increase and diminution, and we call one increasing and the other diminishing?'

'Yes,' he said.

'And being separated and mingled, growing cold and growing hot, and so with all; even if we have sometimes no names for them, yet in fact at least it must be the same everywhere, that they come into being from each other, and that there is a becoming from one to the other?'

'Certainly,' said he (Warmington and Rouse, 1956:475–476).

Samuel Butler expressed a similar conception of polarities in *The Way of All Flesh:*

> People divide off vice and virtue as though they were two things, neither of which had with it anything of the other. This is not so. There is no useful virtue which has not some alloy of vice, and hardly any vice, if any, which carries not with it a little dash of virtue; virtue and vice are like life and death, or mind and matter— things which cannot exist without being qualified by their opposite (Butler, 1943:80).

The one and the many is just such a set of unified opposites and partakes in the nature of opposites. Each system, as the observer recognizes it and separates it from its environment, is simultaneously part/whole or one/many (i.e., holon) and contains a duality within itself; it can also be viewed as one pole of a larger duality. Again, it should be stressed that these are ways of thinking, not descriptions or discoveries of "reality."

It follows, then, that controversies over whether it is better to work toward changing individuals (the one) or to work toward changing society (the many) are of little practical consequence unless the inseparability is fully taken into account. When that is so, it becomes apparent that both (one and many) are inextricably responsible for change. Systems thinking provides a means to observe, understand, and intervene into these interactive processes.

II. IMPLIED VALUE AND ETHICAL POSITIONS

Most of the recurring questions about our social systems approach have had to do with values and ethics. Are there implicit values that should be explicated? Can a perspectivistic model be value free? Does a social systems approach remain at a descriptive level and thus mitigate against change? Does it foster maintenance of status quo?

In our judgment, there are certain value stances implicit in a social systems perspective. Holding no brief for the specific labels, we will discuss five aspects under the following rubrics:

1. interdependence
2. interaction
3. conservation and conflict
4. change
5. egalitarianism

A. Interdependence

The systems view presented in this book begins with the postulate that each human or social entity exists and thrives as both whole and part. It cannot continue existence in isolation and therefore must participate in interdependent relatedness with other entities.

A dramatic example can be drawn from medieval times. The walled castle-keep, surrounded by a moat with a bridge that could be drawn closed and sealed, was designed to protect a community from attack. It often proved to be unassailable with the weaponry available. However, the adversary could simply make sure the boundary was not crossed and that the castle remained isolated to draw the occupants out, for in time the only alternative was death. The modern day naval blockade follows the same strategy. A system then cannot be completely autonomous indefinitely. Neither can it exist without some measure of autonomy. Without some distinguishable quality of separateness it could not be defined or identified within its environment. To deny the quality of autonomy and separateness is to deny human and social existence. "They all look alike to me" is an expression of such denial of humanity. Interdependent relatedness is a melding of dependence and autonomy (independence) and is both desirable and necessary to the well-being of social systems.

B. Interaction

Similarly, interaction is essential and therefore desirable to systems' well-being. Energy exchange and feedback (as a regulatory mechanism) require and depend upon interaction. Furthermore, the quality of mutuality is, and will be, assumed to be a necessary aspect of interaction. Systems interactions are reciprocal and cyclical. That which is valued is mutuality of interaction: systems affecting and being affected by other systems of the same magnitude (horizontal) and differing magnitudes (vertical). Certainly interdependence and interaction are closely related, but they are not identical.

The Old Order Amish continue to employ the social sanction of "shunning" with members who have seriously violated expectation of behavior. The practice of shunning allows the person to remain in the community system but prohibits others from mutual interaction with the person being shunned. Within this custom, the quality of interdependence remains largely unchanged, whereas the quality of mutual interaction is greatly diminished. One of the most severe punishments that can be inflicted on a human being is solitary confinement. This more extreme form of shunning prohibits energy exchange and feedback.

C. Conservation and Conflict

Conservation of system integrity is necessary and desirable to system vitality and well-being. Conservation is defined as "the act of preserving, guarding or protecting; preservation from loss, decay, injury or violation" (Webster's New Twentieth Century Dictionary of the English Language, 1980:389).

Paradoxically, conservation and conflict stem from the same systemic source: A system seeks to protect its integrity in ways that well might interfere with or prevent the protection of another system's integrity. The achievement of synergy, or constructive interchange, occurs only with effort and expenditure of energy. Entropy occurs without effort; conflict requires effort. In those situations where conflict can be avoided, it can be averted only with effort. Conflict, then, is not merely accidental and unfortunate; it is an inherent, legitimate, and frequently unavoidable event that is a direct result of system(s) striving for integrity (i.e., wholeness). As Stafford Beer (1981) puts it, "Resistance is only people continuing to be who they are."

D. Change

Change, too, is necessary and desirable to systems vitality. Without change, systems tend to "feed" on themselves or their environment, depleting the internal or external resources, shrink, and eventually cease to exist (i.e., become entropic). Our view of systems presupposes an interactive balance between change and conservation, the mixture varying according to circumstances. In some instances, conservation requires change, especially for purposes of preservation from decay, injury, or violation. Change is the means to the genesis of "new life" for systems purposes, while conservation maintains or augments the "life stream" of the system.

E. Egalitarianism

Our systems view is permeated by values of equality and equity. Interdependence and mutuality of interaction dictate that systems of varying magnitudes be perceived as being equally necessary to systemic functioning. Within a systems approach, the centrality of the concept of hierarchy strikes some as inimical to an egalitarian value. In point of fact, "hierarchy" is a structural aspect of systems organization that implies no value or power differential.

Egalitarianism does not imply maintenance of a status quo or an absence of conflict. As stated earlier, conflict is inherent within and between systems; and the fact that each system strives to maintain its integrity inevitably leads to conflict. Thus, egalitarianism does not denote absolute equality but rather a recognition that each system possesses its own "will to live," its place in the sun, and thus has, existentially, as much right as any other system, subsystem, or suprasystem to survive. It is the carrying out of this survival that engages the system in other values/ethical positions of interdependence, interaction, conservation, conflict, and change. It could be interpreted as tragedy, in the Greek sense, for in order to preserve itself, any system must risk "losing itself."

This conundrum applies to all systems. In order to thrive, each must change to some degree. This is the ultimate egalitarian imperative of a social systems approach.

Bibliography

Acuña, Rodolpho. 1972. *Occupied America: The Chicano Struggle Toward Liberation.* San Francisco: Canfield.

Adams, Margaret. 1971. "The Compassion Trap-Women Only." *Psychology Today* November:71ff.

Adams, Richard N. 1988. *The Eighth Day: Social Evolution as the Self-organization of Energy.* Austin: University of Texas Press.

Agger, Robert E. 1978. *A Little White Lie.* New York: Elsevier.

Anderson, Ralph E. 1981. Book Review of Jeremy Rifkin, *Entropy.* In *Social Development* Issues, Vol. 5, No. 1.

Ahrons, Constance R. 1987. The Binuclear Family: Two Households, One Family." Paper presented at the Sixth Annual Conference of the Stepfamily Association of America, Lincoln, NE.

Ahrons, Constance R., and Roy H. Rodgers. 1987. *Divorced Families.* New York: Norton.

Ainsworth, Mary D. Salter. 1969. "Object Relations, Dependency and Attachment: A Theoretical Review of the Infant–Mother Relationship." *Child Development* 40(4):969–1025.

Albee. Edward. 1963. *Who's Afraid of Virginia Wolfe?* New York: Pocketbook Cardinal.

Alissi, Albert S. 1980. *Perspectives on Social Group Work Practice.* New York: The Free Press.

Andreski, Stanislav. 1973. *The Prospects of a Revolution in the U.S.A.* New York: Harper Colophon Book.

Angier, Natalie. 1982. "The Organic Computer," *Discover* 3(5):76–79.

Ardrey, Robert. 1966, 1971. *The Territorial Imperative.* New York: Atheneum.

———. 1980. 1970. *The Social Contract.* New York: Atheneum.

Arendt, Hannah. 1962. *The Origins of Totalitarianism.* Cleveland: World Publishing Company.

Argyris, Chris. 1968. "Personal vs. Organizational Goals." In *Human Relations in Administration,* third edition, edited by Robert Dubin. Englewood Cliffs, NJ: Prentice-Hall.

Asimov, Isaac. 1970. "In the Game of Energy and Thermodynamics You Can't Break Even." *Smithsonian* August.

Auger, Jeanine Roose. 1976. *Behavioral Systems and Nursing*. Englewood Cliffs, NJ: Prentice-Hall.

Bahm, Archie. 1977. *The Specialist: His Philosophy, His Disease, His Cure*. Madras, India: The MacMillan Company of India.

Bailey, Joe. 1980. *Ideas and Intervention: Social Theory for Practice*. London: Routledge and Kegan Paul.

Bales, Robert F. 1950. *Interaction Process Analysis*. Cambridge: Addison-Wesley.

Banfield, Edward. 1961. *Political Influence*. New York: The Free Press.

Baratz, Stephen and Joan Baratz. 1971. "Early Childhood Intervention: The Social Science Base of Institutional Racism." In *Majority and Minority*, edited by Norman R. Yetman and C. Hoy Steele. Boston: Allyn and Bacon.

Barnes, John. 1954 "Class and Committees in a Norwegian Island Parish." *Human Relations* 7 (February).

Barnet, Richard, and Ronald Muller. 1974. *Global Reach*. New York: Simon and Schuster.

Beer, Stafford. 1981. "Death is Equifinal." Eighth Annual Ludwig Von Bertalanffy Memorial Lecture. *Behavioral Science* 26:185–196.

Bell, Colin, and Howard Newby. 1972. *Community Studies: An Introduction to the Sociology of the Local Community*. New York: Praeger.

Bellah, Robert N., Richard Madsen, William M. Sullivan, Ann Swidler, and Steven M. Tipton. 1985. *Habits of the Heart*. Berkeley, CA: University of California Press.

Bendix, Reinhard. 1960. *Max Weber: An Intellectual Portrait*. Garden City, NY: Doubleday.

Berger, Brigitte, and Peter Berger. 1983. *The War Over the Family: Capturing the Middle Ground*. Garden City, NY: Doubleday.

Berrien, F.K. 1971. "A General Systems Approach to Human Groups." In *Man in Systems*, edited by Milton D. Rubin. New York: Gordon and Breach.

Bertalanffy, Ludwig Von. 1967. *Robots: Men and Minds*. New York: Braziller.

Bierstedt, Robert. 1961. "Power and Social Organizations." In *Human Relations in Administration*, edited by Robert Dubin. Englewood Cliffs, NJ: Prentice-Hall.

Billingsley, Andrew. 1968. Black Families in White America. Englewood Cliffs, NJ: Spectrum.

———. 1988. *Black Families in White America*. New York: Simon and Schuster.

Bird, Caroline. 1966. *The Invisible Scar*. New York: David McKay.

Birren, James E. 1959. *Handbook of Aging and the Individual*. Chicago, IL: University of Chicago Press.

Blau, Peter. 1956. *Bureaucracy in Modern Society*. New York: Random House.

Bloom, Allan. 1987. *The Closing of the American Mind*. New York: Simon and Schuster.

Boehm, Werner. 1965. "Relationship of Social Work to Other Professions." In *Encyclopedia of Social Work*. New York. National Association of Social Workers.

Boguslaw, Robert. 1965. *The New Utopians*. Englewood Cliffs, NJ: Prentice-Hall.

Boss, Pauline. 1987. "Family Stress." In *Handbook of Marriage and Family*, edited by M.B. Sussman and S.K. Steinman. New York: Plenum.

Boulding, Elise 1972. "The Family as an Agent of Change." *The Futurist* 6(5):186–191.

Bowen, Murray. 1978. *Family Therapy in Clinical Practice.* New York: Jason Aronson.

Bowlby, John. 1962. *Deprivation of Maternal Care.* Geneva: World Health Organization.

Boyd, Robert, and Peter J. Richerson. 1985. *Culture and The Evolutionary Process.* Chicago, IL: University of Chicago Press.

Branch, Taylor. 1988. *Parting The Waters: America In The King Years 1954–63.* New York: Simon and Schuster.

Brill, Charles. 1974. *Indian and Free.* Minneapolis: University of Minnesota Press.

Bringuier, Jean-Claude. 1974, 1980. *Conversations With Jean Piaget.* Chicago, IL: The University of Chicago Press.

Brodey, Warren M. 1977. *Family Dance: Building Positive Relationships Through Family Therapy.* Garden City, NY: Anchor.

Brown, G. Spencer. 1969, 1979. *Laws of Form.* London: Allen & Unwin.

Brown, Roger. 1965. "How Shall a Thing Be Called?" In *Readings in Child Development and Personality,* edited by Paul Musser. New York: Harper and Row.

Bruner, Jerome. 1968. *Toward a Theory of Instruction.* New York: Norton.

Buckley, Walter. 1967. *Sociology and Modern Systems Theory.* Englewood Cliffs, NJ: Prentice-Hall.

———. 1968. *Modern Systems Research for the Behavioral Scientist.* Chicago: Aldine.

Burke, Kenneth. 1935. *Permanence and Change: An Anatomy of Purpose.* New York: New Republic.

Butler, Robert N. 1975. *Why Survive? Being Old in America.* New York: Harper and Row.

Butler, Samuel. 1942. *The Way of All Flesh.* New York: Walter J. Black.

Cahn, Edgar S. 1969. *Our Brother's Keeper: The Indian in White America.* Cleveland: World Publishing.

Cambell, D. T. 1958. "Common Fate, Similarity and Other Indices of the Status of Aggregates of Persons as Social Entities." *Behavioral Science* 3:14–25.

Capelle, Ronald G. 1978. *Changing Human Systems.* Toronto: International Human Systems Institute.

Caplow, Theodore, Howard M. Bahr, Bruce A Chadwick, Reuben Hill, and Margaret Holmes Williamson. 1982. *Middletown Families: Fifty Years of Change and Continuity.* Minneapolis: University of Minnesota Press.

Capra, Fritjof. 1977. *The Tao of Physics.* New York: Bantam Books.

Carse, James P. 1986. *Finite and Infinite Games.* New York: The Free Press.

Carter, Betty, and M. McGoldrick. 1989. *The changing Family Life Cycle,* second edition Boston: Allyn and Bacon.

Carter, E. A., and M. McGoldrick, eds. 1988. *The Family Life Cycle,* revised edition. New York: Gardner.

Cartwright, Darwin and Alvin Zander. 1960. *Group Dynamics.* Evanston, Il.: Row, Peterson.

Caudill, Harry M. 1963. *Night Comes to the Cumberlands.* Boston: Little, Brown.

Chatterjee, Pranab, and Raymond E. Koleski. 1970. "The Concept of Community and Community Organization: A Review." *Social Work* 15(3):82–92.

Christaller, Walter. 1966. *Central Places in Southern Germany.* Englewood Cliffs, N. J.: Prentice-Hall.

Christenson, James A., and Jerry W. Robinson, Jr. 1980. Community Development in America. Ames, Iowa: Iowa State University Press.

———. 1989. *Community Development in Perspective*. Ames, Iowa: Iowa State University Press.

Churchman, C. West. 1968. *The Systems Approach*. New York: Dell.

Cloward, Richard A, and Lloyd Ohlin. (1960). *Delinquency and Opportunity: A Theory of Delinquent Gangs*. Glencoe, II: The Free Press.

Cohen, Bernice. 1988. Global Perspectives: *The Total Culture System in the Modern World*. London: Codek Publications.

Coles, Robert H. 1970. *Erik H. Erikson: The Growth of His Work*. Boston: Little, Brown.

Cooley, Charles Horton. 1967. "Looking Glass Self." In *Symbolic Interaction*, edited by Jerome Manis and Bernard N. Meltzer. Boston: Allyn and Bacon.

Coplon, Jeff. 1988. "Skinhead Nation." *Rolling Stone* 540:54–94.

Corey, Gerald, Marianne Schneider Corey, Patrick J. Callahan, and J. Michael Russell. 1982. *Group Techniques*, Monterey, CA.

Coser, Lewis. 1964. *The Functions of Social Conflict*. New York: The Free Press.

———. 1974. *Greedy Institutions: Patterns of Undivided Commitment*. New York: The Free Press.

Coyle, Dennis J. 1987. *A Critical Theory of Community*. Berkeley, CA: Institute of Governmental Studies, University of California.

Coyle, Grace. 1948. *Group Work with American Youth*. New York: Harper and Row.

Cox, Fred M., et al. 1987. *Strategies of Community Organization: Macro Practice*. Itasca, IL: Peacock.

Curtis, Charles P. Jr., and Ferris Greenslet. 1962. *The Practical Cogitator*. Boston: Houghton Mifflin.

Dahl, Robert A. 1957. "The Concept of Power." *Behavioral Science* 2:201–215.

Davenport, Judith, and Joseph Davenport III. 1982. "Utilizing the Social Network in Rural Communities." *Social Casework* 63(2):106–113.

Dessler, Gary. 1980. *Organization Theory: Integrating Structure and Behavior*. Englewood Cliffs, NJ: Prentice-Hall.

Dewey, John. 1966. *Democracy and Education*. New York: The Free Press

Domhoff, G. William. 1967. *Who Rules America?* Englewood Cliffs, NJ: Prentice-Hall.

———. 1971. *The Higher Circles*. New York: Vintage Books.

———. 1974. *The Bohemian Grove and Other Retreats*. New York: Harper and Row.

Domhoff, G. William, and Thomas R. Dye. 1987. *Power Elites and Organizations*. Newbury Park, CA: Sage Publications.

Dorris, Michael. 1987. *A Yellow Raft in Blue Water*. New York: Warner Books.

Drucker, Peter. 1982. *The Changing World of the Executive*. New York: Truman Talley Books.

Dubin, Robert, ed. 1961. *Human Relations in Administration*, second edition. Englewood Cliffs, NJ: Prentice-Hall.

Dunn, Edgar. 1980. *The Development of the U.S. Urban System*, Volume 1. Baltimore: The Johns Hopkins University Press.

Durkheim, Emile. 1968. "Division of Labor and Interdependence." In *Human Relations in Administration*, third edition edited by Robert Dubin. Englewood Cliffs, NJ: Prentice-Hall.

Durkin, James E. 1981. *Living Groups: Group Psychotherapy and General System Theory*. New York: Brunner/Mazel.

Ehrlich, Elizabeth. 1989. "Is the Mommy Track a Blessing—or a Betrayal?" *Business Week*, 3105, (May 15):98–99.

Elkind, David. 1968. "Giant in the Nursery-Jean Piaget." *New York Times Magazine*, May 26.

Elliot, Faith Robertson. 1986. *The Family: Change or Continuity*. London: Macmillan.

Engel, George. 1977. "The Need for a New Medical Model: A Challenge for Biomedicine." *Science* 196:129–136.

Engels, Friedrich. 1902. *The Origin of The Family, Private Property and the State*. Chicago: C. H. Kerr.

Epstein, Norman. 1982. "A Residence for Autistic and Schizophrenic Adolescents." *Social Casework* 63(4):109–114.

Erdrich, Louise. 1985. *Love Medicine*, second edition. Toronto, New York: Bantam Books.

Erikson, Erik H. 1950. In *Symposium on the Healthy Personality*, edited by M. S. E. Senn. New York: Josiah Macy, Jr. Foundation.

———. 1958. *Young Man Luther*. New York: Norton.

———. 1959. "The Problem of Ego Identity." In *Psychological Issues*, edited by George S. Klein. New York: International Universities Press.

———. 1963. *Childhood and Society*, second edition. New York: Norton.

———. 1964. *Insight and Responsibility*. New York: Norton.

———. 1968. *Identity, Youth and Crisis*. New York: Norton.

———. 1969. *Gandhi's Truth*. New York: Norton.

———. 1974. *Dimensions of a New Identity*. New York: Norton.

———. 1975. *Life History and the Historical Moment*. New York: Norton.

———. 1982. *The Life Cycle Completed: A Review*. New York: Norton.

———. 1985. *Childhood and Society*. 35th anniversary edition. New York: Norton.

Erikson, Erik H., Joan Erikson, and Helen Q. Kivnick. 1986. *Vital Involvements in Old Age*. New York: Norton.

———. 1987. *A Way of Looking at things: Selected Papers from 1930 to 1980*. New York: Norton

Ermarth, Michael. 1978. *Wilhelm Dilthey: The Critique of Historical Reason*. Chicago: The University of Chicago Press.

Etzioni, Amitai. 1964. *Modern Organizations*. Englewood Cliffs, NJ: Prentice-Hall.

Evans, Richard. 1967. *Dialogue with Erik Erikson*. New York: Harper and Row.

Farb, Peter. 1968. *Man's Rise to His Civilization as Shown by the Indians of North America from Primeval Times to the Coming of the Industrial State*. New York: Dutton.

———. 1978. *Man's Rise to Civilization: The Cultural Ascent of the Indians of North America*. New York: Dutton.

Farley, Reynolds. 1984. *Blacks and Whites: Narrowing the Gap?* Cambridge, MA: Harvard University Press.

Feldman, Frances Lomas and Frances H. Scherz. 1967. *Family Social Welfare*. New York: Atherton.

Fellin, Philliip. 1987. *The Community and the Social Worker*. Itasca, IL: Peacock.

Fennell, Graham, Chris Phillipson, and Helen Evers. 1988. *Sociology of Old Age*. Milton Keynes, England: Open University Press.

Fitzgerald, Frances. 1986. *Cities on a Hill*. New York: Simon and Schuster.

Flink, James J. 1976. *The Car Culture*. Cambridge, MA: MIT Press.

French, Robert Mills. 1969. *The Community*. Itasca, IL: Peacock.

Freud, Sigmund. 1949. *An Outline of Psychoanalysis*. Translated by James Strachey. New York: Norton.

Friedenberg, Edgar Z. 1962. *The Vanishing Adolescent*. New York: Dell.

Friedman, Edwin H. 1971. "Family Systems Thinking and a New View of Man." *Central Conference of American Rabbis Journal* 28(1).

Fromm, Erich. 1942. *The Fear of Freedom*. London: Routledge and Kegan Paul.

———. 1955. *The Sane Society*. New York: Rinehart.

———. 1962. "Personality and the Market Place." In Sigmund Nosow and William H. Form (eds.). *Man, Work, and Society*, New York: Basic Books.

Galbraith, John Kenneth. 1968. *The New Industrial State*. New York: Signet Books.

Galper, Jeffry. 1970. "Nonverbal Communication in Groups." *Social Work* 15(2):71–78.

Gardner, Hugh. 1978. *The Children of Prosperity: Thirteen Modern American Communes*. New York: St. Martin's Press.

Garland, James A. 1965. "A Model for States of Development in Social Work Groups." In *Explorations in Group Work*, edited by Saul Bernstein. Boston: Boston University School of Social Work.

Garrow, David J. 1986. *Martin Luther King, Jr., and the Southern Christian Leadership Conference*. New York: Morrow.

Gastil, Raymend D. 1977. *Social Humanities*. San Francisco: Jossey-Bass.

Gemmill, Gary, and George Kraus. 1988. "Dynamics of Covert Role Analysis: Small Groups." *Small Group Behavior* 19:3299–311.

Geyer, Felix and Johannes Van Der Zouwen, Editors. 1986. *Sociocybernetic Paradoxes*. Beverly Hills, CA.: Sage Publications.

Giamatti, A. Bartlett. 1988. *A Free and Ordered Space: The Real World of the University*. New York: Norton.

Giddens, Anthony, and Jonathan Turner. 1987. *Social Theory Today*. Stanford: Stanford University Press.

Gilligan, Carol. 1982. *In a Different Voice: Psychological Theory and Women's Development*. Cambridge, MA: Harvard University Press.

———. 1987. "Adolescent Development Reconsidered." *The Tenth Annual Gisela Konopka Lectures*. May 13, 1987. St. Paul: Center for Youth Development and Research, University of Minnesota.

Gilligan, Carol, Janice Victoria Ward, and Jill McLean Taylor, with Betty Bardige. eds. 1988. *Mapping the Moral Domain: A Contribution of Women's Thinking to Pyschological Theory and Education*. Cambridge, MA: Center for the study of Gender, Education, and Human Development, Harvard University Press.

Giner, Salvador. 1976. *Mass Society*. London: Martin Robertson.

Glasser, Paul, Rosemary Sarri, and Robert Vinter, eds. 1974. *Individual Change Through Small Groups*. New York: Free Press.

Glazer, Nathan, and Daniel P. Moynihan. 1970. *Beyond the Melting Pot*. Cambridge: MIT Press.

Gleick, James. 1987. *Chaos: Making a New Science*. New York: Viking Penguin.

Glick, Paul C. 1989. "Remarried Families, Stepfamilies and Children: A Demographic Profile." *Family Relations* 38(1):24–27.

Goffman, Erving. 1961. *The Presentation of Self in Everyday Life.* Indianapolis: Bobbs-Merrill.

———. 1973. *Asylums: Essays on the Social Situations of Mental Patients and Other Inmates.* New York: Doubleday. (Originally published in 1961 by Aldine.)

Goldberg, Lorna, and William Goldberg. 1982. "Group Work with Former Cultists." *Social Work* 27(2):165–171.

Golembiewski, Robert T., and Arthur Blumberg. 1970. *Sensitivity Training and the Laboratory Approach.* Itasca, IL: Peacock.

Goodman, Ellen. 1989a. "The Mommy Track: Is It Fair?" *Minneapolis Star-Tribune,* March 17.

———. 1989b. "So Long, Feelgood Patriotism." *Minneapolis Star-Tribune,* January 17, 1989.

———1989c. "Abortion and Family Rights"*Chicago Tribune,* February 19.

Goodman, Paul. 1960. *Growing up Absurd.* New York: Random House.

Gouldner, Alvin W. 1961. "Organizational Analysis." in *Human Relations in Administration,* edited by Warren G. Bennis et al., New York: Holt, Rinehart and Winston.

Granovetter, Mark S. 1977. "The Strength of Weak Ties." Pp. 347–367 in *Social Networks,* edited by Samuel Leinhard. New York: Academic Press.

Gray, William, and Nicholas D. Rizzo. 1973. *Unity Through Diversity: a Festschrift for Ludwig von Bertalanffy.* New York: Gordon and Breach Science Publishers.

Gusfield, Joseph R. 1975. *Community: A Critical Response.* New York: Harper and Row.

Hall, Edward T. 1961. *The Silent Language.* Greenwich, CT: Fawcett.

———. 1969. *The Hidden Dimension.* Garden City, NY: Doubleday

———. 1977. *Beyond Culture.* Garden City, NY: Doubleday Anchor Press.

Handy, Charles. 1985. *Understanding Organizations.* Harmondsworth, England: Penguin.

Hare, A. Paul. 1976. *Handbook of Small Group Research.* New York: The Free Press.

Hasenfeld, Yeheskel. 1983. *Human Service Organizations.* Englewood Cliffs, NJ: Prentice-Hall.

Hearn, Gordon, ed. 1969. *The General Systems Approach: Contributions toward an Holistic Conception of Social Work.* New York: Council on Social Work Education.

Herbert, James I. 1989. *Black Male Entrepreneurs and Adult Development.* New York: Praeger.

Hersh, Richard H., Diana Pritchard Paolitto, and Joseph Reimer. 1979, 1983. *Promoting Moral Growth: From Piaget to Kohlberg.* New York: Longman.

Herzberg, Frederick, Bernard Mausner, and Barbara Bloch Snyderman. 1959. *The Motivation to Work.* New York: Wiley.

Hewitt,John P. 1979. *Self and Society,* second edition. Boston: Allyn and Bacon.

Hillery, George A., Jr. 1968. *Communal Organizations: A Study of Local Societies.* Chicago: University of Chicago press.

Hirowkawa, Randy Y., Dennis S. Gouran, and Amy E. Martz. 1988. "Understanding the Sources of Faulty Group Decision Making: A Lesson from the Challenger Disaster." *Small Group Behavior.* 19(4):411–433.

Hofstadter, Daniel, and Daniel C. Dennett. 1982. *The Mind's I.* New York: Bantam Books.

Hollingshead, August. 1969. *Elmtown's Youth*. New York: Wiley.

Homans George. 1950. *The Human Group*. New York: Harcourt, Brace and World.

House, R. J. 1975. "Etzioni's Theory of Organizational Compliance." Pp. 74–80 in *Theories of Organization*, edited by Henry L. Tosi. Chicago: St. Clair Press.

Hunter, Floyd. 1953. *Community Power Structure*. Chapel Hill: University of North Carolina Press.

Huxley, Julian. 1964. *Man in the Modern World*. New York:Mentor Books.

Ichheiser, Gustav. 1949. "Misunderstandings in Human Relations: A Study in False Social Perception." *American Journal of Sociology* 55(2).

Illich, Ivan. 1973. *Tools for Conviviality*. New York:Harper and Row.

Jackson, Don. 1970. "The Study of the Family." in *Family Process*, edited by Nathan W. Ackerman. New York: Basic Books.

Johnson, David W., and Frank P. Johnson. 1982 1987. *Joining Together: Group Theory and Group Skills*. Englewood Cliffs, NJ: Prentice-Hall

Jones, W.H.S. translator. 1923. *Hippocrates: With an English Translation*. London: William Heinemann.

Juario, Rolf. 1989. "Secrets to Your Success," *Etc.* 6(7):7.

Kahn, Alfred J. 1969. *Theory and Practice of Social Planning*. New York: Russell Sage Foundation.

Kanter, Rosabeth Moss. 1970. "Communes." *Psychology Today* 3(2):53ff.

Katz, Alfred H., and Eugene I. Bender. 1976. *The Strength in Us*. New York: New Viewpoints.

Kelly, James, and Pamela Sykes. 1989. "Helping the Helpers: A Support Group for Family Members of Persons With AIDS." *Social Work* 34(3)239–242.

Keniston, Kenneth. 1970. "Youth: A 'New' Stage of Life." *The American Scholar* 39(4):631–654.

Kephart, William M. 1976, 1982. *Extraordinary Groups: The Sociology of Unconventional Lifestyles*. New York: St. Martin's Press.

Kimberly, John R., and Robert H. Miles and Associates. 1981. *The Organizational Life Cycles*. San Francisco: Jossey-Bass.

Kinkade, Kathleen. 1973. *A Walden Two Experiment: The First Five Years of Twin Oaks Community*. New York: Morrow.

Kleiman, Carol. 1980. *Women's Networks*. New York: Ballantine Books.

Knowles, Louis L., and Kenneth Prewitt (eds.) (1969). *Institutional Racism in America*. Englewood Cliffs, NJ: Prentice-Hall.

Koestler, Arthur. 1967. *The Act of Creation*. New York: Dell.

———. 1979 *Janus: A Summing Up*. New York: Random House.

Koestler, Arthur, and J. R. Smythies eds., 1971. *Beyond Reductionism: New Perspectives in the Life Sciences*. Boston: Beacon.

Kohlberg, Lawrence. 1984. *The Psychology of Moral Development*. San Francisco: Harper & Row.

———. 1987. *Child Psychology and Childhood Education: A Cognitive-Developmental View*. New York: Longman.

Kovel, Joel. 1976. *A Complete Guide to Therapy: From Psychoanalysis To Behavior Modification*. New York: Pantheon Books.

Kranichfeld, Marion L. 1988. "Rethinking Family Power." In *Family Relations,* edited by Norval D. Glenn and Marion Tolbert Coleman Chicago: Dorsey Press.

Kroeber, Alfred Louis, and Clyde Kluckholn. 1952 *Culture: A Critical Review of Concepts and Definations.* Cambridge, MA: The Museum.

Ktsanes,Thomas. 1965. "Adolescent Educational Values and Their Implications for the Assumption of the Adult Role. In *Adolescence: Pivotal Period in the Life Cycle.* Tulane Studies in Social Welfare,8.

Kuhn, Thomas S. 1970. *The Structure of Scientific Revolutions,* second edition. Chicago: University of Chicago Press.

Kvaraceus, William C. 1959. *Delinquent Behavior, Culture and the Individual.* Volume 1. Washington, DC: National Education.

LaBarre, Weston. 1954. *The Human Animal.* Chicago: University of Chicago Press.

Larwood, Laurie. 1984. *Organizational Behavior and Management.* Boston: Kent Publishing.

Lasch, Christopher. 1979. *Haven in a Heartless World: The Family Besieged.* New York: Basic Books.

Laslett, Peter. 1971. *The World We Have Lost.* New York: Charles Scribner's Sons. Second Edition.

———. ed. 1974. *Household and Family in Past Time.* Cambridge: Cambridge University Press.

Laszlo, Ervin. 1972. *The Systems View of the World.* New York: Braziller.

Lau, Siu-Kai. 1978. *Utilitarianistic Familism: The Basis of Political Stability in Hong Kong.* Hong Kong: Social Research Centre. The Chinese University of Hong Kong.

Lauffer, Armand. 1984. *Understanding Your Social Agency.* Beverly Hills, CA: Sage Publications.

Lenski, Gerhard. 1970. *Human Societies.* New York: McGraw-Hill.

Leslie, Gerald. 1967. *The Family in Social Context.* New York: Oxford University Press.

Leslie, Gerald, and Sheila Korman. 1989. *The Family in Social Context.* New York: Oxford University Press.

Lidz, Theodore. 1963. *The Family and Human Adaptation.* New York: International Universities Press.

Lincoln, Yvonna S., and Egan G. Guba. 1985. *Naturalistic Inquiry.* Beverly Hills, CA: Sage Publications.

Linton, Ralph. 1945. *The Cultural Background of Personality.* New York: Appleton-Century-Crofts.

Lipset, David. 1980. *Gregory Bateson: The Legacy of a Scientist.* Englewood Cliffs, NJ: Prentice-Hall

Loeb, Martin. 1961. "Social Class and the American Social System." *Social Work* 6(2):12–18.

Loomis, Charles P., and Zona K. Loomis. 1961. *Modern Social Theories.* Princeton, NJ: Van Nostrand.

Lorenz, Konrad. 1963. *On Aggression.* New York: Harcourt, Brace and World.

Lyman, Stanford M., and Marvin B. Scott. 1967. "Territoriality: A Neglected Sociological Dimension." *Social Problems* 15:236–245.

Lynd, Robert S. and Helen Merrell Lynd. 1929. *Middletown.* New York: Harcourt, Brace and World.

————. 1937. *Middletown in Transition*. New York: Harcourt, Brace and World.

Maier, Henry W. 1988. *Three Theories of Child Development*, third edition. Lanham, MD: University Press of America.

Malcolm X. (with Alex Haley). 1966. *The Autobiography of Malcolm X*. New York: Grove.

March, James G., and Herbert A. Simon. 1968. "Significance of Organizations." In *Human Relations in Administration*, third edition, edited by Robert Dubin. Englewood Cliffs, NJ: Prentice-Hall

Marrow, Alfred J. 1969. *The Practical Theorist: The Life and Work of Kurt Lewin*. New York: Basic Books.

Marshall, T. H. 1964. *Class, Citizenship, and Social Development*. New York: Doubleday.

Maruyama, Magorah. 1966. "Monopolarization, Family and Individuality." *Psychiatric Quarterly* 40(1):133–149.

Maslow, Abraham. 1964. "Synergy in the Society and in the Individual." *Journal of Individual Psychology* 20:153–164.

———— 1968. *Toward a Psychology of Being*. Princeton: Van Nostrand.

Matejko, Alexander J. 1986. *In Search of New Organizational Paradigms*. New York: Praeger.

Maturana, Humberto R., and Francisco J. Varela. 1980. *Autopoiesis and Cognition*. Dordrecht, Holland: D. Reidel.

May, Rollo. 1969. *Love and Will*. New York: Norton.

Mayer, Milton. 1969. *On Liberty: Man vs. the State*. Santa Barbara, CA: The Center for the Study of Democratic Institutions.

Mayo, Elton. 1945. *The Social Problems of an Industrial Civilization*. Boston: Harvard University Press.

McGrath, Joseph E. 1984. *Groups: Interaction and Performance*. Englewood Cliffs, NJ: Prentice-Hall.

McIntyre, Eilene L. G. 1986. "Social Networks: Potential for Practice." *Social Work* 31(6):421–426.

McLuhan, Marshall. 1965. *Understanding Media: The Extensions of Man*. New York: McGraw-Hill.

McRobie, George. 1981. *Small is Possible*. New York: Harper and Row.

Mead, Margaret. 1970. *Culture and Commitment*. Garden City, NY: Natural History Press.

————. 1972. *Blackberry Winter*. New York: Simon and Schuster.

Meadows, Donella H., Dennis L. Meadows, Jorgen Randers, and William W. Behrens III. 1972. *Limits to Growth*. New York: Universe Books.

Meenaghan, Thomas M. 1972. "What Means 'Community'?" *Social Work* 17(6):94–98.

Meltzer, Bernard N. 1967. "Mead's Social Psychology," In *Symbolic Interaction*, edited by Jerome G. Manis and Bernard N. Meltzer. Boston: Allyn and Bacon.

Menninger, Karl. 1963. *The Vital Balance*. New York: Viking.

Merton, Robert K. 1957. *Social Theory and Social Structure*, revised edition. New York: The Free Press.

Miller, Arthur. 1955. *Death of a Salesman*. New York: Bantam.

Miller, James G. 1955. "Toward a General Theory for the Behavioral Sciences." *American Psychologist* 10:513–531.

————. 1965. "Living Systems: Basic Concepts." *Behavioral Science* 10:193–237.

———. 1972. "Living Systems: The Organization." *Behavioral Science* 17(1):1–182.

———. 1978. *Living Systems*. New York: McGraw-Hill.

Mills, C. Wright. 1948. *The New Men of Power*. New York: Harcourt, Brace and World.

———. 1951. *The Power Elite*. New York: Oxford University Press.

Mills, Theodore. 1967. *The Sociology of Small Groups*. Englewood Cliffs, NJ: Prentice-Hall.

Minuchin, Salvador. 1974. *Families and Family Therapy*. Cambridge, MA: Harvard University Press.

Mitchell, Arnold. 1983. *The Nine American Lifestyles: Who Are We and Where Are We Going*. New York: Macmillan.

Monane, Joseph H. 1967. *A Sociology of Human Systems*. New York: Appleton-Century-Crofts.

Monge, Peter R. 1977. "The Systems Perspective as a Theoretical Basis for the Study of Human Communication." *Communication Quarterly* 25(1):19–29.

Moore, Barrington. 1958. *Political Power and Social Theory*. Cambridge, MA: Harvard University Press.

Mumford, Lewis. 1970. *The Myth of the Machine: II. The Pentagon of Power*. New York: Harcourt Brace Jovanovich.

Munch, Richard. 1987. "Parsonian Theory Today: In Search of a New Synthesis." In *Social Theory Today*, edited by Anthony Giddens and Jonathan H. Turner. Stanford, CA: Stanford University Press.

Nisbet, Robert A. 1966. *The Sociological Tradition*. New York: Basic Books.

Northen, Helen. 1969,1988. *Social Work with Groups*. New York: Columbia University Press.

Olmsted, Michael. 1959,1978. *The Small Group*. New York: Random House.

Olsen, Marvin. 1968,1978. *The Process of Social Organization*. New York: Holt, Rinehart, and Winston.

Olson, David. 1983. *Families: What Makes Them Work*. Beverly Hills, CA: Sage Publications.

Olson, David H., Yoav Lavee, and Hamilton I. McCubbin. 1988. "Types of Families and Family Responses to Stress Across the Family Life Cycle," In *Social Stress and Family Development*, edited by David Klein and Joan Aldous. New York: Guilford.

Ouchi, William G. 1981a. "A Framework for Understanding Organizational Failure." In *The Organizational Life Cycle*, edited by John R. Kimberly, Robert H. Miles, and Associates. San Francisco: Jossey-Bass.

———. 1981b. *Theory Z: How American Business can Meet the Japanese Challenge*. Reading, MS: Addison-Wesley.

Papademetrious, Marguerite. 1971. "Use of a Group Technique with Unwed Mothers and Their Families." *Social Work*, 16(4):85–90.

Park, Robert E. 1952. *Human Communities*. Glencoe., IL: The Free Press.

Parsons, Talcott. 1960. *Structure and Process in Modern Societies*. New York: The Free Press.

———. 1964a. "The Normal Family." *Family Mental Health Papers*. Los Angeles, CA: County Bureau of Public Assistance.

———. 1964b. *The Social System*. New York: The Free Press.

Parsons, Talcott, R. F. Bales, and E. A. Shils. 1953. *Working Papers in the Theory of Action*. New York: The Free Press.

Pasley, B. Kay, and Marilyn Ihinger-Tallman. 1989. "Boundary Ambiguity in Remarriage: Does Ambiguity Differentiate Degree of Marital Adjustment and Integration?" *Family Relations* 38(1):46–52.

Peck, M. Scott. 1987. *The Different Drum.* New York: Simon and Schuster.

Pei, Mario. 1966,1984. *The Story of Language.* New York: Mentor Book.

Pharand, Gisèle R., Maria L. Sudermann, and Ray DeV. Peters. 1988. "Comprehensive Assessment of Family Functioning." In *Social Learning and Systems Approaches to Marriage and the Family,* edited by Ray DeV. Peters and Robert J. McMahon New York: Brunner/Mazel.

Phillips, John L. Jr. 1969. *The Origins of Intellect: Piaget's Theory.* San Francisco: Freeman.

Piaget, Jean. 1932. *The Moral Judgement of the Child.* Translated by Marjorie Gabian. London: Kegan Paul.

———. 1970. *Genetic Epistemology.* Translated by Eleanor Duckworth. New York: Coumbia University Press. (with E. Ackerman-Vailadao, et al.)

———. 1987. *Possibility and Necessity.* Minneapolis: University of Minnesota Press.

Pirsig, Robert M. 1975. *Zen and The Art of Motorcycle Maintenance.* New York: Bantam Books.

Plath, Sylvia. 1966 "Tulips." In *Ariel.* New York: Harper and Row.

Popenoe, David. 1988. *Disturbing the Nest.* New York: Aldine de Gruyter.

Presthus, Robert. 1962. *The Organization Society: An Analysis and a Theory.* New York: Vintage Books.

———. 1964. *Men at the Top.* New York: Oxford University Press.

Ramsoy, Ødd. 1962. *Social Groups: As System and Subsystem.* Oslo: Norwegian Universities Press.

Reeves, Richard. 1989. "Following the Potomac," *Travel and Leisure,* March 26.

Reik, Theodor. 1948. *Listening with the Third Ear.* New York: Farrar Strauss.

Robbins, William G. 1988. *Hard Times in Paradise: Coos Bay, Oregon, 1850–1986.* Seattle: University of Washington Press.

Roberts, Robert W. and Helen Northen eds. 1976. *Theories of Social Work with Groups.* New York: Columbia University Press.

Rodman, Hyman ed. 1966. *Marriage, Family and Society.* New York: Random House.

Roethlisberger, F. J., and W. L. Dickson. 1947. *Management and the Worker.* Cambridge, MA: Harvard University Press.

Rogers, Carl. 1970. *Carl Rogers on Enounter Groups.* New York: Harper and Row.

Rose, Arnold M. 1967. *The Power Structure.* New York: Oxford University Press.

Rose, Reginald. 1955. *Twelve Angry Men.* Chicago: Dramatics Publications Co.

Rosen, Hugh. 1980. *The Development of Sociomoral Knowledge.* New York: Columbia University Press.

Ross, Murray G. 1955. *Community Organization.* New York: Harper and Row.

Ross, Murray, and Charles Hendry. 1957. *New Understandings of Leadership.* New York: Association Press.

Rowan, John. 1978. *The Structured Crowd.* London: Davis Poynter.

Rushdie, Salman. 1989. *The Satanic Verses.* New York: Viking.

Rutherfurd, Edward. 1987. *Sarum.* New York: Ivy Books.

Sager, Clifford, and Helen Singer Kaplan eds. 1972. *Progress in Group and Family Therapy.* New York: Brunner/Mazel.

Sale, Kirkpatrick. 1980. *Human Scale*. New York: Coward, McCann and Geoghegan.

Salzinger, Suzanne, John Antrobus, and Muriel Hammer. 1988. *Social Networks of Children, Adolescents, and College Students*. Hillsdale, NJ: Lawrence Erlbaum Associates.

Sandburg, Carl. 1955. "Chicago." In edited by Oscar Williams. *The New Pocket Anthology of American Verse*, New York: The Pocket Library.

Sarri, Rosemary C., and Meade J. Galinsky. 1967. "A Conceptual Framework for Group Development." In *Readings in Group Work Practice*, edited by Robert D. Vinter. Ann Arbor: Campus Publishers.

Saxton, Dolores F., et al., eds. 1977 *Mosbys' Comprehensive Review of Nursing*, ninth edition. St. Louis, MO: The C. V. Mosby Co.

Schumacher, E. F. 1973. *Small is Beautiful: Economics as if People Mattered*. New York: Harper and Row.

Scott, William G., and David K. Hart. 1980. *Organizational America*. Boston: Houghton Mifflin.

Scott, W. Richard. 1987. *Organizations: Rational, Natural, and Open Systems*, second edition. Englewood Cliffs, NJ: Prentice-Hall.

Sennett, Richard. 1974. *Families Against the City*. New York: Vintage Books.

Shaw, Marvin E. 1981. *Group Dynamics: The Psychology of Small Group Behavior*, third edition. New York: McGraw-Hill.

Sheehy, Gail. 1976. *Passages*. New York: Dutton.

Shepard, Clovis R. 1964. *Small Groups*. San Francisco: Chandler.

Shilts, Randy. 1988. *And the Band Played On: Politics, People and the AIDS Epidemic*. New York: Penguin.

Silk, Leonard, and Mark Silk. 1981. *The American Establishment*. New York: Avon Books.

Simon, H. A. 1945. *Administrative Behavior*. New York: Macmillan.

Simon, Paul. 1966. *I Am A Rock*. New York: Charing Cross Music.

Skinner, B. F. 1948. *Walden Two*. New York: Macmillan.

Slater, Philip. 1974. *Earthwalk*. New York: Anchor.

Southey, Robert . 1959. "The Doctor." In *Oxford Dictionary of Quotations*, second edition. London: Oxford University Press.

Spitz, René. 1965. *The First Year of Life*. New York: International Universities Press.

Stack, Carol B. 1974. *All Our Kin: Strategies for Survival In Two Black Families*. New York: Harper and Row.

Stein, Maurice R. 1960. *The Eclipse of Community*. Princeton, NJ: Princeton University Press.

Steiner, Gilbert. 1981. *The Futility of Family Policy*. Washington, DC: The Brookings Institution.

Stivers, Richard. 1982. *Evil in Modern Myth and Ritual*. Athens, GA: The University of Georgia Press.

Sweet, James A., and Larry L. Bumpass. 1987. *American Families and Households*. New York: Russell Sage Foundation.

Szent-Gyorgyi, Albert. 1963. *Science, Ethics and Politics*. New York: Vantage Press.

———. 1977 "Drive in Living Matter to Perfect Itself." *Synthesis* I:14–36.

Tarrytown Newsletter. 1982. "Virginia Hine: Complete at Last." No. 14, April.

Tausky, Curt. 1970. *Work Organizations: Major Theoretical Perspectives*. Itasca, IL: Peacock.

Terkel, Studs. 1975. *Working*. New York: Avon.

Thorne, Barrie, and Marilyn Yalom eds. 1982. *Rethinking the Family*. New York: Longman.

Toffler, Alvin. 1970. *Future Shock*. New York: Random House.

Tönnies, Ferdinand. 1957. *Community And Society*, Translated by Charles P. Loomis. East Lansing: Michigan State University Press.

Trecker, Harleigh. 1955. *Social Group Work Principles and Practices*. New York: Whiteside.

Tropp, Emanuel. 1976. "A Developmental Theory." In *Theories of Social Work with Groups*, edited by Robert W. Roberts and Helen Northen. New York: Columbia University Press.

Van Maanen, John. 1988. *Tales of the Field*. Chicago: University of Chicago Press.

Vattanno, Anthony J. 1972. "Power to the People: Self-Help Groups." *Social Work* 17(4):7–15.

Vaux, Alan, 1988. *Social Support: Theory, Research, and Intervention*. New York: Praeger.

Veninga, Robert, and James P. Spradley. 1981. *The Work-Stress Connection*. Boston: Little, Brown.

Vidich, Arthur J., and Joseph Bensman. 1958. *Small Town in Mass Society*. Princeton, NJ: Princeton University Press.

Vigil, James Diego. 1988. *Barrio Gangs*. Austin, TX: University of Texas Press.

Vogel, Ezra, and Norman Bell. 1960. *A Modern Introduction to the Family*. New York: The Free Press.

Voiland, Alice L., and Associates. 1962. *Family Casework Diagnosis*. New York: Columbia University Press.

Warmington, Eric H., and Philip Rouse. 1956. *Great Dialogues of Plato*, translated by W. H. D. Rouse. New York: American Library of World Literature.

Warren, Roland L. 1963, 1978. *The Community in America*. Chicago: Rand McNally.

———. 1977. *New Perspectives on the American Community: A Book of Readings*, third edition. Chicago: Rand McNally.

Washburne, Norman F. 1964. *Interpreting Social Change in America*. New York: Random House.

Wasow, Mona. 1986. "Support Groups for Family Caregivers of Patients With Alzheimer's Disease." *Social Work* 31(2):93–97.

Watts, Alan. 1966. *The Book: On the Taboo Against Knowing Who You Are*. New York: Pantheon Books.

Watzlawick, Paul. 1976. *How Real is Real?* New York: Random House.

Watzlawick, Paul, Janet Helmick Beavin, and Don Jackson. 1967. *Pragmatics of Human Communication: A Study of Interactional Patterns, Pathologies, and Paradoxes*. New York: W. W. Norton.

Webster's New Twentieth Century Dictionary of the English Language. 1980. Unabridged second edition. Cleveland: William Collins Publishers, Inc.

Weisman, Celia B. 1963. "Social Structures as a Determinant of the Group Worker's Role." *Social Work* 8(3):87–94.

Welch, Mary Scott. 1981. *Networking*. New York: Warner Books.

Whorf, Benjamin Lee. 1956. *Language, Thought and Reality*. New York: Wiley/
Technology Press.

Whyte, Lancelot Law, Albert G. Wilson, and Donna Wilson. 1969. *Hierarchical
Structures*. New York: American Elsevier Publishing Company.

Whyte, William Foote. 1955, 1981. *Street Corner Society*, second edition. Chicago:
University of Chicago Press.

Woodruff, John. 1989. *China in Search of Its Future: Years of Great Reform; 1982-
1987*. Seattle: University of Washington Press.

Woodward, Bob, and Scott Armstrong. 1981. *The Brethren*. New York: Avon.

Work in America. 1973. *Report of a Special Task Force to the Secretary of Health, Education, and Welfare*. Cambridge, MA: MIT Press.

World of Work Report. 1977. "Britain's Longtime Unemployed: Most Prefer Work
over State Aid." Vol. 2(2)24.

Wright, J. Patrick. 1979. *On a Clear Day You can See General Motors*. New York:
Avon.

Wuthnow, Robert, James Davison Hunter, Albert Bergesen, and Edith Kurzweil. 1984. *Cultural Analysis: The Work of Peter L. Berger, Mary Douglas, Michel
Foucault, and Jurgen Habermas*. Boston/London: Routledge and Kegan Paul.

Zalenznik, Abraham, and Anne Jardim, 1967. "Management." In *The Uses of
Sociology*, edited by Paul F. Lazersfield. New York: Basic Books.

Zimmerman, Carle. 1947. *Outline of the Future of the Family*. Cambridge: The Phillips Book Store.

Zukav, Gary. 1979. *The Dancing Wu Li Masters*. New York: William Morrow.
(Also available in Bantam edition).

Literary Sources

Anderson, Robert Woodruff, 1968. *I Never Sang for My Father*. New York: Random House.

Bergman, Ingmar. 1960. "Wild Strawberries." In *Four Screenplays*. New York: Simon and Schuster.

Branch, Taylor. 1988 *Parting the Waters: America in the King Years 1954–1963*. New York: Simon and Schuster.

Dorris, Michael. 1987. *A Yellow Raft in Blue Water*. New York: Warner.

Erdrich, Louise. 1985. *Love Medicine*. Toronto, New York: Bantam Books.

Forster, E. M. 1954. *Howards End*. New York: Random House. (Originally published in 1921 by Vintage Books.)

Golding, William. 1959. *Lord of the Flies*. New York: Capricorn Books/Putnam.

Guest, Judith, 1976. *Ordinary People*. New York: Viking.

Keillor, Garrison. 1985. *Lake Wobegon Days*. New York: Viking.

Kesey, Ken. 1962. *One Flew Over the Cuckoo's Nest*. New York: New American Library.

Lee, Harper. 1960. *To Kill a Mockingbird*. Philadelphia: Lippincott.

Mailer, Norman. 1979. *The Executioner's Song*. New York: Warner Books.

Malcolm X (with Alex Haley). 1966. *The Autobiography of Malcolm X*. New York: Grove Press.

McCullers, Carson. 1940. *The Heart Is a Lonely Hunter*. Boston: Houghton Mifflin.

Miller, Arthur. 1949. *Death of a Salesman*. New York: Bantam Books.

Olsen, Tillie, 1976. *Tell Me a Riddle*. New York: Dell/Laurel Edition.

Pa Chin. 1972. *Family*. Garden City, NY: Anchor.

Romains, Jules. 1961. *Death of a Nobody*. New York: New American Library.

Rose, Reginald. 1955. *Twelve Angry Men*. Chicago: Dramatics Publications Co.

Thompson, Ernest. 1979. *On Golden Pond*. New York: Dodd, Mead.

Warren, Robert Penn. 1946, 1982. *All the King's Men*. New York: Harcourt, Brace, Jovanovich.

Zindel, Paul. 1970. *The Effect of Gamma Rays on Man-in-the-Moon Marigolds*. New York: Harper and Row.

Glossary

Accommodation. Modification of the system to adapt to environmental conditions. See ADAPTATION, ASSIMILATION.

Adaptation. Action by the system to secure or conserve energy from the environment. Parsons' use of this term includes this as well as the achievement of goals in the environment. See ACCOMMODATION, ASSIMILATION, FUNCTIONAL IMPERATIVES.

Alienation. This term has a wide variety of definitions. We consider that, fundamentally, it describes a state in which a person does not experience a synergistic linkage with a system (or component) that is significant to the person.

Assimilation. A form of adaptation in which incoming information is interpreted as being similar to previous information (i.e., fitted into old schemas). See ACCOMMODATION, ADAPTATION.

Autonomy. Independence from other components within a system. The components are related to a common suprasystem but are largely or entirely separate from each other.

Autopoiesis. Literally (from Greek), "self-powered;" self-development and self-creation.

Behavior. Short-term exchanges between components or systems that accomplish specific goals for the system. This includes socialization, communication, and social control. See EVOLUTION, STRUCTURE.

Body Language. Communication of a nonvocal nature expressed through touch, posture, facial expression, and movement.

Bond. The common interest, identification, or feeling of "we-ness' among members of a group that permits the group to exist as a system. See BOUNDARY.

Boundary. The limits of the interaction of the components of a system with each other or with the environment. It is usually defined by intensity or frequency of interaction between systems and components.

Bureaucracy. A distinct form of organization in which there is a relatively high degree of administrative centralization, hierarchical control, specificity of rules, and clearly identified role expectations. This form of organization is usually found in cultures that are highly elaborated, and it usually serves social control functions in the society.

Chaos Theory. This new conception of natural events holds that events occur in nonlinear fashion, due to extreme sensitivity to initial conditions, and that variations (or perturbations) are random, but occur within some clear parameters. The infinite variations of snowflakes, e.g., and of human events have brought the natural sciences and social sciences closer in recognizing and accounting for complexity and uncertainty.

Class. A scheme of classification of a particular society. Usually ordered by indices such as income, occupation, and education. See ROLE, STATUS.

Communication. In a narrow sense, the transportation of information between or within systems; in a broader sense, the transportation of energy also. In this broader sense, information is considered a special form of energy (see Monane, 1967, Chapter 2, for his use of these terms).

Component. Synonymous with "part" (a part of a system). It may or may not be a system in itself, in contrast to a subsystem, which is a system. See SUBSYSTEM.

Differentiation. Selectivity of function or activity among components of a system. "Division of labor" is one example. A function or activity is performed by one, or some, components and not others. This differs from specialization in that the component may perform other functions or activities in addition to the assigned, differentiated one. See SPECIALIZATION.

Disintegration. "Disintegration means systemic death. With it, components *De*-sys-tematize. It is a movement away from organization into entropy and randomness" (Monane, 1967:159). See ENTROPY, ORGANIZATION.

Ecological Approach. This is an approach that is virtually synonymous with a systems approach. Specifically, it refers to "nested" systems, that is, from component to subsystem to system to suprasystem, and specifically with the relationships between humans and their environments. It is based on Lewin's field theory. See ECOLOGICAL SYSTEMS.

Ecological Systems. A term used by some systems writers in the broad sense of systems that are hierarchically related. In biology and ecology, the term refers to living organisms in the earth's biosphere that are hierarchically related. See ECOLOGICAL APPROACH.

Elaboration. Used in reference to evolution of groups, this denotes increasing complexity and multiplication of parts of the system.

Energy. Capacity for action; action; or power to effect change. We use this term much as Parsons used action. As increased interaction occurs, there is greater available energy. Richard Adams (1988) prefers the term, "energy forms," which is a useful concept. See ENTROPY, POWER, SYNERGY, SYNTROPY.

Entropy. "The quantity of energy *not* capable of conversion into work" (Asimov, 1970:8). Entropy is the tendency of systems to "run down," to distribute energy randomly so that it becomes less accessible; the system therefore becomes less capable of organized work. Some argue that open systems are not subject to the law of entropy. Rudolph Clausius is credited with the origin of the concept in 1865. See ENERGY, NEGENTROPY, ORGANIZATION SYNTROPY.

Environment. Anything not included within the interaction of the components of a system but that affects the system. It may also be considered as anything that affects the system but over which it has no control (Churchman, 1968:50).

Equifinality. The term derives from systems theory; it means that two different systems, if they receive similar inputs, will arrive at similar end states even though they had different initial conditions. One illustration is that although two children may grow differently, one "undershooting" and the other "overshooting" initially, both will arrive at adulthood in good health and normal size If they are fed similarly and adequately.

Equilibrium. Fixed balance in a relatively closed system characterized by little interchange with the environment and avoidance of disturbance. See HOMEOSTASIS, STEADY STATE.

Ethology. The study of animal behavior, especially of innate patterns. In the past two decades, writings of ethologists, including Konrad Lorenz, Desmond Morris, Lionel Tiger and Robin Fox, have gained popularity. See TERRITORIALITY.

Evolution. Change in a system's structure and behavior from one time to another. This term describes which relationships have altered (and which have remained the same) and in what manner a system's functions are being performed differently at the end of some particular period of time. See BEHAVIOR, STRUCTURE.

Feedback. The process in which a system receives internal or environmental responses to its behavior and, in turn, reacts to these received responses by accommodating and assimilation the information or energy received. See ADAPTATION, COMMUNICATION.

Focal system. This refers to the system that is the object of attention at a particular moment. It must be specified in order to be consistent with the demand that the perspective of the viewer should be stated. Systems analysts frequently label this the TARGET SYSTEM if the focal system is the system in which change is to be achieved. See HOLON, PERSPECTIVISM.

Functional Imperatives. Parsons specified four functions that are necessary in a system. These are ADAPTATION, GOAL -DIRECTED ACTIVITY, INTEGRATION and PATTERN MAINTENANCE. We identify other energy functions that we consider more descriptive.

Goal. A desired steady state to be achieved by fulfilling a specific function of the system within some relatively short period of time. See PURPOSE.

Goal-Directed Activity (GE and GI functions). One of two kinds of energy functions, the other being SECURING AND CONSERVING ENERGY. The process is the expenditure of energy to achieve system goals, either internally or externally.

Hierarchy. A form of organization that characterizes all viable systems. Hierarchy is a superordinate-subordinate relationship between systems in which any unit is dependent upon its suprasystem for performance of energy functions and must provide direction to its subsystems. See HOLON.

Holon. Arthur Koestler's term, denoting that a system is both a part of a larger suprasystem and is itself a suprasystem to other systems. See FOCAL SYSTEM, SUBSYSTEM, SUPRASYSTEM.

Homeostasis. Fixed balance in a partially open system, characterized by very limited interchange with the environment and by maintenance of the system's present structure. See EQUILIBRIUM, STEADY STATE.

Identity. Erikson defines this in several variations. The central idea is integration of the components of the personality, along with validation through interaction with the social environment. The result of these is ego identity, which is inner assurance of congruence between one's own feelings about self and others' feelings about oneself. The concept has been loosely applied to other systems such as "national identity" and "racial identity." Identity is a steady state of the personality system but is richer in its meaning than steady state. See STEADY STATE, SYNTALITY, SYNERGY.

Information. The content of feedback and communication. In a narrow sense, information includes signs and symbols that are communicated. In a broader sense, information could include energy interchange itself. See COMMUNICATION, FEEDBACK.

Institutionalization. One form of differentiation in which some component or system is assigned responsibility to perform specific major functions for the system (usually a culture, society or community but, in a broader sense, in microsystems as well). The differentiated component or system may specialize in this function. A new component or system may be created to carry out the function, or the assignment may be given to an existing component or system. See DIFFERENTIATION, SPECIALIZATION.

Integration. One of Parsons' four functional imperatives. A system must ensure the harmonious interaction of its components in order to prevent entropy and in order to secure and conserve internal energy sources.

Isomorphic. Similarity of form or function between systems or components of systems. "Isomorph" is used in this book to point to similarities between the behaviors and structures of different levels of systems. For example, "feedback cycle" is applicable to all levels of systems from person to culture and thus can be termed "isomorphic."

Linkage. Energy exchange among and between components and systems.

Loop. This term is from engineering and cybernetics. It is a specific form of feedback in which a system's output becomes input that modifies the system's functioning. That is, the system's own behavior supplies stimuli for system modification. See FEEDBACK

Mission. See PURPOSE.

Morphogenesis. A system tending toward structural change. In actuality, all systems must simultaneously maintain and change a shifting balance between morphogenesis and morphostasis. See MORPHOSTASIS.

Morphostasis. A system tending toward maintenance of the status quo structurally. See MORPHOGENESIS.

Negentropy. The word is a contraction of "negative entropy," meaning the reduction of randomized, unavailable energy via importing energy from outside the system. See ENERGY, ENTROPY, SYNERGY, SYNTROPY.

Network. A set of persons linked together, although not all to every other. As McIntyre said (1986:422; see p.72), a network includes indirect links, different from a group, which has only direct, face-to-face linkage between members. "Networking" is the usage or exploitation of such linkages to achieve specific, desired results. See BOND.

Open or Closed System. "Open" denotes energy exchange across a system's boundaries. "Closed" denotes lack of energy exchange across boundaries.

Organization. The process of structuring the exchange of energy in a system.

Persistent regularities of relationship between components make up the structure, or organization, of the system. See DIFFERENTIATION, SPECIALIZATION.

Pattern Maintenance. One of Parsons' four functional imperatives. This refers to the necessity of the system to regulate and enforce legitimized behaviors in order to conserve energy and achieve goals. We consider this to include our SI and GI functions.

Perspectivism. In the systems approach, this means that any description or definition of a system must include an explicit statement of one's own position or intention with regard to that system and an explicit identification of the system that one is identifying as the focal system. Philosophically, the term denotes that any viewpoint is relative to one's own perceptions and relations to the system being described or defined and to its environment.

Polarities. Opposite or contrasting qualities. Many of the systems ideas are conceived as polarities at opposite ends of a continuum. Any system at any time is a mixture or ratio of two polar qualities, such as task vs. sentiment, adaptation vs. integration, basic trust vs. basic mistrust. Polarities are opposites that define each other and together form a single quality.

Power. The capacity to achieve goals by the application or deprivation of energy to another system so as to affect its functioning.

Psychosexual. Generally, refers to the Freudian stages of personality development (i.e., oral, anal, phallic, and genital). See PSYCHOSOCIAL.

Psychosocial. Generally, refers to the Eriksonian life cycle formulation of personality development. This is a modification and extension of the psychosexual, with emphasis on the social and cultural influences. See PSYCHOSEXUAL.

Purpose. A desired steady state achieved by assignment of goal(s) to a subsystem and completion of the goal(s). "Goal" denotes that the system itself will be the object of change; "Purpose" that the suprasystem will be the object of change. Systems analysts frequently use "mission" to mean the same as purpose. See GOAL.

Role. A set of expectations regarding behavior that can be fulfilled by a person. It carries with it expectations of behavior that are defined and sanctioned by significant environmental systems. The role occupant generally has some leeway in interpretation of assigned behaviors. This is analogous to the theater, in which the playwright prescribes the role but the artist interprets through the performance. See STATUS.

Schema. Precisely used, this is Piaget's term for a single complex, or nexus, or associated responses a person is capable of making. We use the term in a broader sense to emphasize its applicability to systems other than a person (e.g., the repertoire of responses that an organization or community is capable of making). We also use the term to mean the integrated knowledge, experience, and interpretations that underlie a system's responses.

Securing and Conserving Energy. We designate this as one of two kinds of energy functions in a system (the other is GOAL-DIRECTED ACTIVITY). The process is one of expending energy to secure further energy or to reduce the expenditure of energy, as in minimizing intrasystem conflict.

Social Control. The use of energy by a system to assure that its components fulfill assigned functions (see PURPOSES and GOALS). Such activity includes socialization and enforcement of norms of behavior. Enforcement may entail persuasion, authority, or force. The purpose of social control is to permit continued functioning of the system through reducing or preventing deviance among the components. See SOCIALIZATION.

Socialization. One form of social control intended to assure the availability of components' energies to the system. The means to achieve this are primarily through assimilating the culture. Hence education, indoctrination, and enculturation are forms of socialization. See SOCIAL CONTROL.

Specialization. Performance of a function or activity to the exclusion of other functions or activities by a component or part of a system. A system may differentiate its components by allocating functions or activities among them; some perform certain functions, whereas others do not perform the same functions. If the part performs *only* the differentiated function, then it has specialized; if it performs other functions as well, it is differentiated but not specialized. The two are separate. See DIFFERENTIATION.

Status. A vertical dimension of ranking. May be ascribed (assigned by society) or achieved (attained by dint of individual or group activity). See CLASS, ROLE.

Steady State. A total condition of the system in which it is in balance both internally and with its environment but is at the same time undergoing some degree of change (i.e., it is not static). The word "Steady" fails to connote the dynamic nature of systems, while the word "State" fails to connote a succession of conditions of the system. Used fairly loosely and somewhat interchangeably with equilibrium and homeostasis but distinct from them. See EQUILIBRIUM, HOMEOSTASIS.

Structure. The most stable relationships between systems and components (i.e., with the slowest rate of change). This states which components or systems are related to each other during a given time period but does not necessarily give details of the amount of energy exchange, or in what direction, or the functions being performed for each party to the relationship. It is thus a "snapshot," frozen in time, not a "movie". See BEHAVIOR, EVOLUTION.

Subsystem. A component of a system that is itself a system. It is one kind of component. See COMPONENT, SUPRASYSTEM, SYSTEM.

Suprasystem. A larger system that includes the focal system; a "whole" of which the focal system is a "part."

Symbolic Interaction. A theoretical perspective within social psychology that seeks to understand human behavior through study of the "social act." Such study attends to overt behavior and what the act symbolizes within the social context.

Synergy. Increasing the amount of available energy in a system through increased interaction of the components. Loosely, it may be described as the creation of new energy through compounding the actions of the parts, but this is a moot point in the systems approach. See ENERGY, ENTROPY, NEGEN TROPY, SYNTROPY.

Syntality. This is the unique character of a group; analogous to the "personality" of a person.

Syntropy. An innate drive in living matter to protect itself, to seek synthesis and wholeness. See ENERGY, ENTROPY, NEGENTROPY, SYNERGY.

System. An organized whole made up of components that interact in a way distinct from their interaction with other entities and which endures over some period of time. See COMPONENT, SUBSYSTEM, SUPRASYSTEM.

Territoriality. Refers to the proclivity of organisms, including, humans, to seek, obtain, and defend an area of space or action. This serves to order and stabilize behavioral space. See ETHOLOGY.

Name Index

Subject Index

42